North Brittany

NORTH BRITTANY

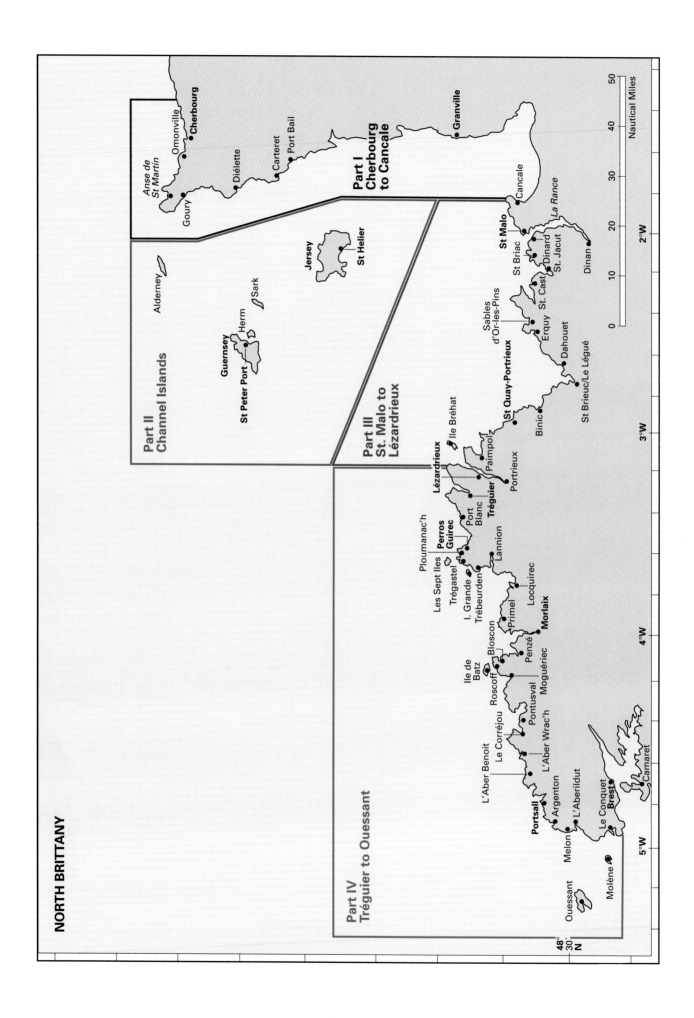

Part I
Cherbourg
to Cancale

Part II
Channel Islands

Part III
St. Malo to
Lézardrieux

Part IV
Tréguier to Ouessant

Cherbourg
Omonville
Anse de
St Martin
Goury
Diélette
Carteret
Port Bail
Granville

Alderney

Jersey
St Helier

Sark
Herm
Guernsey
St Peter Port

Cancale
St Malo
St Briac
Dinard
St. Cast
St. Jacut
La Rance
Dinan
Erquy
Sables
d'Or-les-Pins
Dahouet
St Quay-Portrieux
Binic
St Brieuc/Le Légué

Ile Bréhat
Lézardrieux
Paimpol
Tréguier
Portrieux
Port
Blanc
Perros
Guirec
Ploumanac'h
Les Sept Iles
Trégastel
I. Grande
Trébeurden
Lannion
Locquirec
Primel
Morlaix
Penzé
Moguériec
Bloscon
Ile de
Batz
Roscoff
Pontusval
Le Corréjou
L'Aber Wrac'h
L'Aber Benoit
Argenton
L'Aberildut
Portsall
Melon
Le Conquet
Brest
Camaret
Molène
Ouessant

48°
30'
N

5°W   4°W   3°W   2°W

0   10   20   30   40   50
Nautical Miles

North Brittany

Cherbourg to Ouessant and the Channel Islands

ROYAL CRUISING CLUB
PILOTAGE FOUNDATION

John Lawson

Imray Laurie Norie & Wilson

Published by
Imray Laurie Norie & Wilson Ltd
Wych House The Broadway St Ives
Cambridgeshire PE27 5BT England
☎ +44 (0)1480 462114
Fax +44 (0)1480 496109
Email ilnw@imray.com
www.imray.com
2008

First edition 2001
Second edition 2008

ISBN 978 184623 069 1

British Library Cataloguing in Publication Data.
A catalogue record for this title is available from the British Library.

Printed in Singapore by Star Standard Industries Ltd

CORRECTIONAL SUPPLEMENTS

This pilot book may be amended at intervals by the issue of correctional supplements. These are published on the internet at our website www.imray.com and also via www.rccpf.org.uk and may be downloaded free of charge. Printed copies are also available on request from the publishers at the above address. Like this pilot, supplements are selective. Navigators requiring the latest definitive information are advised to refer to official hydrographic office data.

The Pilotage Foundation's website www.rccpf.org.uk includes book support files including waypoint lists, access to Google maps, mid-season updates and additional photographs.

CAUTION

Whilst every care has been taken to ensure that the information contained in this book is accurate, the RCC Pilotage Foundation, the authors and the publishers hereby formally disclaim any and all liability for any personal injury, loss and/or damage howsoever caused, whether by reason of any error, inaccuracy, omission or ambiguity in relation to the contents and/or information contained within this book. The book contains selected information and thus is not definitive. It does not contain all known information on the subject in hand and should not be relied on alone for navigational use: it should only be used in conjunction with official hydrographic data. This is particularly relevant to the plans, which should not be used for navigation.

The RCC Pilotage Foundation, the authors and publishers believe that the information which they have included is a useful aid to prudent navigation, but the safety of a vessel depends ultimately on the judgment of the skipper, who should assess all information, published or unpublished.

WAYPOINTS

This edition of the *North Brittany and the Channel Islands* pilot includes the introduction of waypoints. The RCC PF consider a waypoint to be a position likely to be helpful for navigation if entered into some form of electronic navigation system for use in conjunction with GPS. All waypoints are given to datum WGS 84 and every effort has been made to ensure their accuracy. Nevertheless, for each individual vessel, the standard of onboard equipment, aerial position, datum setting, correct entry of data and operator skill all play a part in their effectiveness. In particular it is vital for the navigator to note the datum of the chart in use and apply the necessary correction if plotting a GPS position on the chart.

We emphasise that we regard waypoints as an aid to navigation for use as the navigator decides. We hope that the waypoints in this pilot will help ease that navigational load.

POSITIONS
Positions given in the text and on plans are intended purely as an aid to locating the place in question on the chart.

PLANS
The plans in this guide are not to be used for navigation – they are designed to support the text and should always be used together with navigational charts. Every effort has been made to locate harbour and anchorage plans adjacent to the relevant text.

All bearings are given from seaward and refer to true north. Scales are indicated on the plans. Symbols are based on those used by the British Admiralty – users are referred to *Symbols and Abbreviations (5011)*.

Contents

In 1976 an American member of the Royal Cruising Club, Dr Fred Ellis, indicated that he wished to make a gift to the Club in memory of his father, the late Robert E Ellis, of his friends Peter Pye and John Ives and as a mark of esteem for Roger Pinckney. An independent charity known as the RCC Pilotage Foundation was formed and Dr Ellis added his house to his already generous gift of money to form the Foundation's permanent endowment. The Foundation's charitable objective is 'to advance the education of the public in the science and practice of navigation', which is at present achieved through the writing and updating of pilot books covering many diffent parts of the world.

The Foundation is extremely grateful and privileged to have been given the copyrights to books written by a number of distinguished authors and yachtsmen including the late Adlard Coles, Robin Brandon and Malcolm Robson. In return the Foundation has willingly accepted the task of keeping the original books up to date and many yachtsmen and women have helped (and are helping) the Foundation fulfil this commitment. In addition to the titles donated to the Foundation, several new books have been created and developed under the auspices of the Foundation. The Foundation works in close collaboration with three publishers – Imray Laurie Norie and Wilson, Adlard Coles Nautical and On Board Publications – and in addition publishes in its own name short run guides and pilot books for areas where limited demand does not justify large print runs. Several of the Foundation's books have been translated into French, German and Italian.

The Foundation runs its own website at www.rccpf.org.uk which not only lists all the publications but also contains free downloadable pilotage information.

The overall management of the Foundation is entrusted to trustees appointed by the Royal Cruising Club, with day-to-day operations being controlled by the Director. All these appointments are unpaid. In line with its charitable status, the Foundation distributes no profits; any surpluses are used to finance new books and developments and to subsidise those covering areas of low demand.

PUBLICATIONS OF THE RCC PILOTAGE FOUNDATION

Imray
The Baltic Sea
Norway
North Brittany and the Channel Islands
Faroe, Iceland and Greenland
Isles of Scilly
The Channel Islands
North Biscay
Atlantic Islands
Atlantic Spain & Portugal
Mediterranean Spain
 Costas del Azahar,
 Dorada & Brava
Mediterranean Spain
 Costas del Sol & Blanca
Islas Baleares
Corsica and North Sardinia
North Africa
Chile

Adlard Coles Nautical
Atlantic Crossing Guide
Pacific Crossing Guide

On Board Publications
South Atlantic Circuit
Havens and Anchorages for the South American Coast

The RCC Pilotage Foundation
RCC PF Website www.rccpf.org.uk
Cruising Guide to West Africa
Web pilots in the South Atlantic
Book support files
Passage planning guides

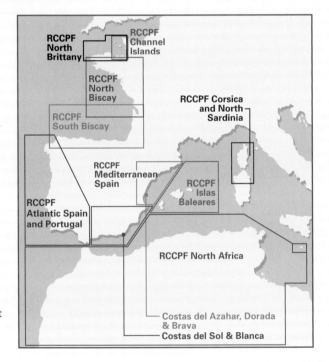

Foreword

The origins of this pilot book go back to 1952 when Blondie Hasler wrote the first *North Brittany Pilot*. This went through six editions, that in 1995 by Nick Heath under the aegis of the RCC Pilotage Foundation. In 2001 John Lawson took on the mantle and included the Channel Islands and the Normandy coast west of Cherbourg, to accommodate the large number of yachts following the route from the Solent and the East. Alderney, Guernsey, Herm, Sark and Jersey are covered but those wishing to visit Les Ecrehous, Les Minquiers and Iles Chausey, or indulge in serious rock hopping outside the main Channel Island ports and anchorages, should consult *The Channel Islands* by Peter Carnegie and the RCC Pilotage Foundation.

This book is in a new format, which John Lawson first adopted for his book *South Biscay*. Where possible pilotage directions are on the same pages as the plans of the routes or ports, and waypoints are positioned to lead straight in to the pilotage phase. Fuller lists of lights, waypoint details, charts and the Breton language glossary are given in Appendices.

There have been a number of changes on the coast and in the islands over the past six years. New marinas have appeared, more are in build, and there are many minor additions to harbours, anchorages and facilities ashore.

Sadly John Lawson died shortly after preparing this work. Subsequent ground recces have been carried by Peter Taylor and Robin Rundle whose meticulous work on their visits to the French coast line produced many photographs and brought the book up to date for publication. Martin and Elizabeth Walker similarly recced the Normandy coast and Peter Carnegie flew many hours to check or update many of the air photographs. Many of Nick Heath's 1995 photographs remain relevant and have been retained.

The Pilotage Foundation is grateful to the many contributors over the years, to those who have completed John Lawson's work and to Willie Wilson and his crew at Imray; also to William Bourne, Peter Carnegie, Graham Adam and Ros Hogbin for their assistance with proof reading.

This book covers a wonderful area for cruising but to quote from John Lawson's notes – 'There is a multitude of first class visual aids to navigation on the French and Channel Island coasts. These are essential for safety in these rock strewn areas with exceptional tidal range swept by fierce tidal streams. Modern electronic means and equipment help the navigator greatly but it is an unwise mariner who neglects his traditional pilotage in the final stages of an approach to the coast.'

The Pilotage Foundation welcomes feedback from yachtsmen and issues updating supplements as appropriate via the Publisher. Additional supporting files – including waypoint lists and further photographs, may be found at www.rccpf.org.uk.

M R Walker, Honorary Director
RCC Pilotage Foundation
March 2008

Captain J A F Lawson RN

The RCC Pilotage Foundation has charitable status and relies on yachtsmen to give their time to help in the production of pilot books and other aids to navigation. John Lawson was ideally suited for this. His long career in the Royal Navy, followed by years as skipper of a sail training vessel and a lifetime of sailing his own boat, gave him a deep practical knowledge. His contribution matched his enthusiasm and was considerable. It included authorship of *South Biscay, North Brittany and the Channel Islands,* and revision of *The Atlantic Crossing Guide.* He produced an innovative series of Passage Planning Guides, which are available without charge on the RCCPF website, and he continued to pass on his expertise to current yachtsmen right up to the time of his death.

Key to symbols used on the plans

⚓	harbour office
⛽	fuel (diesel, petrol)
⛴ (25T)	travel-lift
⚑	yacht club
⚓	anchorage
Ⓥ	visitors' moorings
►	slipway

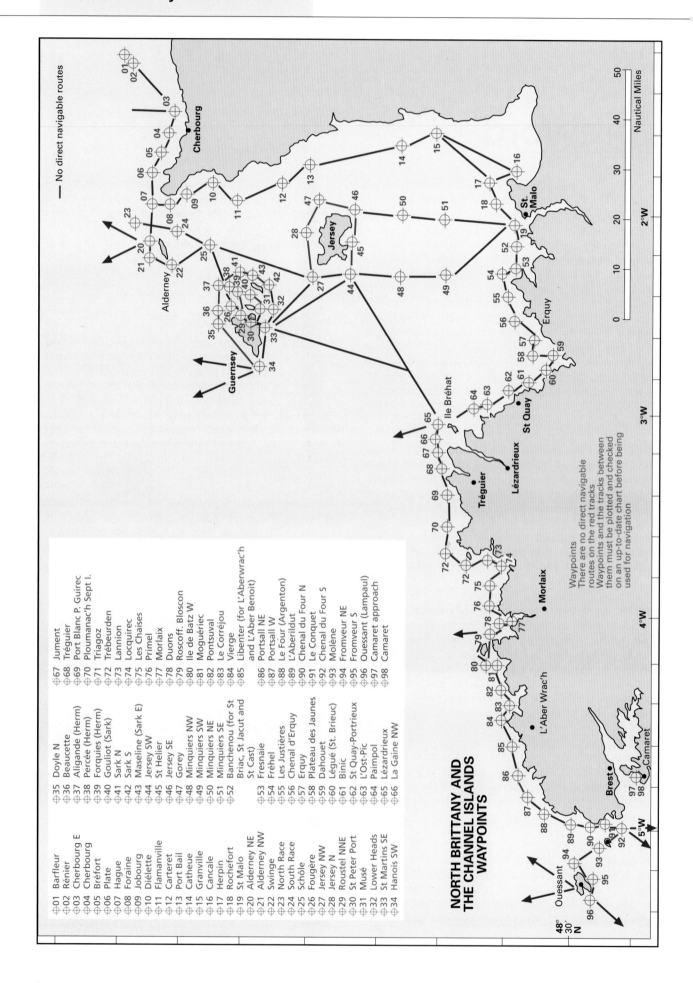

NORTH BRITTANY AND THE CHANNEL ISLANDS WAYPOINTS

— No direct navigable routes

Waypoints
There are no direct navigable routes on the red tracks
Waypoints and the tracks between them must be plotted and checked on an up-to-date chart before being used for navigation

Nautical Miles

⊕01 Barfleur
⊕02 Rénier
⊕03 Cherbourg E
⊕04 Cherbourg
⊕05 Bréfort
⊕06 Plate
⊕07 Hague
⊕08 Foraine
⊕09 Jobourg
⊕10 Diélette
⊕11 Flamanville
⊕12 Carteret
⊕13 Port Bail
⊕14 Catheue
⊕15 Granville
⊕16 Cancale
⊕17 Herpin
⊕18 Rochefort
⊕19 St Malo
⊕20 Alderney NE
⊕21 Alderney NW
⊕22 Swinge
⊕23 North Race
⊕24 South Race
⊕25 Schôle
⊕26 Fougère
⊕27 Jersey NW
⊕28 Jersey N
⊕29 Roustel NNE
⊕30 St Peter Port
⊕31 Musé
⊕32 Lower Heads
⊕33 St Martins SE
⊕34 Hanois SW

⊕35 Doyle N
⊕36 Beaucette
⊕37 Aligande (Herm)
⊕38 Percée (Herm)
⊕39 Forquies (Herm)
⊕40 Gouliot (Sark)
⊕41 Sark N
⊕42 Sark S
⊕43 Maseline (Sark E)
⊕44 Jersey SW
⊕45 St Helier
⊕46 Jersey SE
⊕47 Gorey
⊕48 Minquiers NW
⊕49 Minquiers SW
⊕50 Minquiers NE
⊕51 Minquiers SE
⊕52 Banchenou (for St Briac, St Jacut and St Cast)
⊕53 Fresnaie
⊕54 Fréhel
⊕55 Les Justières
⊕56 Chenal d'Erquy
⊕57 Erquy
⊕58 Plateau des Jaunes.
⊕59 Dahouet
⊕60 Légué (St. Brieuc)
⊕61 Binic
⊕62 St Quay-Portrieux
⊕63 L'Ost-Pic
⊕64 Paimpol
⊕65 Lézardrieux
⊕66 La Gaine NW

⊕67 Jument
⊕68 Tréguier
⊕69 Port Blanc P. Guirec
⊕70 Ploumana'ch Sept I.
⊕71 Triagoz
⊕72 Trébeurden
⊕73 Lannion
⊕74 Locquirec
⊕75 Les Chaises
⊕76 Primel
⊕77 Morlaix
⊕78 Duons
⊕79 Roscoff. Bloscon
⊕80 Ile de Batz W
⊕81 Moguériec
⊕82 Pontsuval
⊕83 Le Corréjou
⊕84 Vierge
⊕85 Libenter (for L'Aberwrac'h and L'Aber Benoit)
⊕86 Portsall NE
⊕87 Portsall W
⊕88 Le Four (Argenton)
⊕89 L'Aberildut
⊕90 Chenal du Four N
⊕91 Le Conquet
⊕92 Chenal du Four S
⊕93 Molène
⊕94 Fromveur NE
⊕95 Fromveur S
⊕96 Ouessant (Lampaul)
⊕97 Camaret approach
⊕98 Camaret

Introduction

Cruising in Normandy and Brittany

Cruising conditions vary appreciably if not dramatically between the sandy and low-lying shores of the Cotentin peninsula in the east, to the rock-strewn and iron-bound coasts of the west. The whole area is subject to strong tidal streams and a great range of tide in the south east and in the Channel Islands, which gradually decreases as westing is made. The likelihood of swell and fog increases at the western end and accurate navigation is always of importance in the whole area where mistakes in narrow channels and rocky areas can have severe consequences.

GPS can be a great comfort with enhanced accuracy if using DGPS or other systems such as EGNOS. However although British Admiralty (BA) charts have now almost all been changed to WGS84 datum in these areas, a lot of French (SHOM) charts and some privately produced charts have not yet been converted. The process of conversion will be continuing for some time yet so the datum of the chart should always be checked before use and a correction applied if necessary. Also while GPS allows for accurate navigation to the outer end of a narrow channel or entrance (a summary sheet is given on page viii) leading marks or lines are still essential for safe navigation. These are given for each port or anchorage where they exist. A well-operated radar set can also be a very useful navigational aid in poor visibility. Having said that, the coast is well endowed with lights, beacons and buoys and even insignificant harbours may have well-lit and well-marked leading lines.

A successful and quick passage will often depend on timing to make the tidal streams work in one's favour. While this is relatively easy when going E or W along the N coast of Brittany, it can be confusing

The rock-strewn, iron-bound coast of west Brittany

in the Channel Islands. This section makes recommendations on optimum departure times to proceed in any direction from each port.

Marinas or harbours specifically for yachts are spaced at convenient distances throughout the area. For those unwilling to pay for these facilities, there are hundreds of anchorages in sheltered or not so sheltered surroundings, many of which have been included.

The Bretons and Channel Islanders may have their occasional differences over fishing rights but they are both friendly and helpful to visiting yachtsmen. The Celtic ties between the Welsh, Cornish and Bretons precede Roman times and are maintained today in many exchange visits and folk festivals. The Channel Islands have been part of the United Kingdom since William the Conqueror brought them as part of the Kingdom of Normandy in 1066, the only break being the German occupation during the second world war.

Tides and tidal streams

The range of tides is the highest in European waters in the Baie de Mont St Michel where the highest spring tide can reach 13m with a range of 12m. These decrease at the W and E ends of the area (around 6m at Ouessant and Cherbourg but the tidal streams increase dramatically to 9 knots or more in the choke points of Passage du Fromveur (inside Ouessant) and the Alderney Race by Cap de la Hague. Tides and their streams are always a factor to be considered on these coasts even at neaps. Tidal Stream diagrams are given on pages 6 and 7 and tidal information is shown on a blue blackground in the text.

Spring tides can reach 13m (St Jacut)

Provisions and shopping

Most villages now have their own *supermarché* but there are a number of harbours where these are some distance from the landing and all that can be obtained within a short walk are bread and milk. Details are noted for each place; generally shopping for food and drink becomes more of an exercise the further W one gets and a bicycle becomes more necessary for the less energetic. Shops selling bread open early and most close mid-morning. French bread does not keep but may be revived by a short spell in the oven after 24 hours. Ask for *pain complet* for longer lasting and wholemeal bread. Fish and crustaceans can be found readily along the coast and it is often possible to buy direct from the fishing facility in the fishing ports.

Yacht chandlers will be found only in the major marinas (Cherbourg, Granville, St Malo, St Quay and the Channel Islands but ironmongers selling some chandlery, or fishing or commercial chandlers will be found elsewhere.

Formalities

An ensign should be flown from 0800 to 2100 and a French courtesy flag up to 12M from the coast.

It is essential that a Certificate of Registry, or for British yachts the Small Ships Registry document is carried on board and produced on demand to the authorities. Photocopies are NOT acceptable and failure to produce the originals is likely to lead to a fine on the spot.

The following documents should also be carried:

- RYA Certificate of Competence at least for the skipper.
- Insurance Certificate for the yacht (NOT a copy).
- Passports for all on board. These are likely to be demanded if boarded by the Customs, will be needed for return to the UK by other means and are useful as a means of identification.

Yachts registered in an EU country arriving in French waters need not complete any formalities (and should not fly a Q flag) unless they are carrying goods dutiable in France or they have non-EU residents on board. In these cases entry should be made at a port with a Customs office (noted in the text) and a Q flag flown until cleared. The Channel Islands are not part of the EU.

Money

Cash machines can be found in unexpected places and are not confined to banks. All but the smallest Post Office will advance cash against a card. Travellers' cheques are negotiable.

Value Added Tax (VAT)

The RYA issues a guide on VAT for yachts and this should be consulted if in doubt. In general, EU yachts must be able to demonstrate that they have paid VAT in order to enjoy freedom of movement within the EU. A VAT receipt issued by the builder should satisfy French Customs, and a Bill of Sale and Registration Document issued in the UK may do so particularly for an older yacht. A yacht built, or first registered before the first introduction of VAT in the UK and which cannot produce a VAT receipt may have a problem. Failure to carry the correct documentation may result in a non-negotiable demand for the tax to be paid immediately at the French rate which is currently above the UK one of 17½%.

Glorious beaches abound along the whole coast, Anse de Porsmoguer *Peter Taylor*

Yachts registered outside the EU, on which VAT has not been paid, may be temporarily imported into the Union tax-free by non-EU nationals. At present the time limit for importation is six months but this may be increased. In the past it has sometimes been possible to obtain an extension to the permitted length of stay if a yacht has been laid up in the EU while the owners return to their home country.

New yachts, exported VAT-free from the UK and calling in France en route to a non-EU destination are a special case on which early advice should be taken regarding the current time limits that apply to them.

The penalties of poor pilotage on a rocky coast are remembered at Cap de la Hague

Search and Rescue

The *Centres Régionaux Opérationels de Surveillance et de Sauvetage* (CROSS) are Maritime Rescue Co-ordination Centres (MRCCs). CROSS Joburg (near Cap de la Hague) covers the area from Cherbourg to Granville with a sub-station at Granville. CROSS Corsen (near Le Conquet) covers the area from Granville to Ile d'Ouessant with sub-stations at Cap Fréhel, Bodic (near Lézardrieux), Ile de Batz (near Roscoff) and Le Stiff (Ouessant). They will respond to COSPAS/SARSAT emergency transmissions on EPIRBs, to DSC activation of Ch 70 and to emergency calls on Ch 16. VHF coverage of the whole area is total. Medical advice can be given from both MRCCs.

Telephones

The telephones accept cards and not cash. These telephone cards may be obtained from Post Offices, tobacconists, newsagents and some cafés/bars. Mobile coverage coastwise is good.

Yacht Clubs

There are yacht clubs and sailing schools in most French harbours; they are invariably hospitable to visitors. Assistance or advice is readily given and there are often showers available.

Inland waterways

The only access to the French inland waterways in this pilot is from St Malo, La Rance and Dinan but there are many attractive estuaries.

Lights

A brief description of all lights whether ashore or on buoys is given in the pilotage directions for each port and shown on the plans. Full descriptions of the lights are shown in the Light List at Appendix 1. Both follow the conventions in *Admiralty List of Lights*. This section of the French coast is covered by light numbers 1469 to 1524, and from 1632 to 1886 (NP 74 Vol A).

Beacon towers and beacons

Beacons usually consist of a single, spindly post with or without a topmark. Beacon towers are substantial structures usually of masonry that may or may not have a light.

Fishing

Nearly every port or harbour in this book has its fishing fleet from a few inshore open boats to sea-going fleets that are often away for weeks at a time. There are only a few ports where yachts and fishing boats are not mutually catered for and the French usually manage to accommodate the needs of both users in one port. The fishermen are friendly to yachtsmen but berths alongside fishing boats should always be sought rather than taken.

There is a lot of lobster and crab potting along the coast and a sharp lookout should be kept for their markers which are often awash or just under the surface in the strong streams.

It is not all rocks, swell and strong tidal streams in North Brittany. There are many attractive estuaries. Château Roche Jagu up river from Lézardrieux

Many of the estuaries and rivers have oyster and shellfish beds, and fish farms continue to appear in the bays. Anchoring is prohibited in these areas.

Laying up

There are many ports and marinas where yachts may be hauled out and/or laid up where the prices are cheaper than in the UK. Details and suitability are noted in the text for each port where applicable.

Travel and crew changes

Road, rail and air communications are good all along the coast to the rest of France and to the UK, mostly via the Channel Islands but direct and frequent ferries run to England from Cherbourg, St Malo and Roscoff. The various small airfields connect with Paris but Dinard connects with the Channel Islands, and Cherbourg with the UK and Channel Islands. There may be budget air routes to airfields. Details may be found in each port.

The radio watchtower on Ouessant which is part of the CROSS Corsen MRCC. Le Stiff lighthouse on the right

Technical and navigational information

Harbour plans

The plans have been drawn solely to illustrate the pilotage directions on the same page. They should not be used directly for navigation but only as a means to follow the pilotage directions.

Chart datum and tidal heights

Chart Datum (CD) is fixed at a level below which the sea level will not fall in normal circumstances, but it may do so under extreme meteorological conditions. The chart datum of the French charts is the same as the British Admiralty (BA) charts. The figures on the charts and plans of soundings and drying heights are both related directly to CD.

Predicted heights of tides have been taken from *Admiralty Tide Tables Vol I* and are related to CD and to times of HW and LW at Cherbourg, St Helier or Brest; the same times for St Malo are only referred to for ports and places between Cancale and Chenal d'Erquy including La Rance. Simplified conversion figures for times and heights in relation to these standard ports are shown for most of the minor ports; these figures are within 15 minutes and 0.2m of the given figures.

The coast is well endowed with lighthouses. Les Heaux between Tréguier and Lézardrieux

Bearings

Bearings are given in degrees True from seaward. Magnetic variation is about 3¼°W throughout the area (2006) decreasing about 8′ annually. Magnetic bearings in compass points are used for photographic views and sometimes in the text to express direction.

Heights

On BA charts these are above MHWS and apply to air clearances under bridges or overhead obstructions. French charts use a different datum for these clearances which will appear greater than the ones on BA charts.

Horizontal chart datum – satellite derived positions

Positions derived from GPS are usually expressed in relation of WGS84. While all BA charts in this area are now converted to this, some French (SHOM) and private charts are not yet. Note should be taken on SHOM and private charts of any correction that should be applied to equate to WGS84. This caution applies to some electronic (but not to ARCS) as well as paper charts.

Caution should be exercised if using pre-metric BA or old SHOM or private charts which do not show any correction. There may be significant discrepancies between the latitude and longitude on the chart and that shown by GPS set to any datum.

Charts

Details of BA and Imray charts are shown in Appendix 3 on page 197. They are also shown in the text for each port. BA charts in paper, ARCS form or Small Craft (SC) editions may be obtained from any chart agent and are corrected up to the date of purchase. They may be kept corrected at no cost from www.nmwebsearch.com or by buying the weekly paper *Notices to Mariners*. ARCS charts carry the same numbers as paper charts.

Details of SHOM charts may be found from www.shom.fr under *cartes* and *catalogue*. SHOM charts may be ordered through Imray, Laurie, Norie and Wilson Ltd, Wych House, The Broadway, St Ives, Huntingdon, Cambridgeshire PE 27 5BT. ☎ +44(0)1480 462114; *Fax* +44(0)1480 496109; www.imray.com or from the French chart agents in the principal ports. Some chandlers hold a small stock of local charts. SHOM charts with the suffix P are printed on waterproof paper and folded like a map for small craft.

The French also produce the Fluviacarte series of charts to a scale of 1:50,000 with large scale inserts specifically for yachtsmen. These may also be obtained from Imray, Laurie, Norie and Wilson.

In general BA charts give an excellent coverage of the area and are increasingly convergent in coverage, scale and style with the SHOM charts but with slightly different symbols and conventions. The SHOM chart numbers are only given in the text where the scale is substantially larger for a particular port or area.

Weather forecasts
All VHF weather forecasts are in French and English.
ALL TIMES LOCAL
The French forecast areas are:
Cherbourg to Roscoff – CASQUETS
Roscoff to Ouessant - OUESSANT

On Ch 80
From CROSS Joburg At 0715, 1545, 1915
From Granville At 0703, 1533, 1903

On Ch 79
From CROSS Corsen At 0150, 0450, 0750, 1050, 1350,
1650, 1950, 2250
From Cap Fréhel At 0545, 0803, 1203, 1633, 2003
From Bodic At 0533, 0745, 1145, 1615, 1945
From Ile de Batz At 0515, 0733, 1133, 1603, 1933
From Le Stiff At 0503, 0715, 1115, 1545, 1915

Navtex
Niton E 518kHz At 0040, 0840, 2040
I 490kHz. At 0520, 1720
T 490kHz. At 0710, 1910 in French
Corsen A 518kHz. At 0000, 1200
E 490kHz. At 0840, 2040 in French
All *capitaineries* and Marina Offices usually have a daily
weather map available.

Telephone Weather Service (in French)
☎ 008 92 68 08 08 (€0.34 per minute)
www.weatheronline.co.uk provides free synoptic charts
and long range forecasts.
www.theyr.net provides free synoptic charts from actuals
to 3-day forecasts.

Apart from ARCS and ECN there are several commercial electronic chart systems which will have their own followers.

Radio services

Port radios are shown for each harbour where they function. Only aero radio beacons still transmit.

Besides providing a full VHF emergency cover of the area CROSS Joburg and Corsen also provide navigational assistance on request in an emergency on Ch 80 (Joburg) and Ch 79 (Corsen). This is particularly relevant in the Chenal du Four area where fogs are more prevalent.

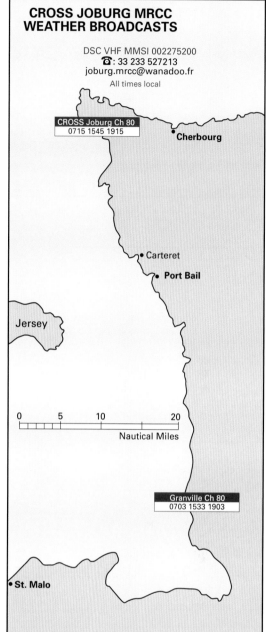

CROSS JOBURG MRCC WEATHER BROADCASTS

DSC VHF MMSI 002275200
☎: 33 233 527213
joburg.mrcc@wanadoo.fr
All times local

CROSS Joburg Ch 80
0715 1545 1915
Cherbourg
Carteret
Port Bail
Jersey

0   5   10   20
Nautical Miles

Granville Ch 80
0703 1533 1903

St. Malo

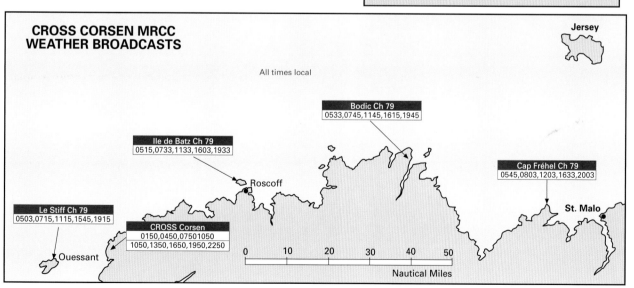

CROSS CORSEN MRCC WEATHER BROADCASTS

Jersey

All times local

Bodic Ch 79
0533,0745,1145,1615,1945

Ile de Batz Ch 79
0515,0733,1133,1603,1933

Cap Fréhel Ch 79
0545,0803,1203,1633,2003

Roscoff

Le Stiff Ch 79
0503,0715,1115,1545,1915

CROSS Corsen
0150,0450,0750,1050
1050,1350,1650,1950,2250

St. Malo

Ouessant

0   10   20   30   40   50
Nautical Miles

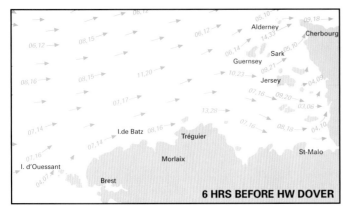

6 HRS BEFORE HW DOVER

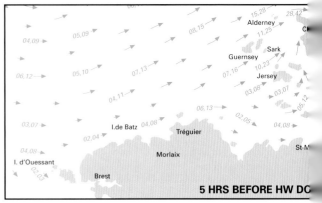

5 HRS BEFORE HW DOVER

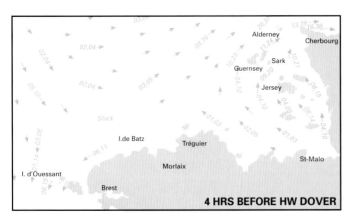

4 HRS BEFORE HW DOVER

3 HRS BEFORE HW DOVER

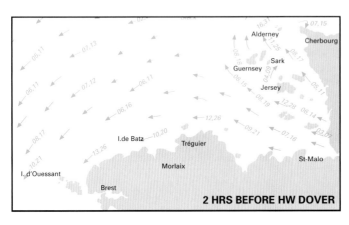

2 HRS BEFORE HW DOVER

1 HR BEFORE HW DOVER

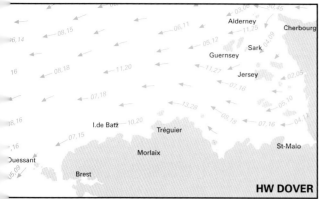

HW DOVER

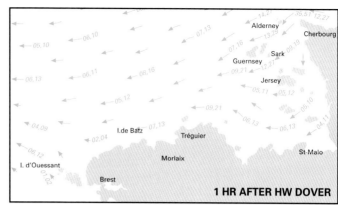

1 HR AFTER HW DOVER

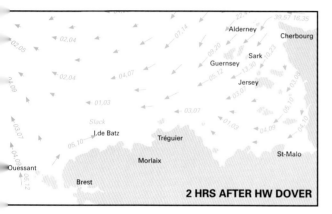

2 HRS AFTER HW DOVER

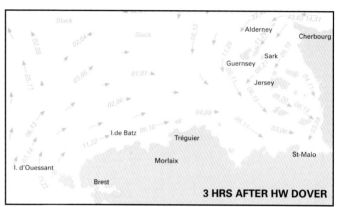

3 HRS AFTER HW DOVER

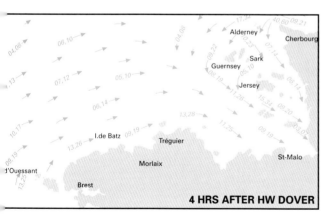

4 HRS AFTER HW DOVER

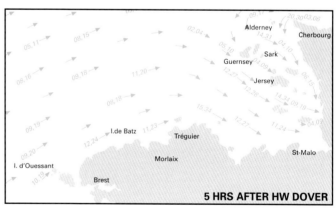

5 HRS AFTER HW DOVER

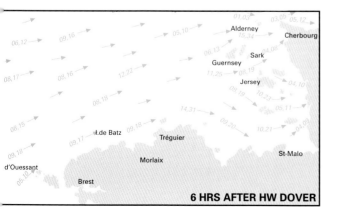

6 HRS AFTER HW DOVER

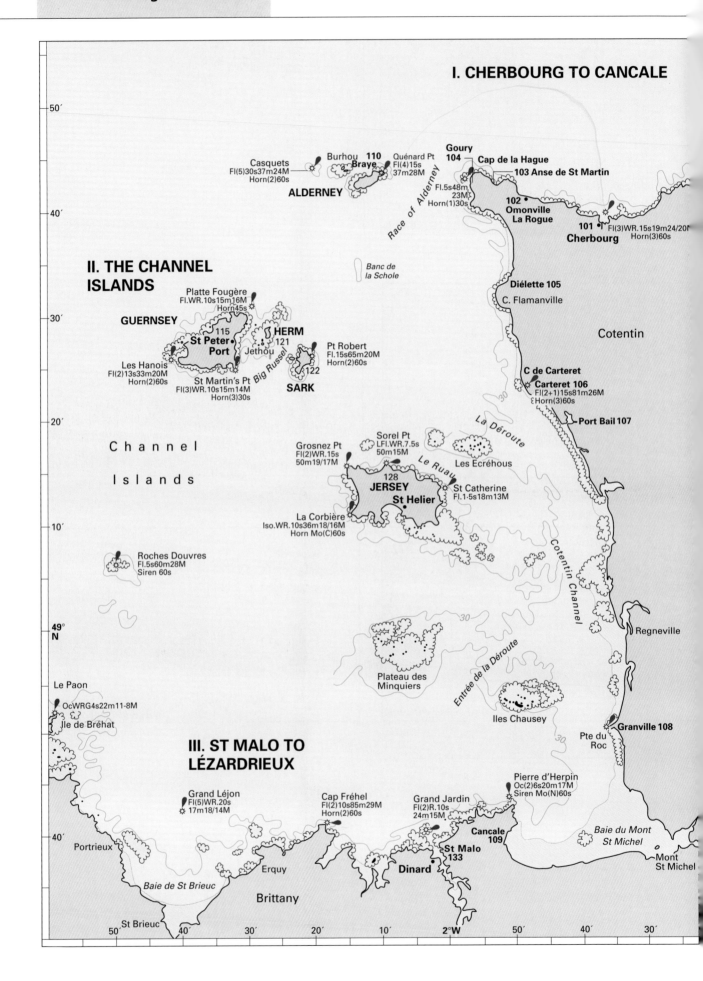

I. CHERBOURG TO CANCALE

Casquets
Fl(5)30s37m24M
Horn(2)60s

Burhou **110**
Braye

ALDERNEY

Quénard Pt
Fl(4)15s
37m28M

Goury
104

Cap de la Hague

103 Anse de St Martin

Fl.5s48m
23M
Horn(1)30s

102
Omonville
La Rogue

101 Fl(3)WR.15s19m24/20M
Horn(3)60s

Cherbourg

Race of Alderney

Banc de
la Schole

Diélette 105
C. Flamanville

Cotentin

II. THE CHANNEL
ISLANDS

Platte Fougère
Fl.WR.10s15m16M
Horn45s

GUERNSEY

115

St Peter
Port

Les Hanois
Fl(2)13s33m20M
Horn(2)60s

HERM

121
Jethou

Big Russel

St Martin's Pt
Fl(3)WR.10s15m14M
Horn(3)30s

122

SARK

Pt Robert
Fl.15s65m20M
Horn(2)60s

C de Carteret
Carteret **106**
Fl(2+1)15s81m26M
Horn(3)60s

Port Bail 107

La Déroute

C h a n n e l

I s l a n d s

Grosnez Pt
Fl(2)WR.15s
50m19/17M

Sorel Pt
LFl.WR.7.5s
50m15M

Le Ruau

Les Ecréhous

128
JERSEY
St Helier

St Catherine
Fl.1.5s18m13M

La Corbière
Iso.WR.10s36m18/16M
Horn Mo(C)60s

Roches Douvres
Fl.5s60m28M
Siren 60s

49°
N

Cotentin Channel

Regneville

Le Paon

OcWRG4s22m11-8M

Ile de Bréhat

Plateau des
Minquiers

Entrée de la Déroute

Iles Chausey

Pte du
Roc

Granville 108

III. ST MALO TO
LÉZARDRIEUX

Pierre d'Herpin
Oc(2)6s20m17M
Siren Mo(N)60s

Grand Léjon
Fl(5)WR.20s
17m18/14M

Cap Fréhel
Fl(2)10s85m29M
Horn(2)60s

Grand Jardin
Fl(2)R.10s
24m15M

Cancale
109

Baie du Mont
St Michel

Portrieux

St Brieuc

Baie de St Brieuc

Erquy

Brittany

St Malo
133

Dinard

Mont
St Michel

I. Cherbourg to Cancale

101 Cherbourg

102 Omonville-la-Rogue

103 Anse de St Martin (Port Racine)

104 Goury

105 Diélette

106 Carteret

107 Portbail

108 Granville

109 Cancale

⊕01	Barfleur	49°42′.90N 01°15′.50W
⊕02	Rénier	49°45′.00N 01°22′.00W
⊕03	Cherbourg E	49°40′.75N 01°35′.40W
⊕04	Cherbourg	49°40′.75N 01°39′.30W
⊕05	Bréfort	49°44′.00N 01°51′.00W
⊕06	Plate	49°44′.40N 01°55′.60W
⊕07	Hague	49°44′.00N 01°58′.00W
⊕08	Foraine	49°43′.00N 01°59′.00W
⊕09	Jobourg	49°38′.80N 01°59′.00W
⊕10	Diélette	49°33′.37N 01°52′.17W
⊕11	Flamanville	49°32′.50N 01°55′.00W
⊕12	Carteret	49°21′.20N 01°48′.06W
⊕13	Port Bail	49°17′.50N 01°45′.40W
⊕14	Catheue	48°57′.80N 01°41′.50W
⊕15	Granville	48°49′.50N 01°37′.70W
⊕16	Cancale	48°40′.06N 01°49′.40W
⊕17	Herpin	48°44′.50N 01°48′.00W
⊕18	Rochefort	48°43′.50N 01°58′.40W

This section of the Normandy coast is included so that those sailing from the Solent or further east can visit ports in France en route, as well as the Channel Islands. However, apart from Cherbourg and three anchorages, access to the other three marinas at Diélette, Carteret and Granville is limited to deep draught vessels for some 2 hours either side of HW.

The coast is sandy and low-lying and is divided by the tidal gate of the Alderney Race off Cap de la Hague. Here the streams can run at up to 10 knots at springs by the Cap and overfalls are dangerous and extensive in wind over tide conditions. Advice for transiting the Race are shown in the Alderney and the Race section on page 37.

There are two anchorages sheltered from the west between Cherbourg and Cap de la Hague; Omonville-la-Rogue and Anse de St Martin – where a favourable stream round the Cap can be awaited.

South and east of Jersey are the extensive rocky areas of the Minquiers and Les Ecréhous both of which are part of Jersey and which have a few houses on the larger rocks. To the west of Granville lie the French Iles Chausey. Reference should be made to the RCC Pilotage Foundation's *The Channel Islands* by Peter Carnegie to navigate these areas.

In the southeast corner lies the wide shallow Baie of Mont St Michel with miles of oyster and shellfish beds and the highest tides in Europe.

Cherbourg marina (and old inner harbour) entrance from Port Chantereyne mole head   *Martin Walker*

HW DOVER

HW St Helier +0500

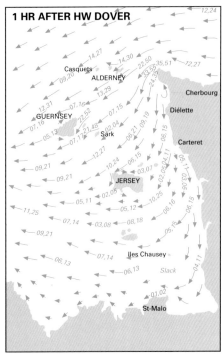

1 HR AFTER HW DOVER

HW St Helier +0600

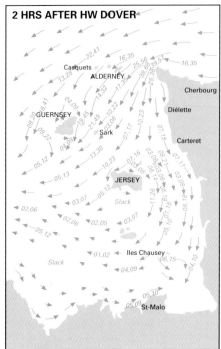

2 HRS AFTER HW DOVER

HW St Helier −0530

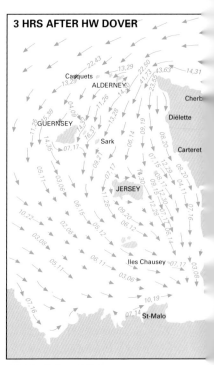

3 HRS AFTER HW DOVER

HW St Helier −0430

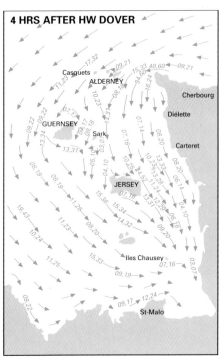

4 HRS AFTER HW DOVER

HW St Helier −0330

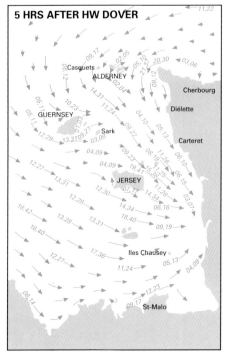

5 HRS AFTER HW DOVER

HW St Helier −0230

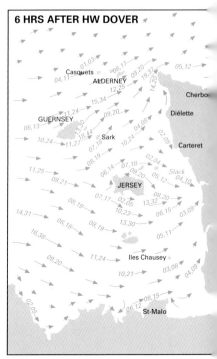

6 HRS AFTER HW DOVER

HW St Helier −0130

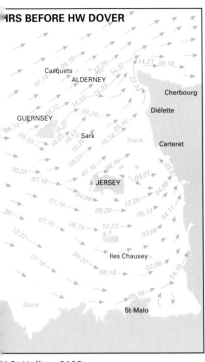

HRS BEFORE HW DOVER

V St Helier –0100

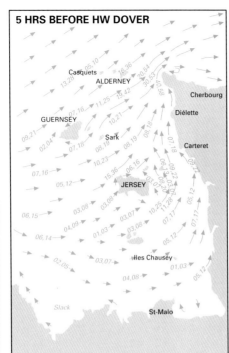

5 HRS BEFORE HW DOVER

HW St Helier

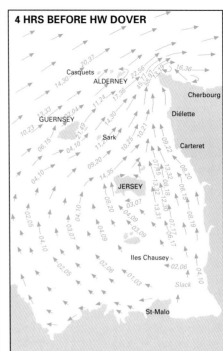

4 HRS BEFORE HW DOVER

HW St Helier +0100

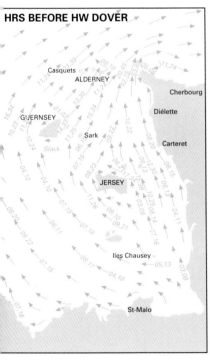

HRS BEFORE HW DOVER

HW St Helier +0200

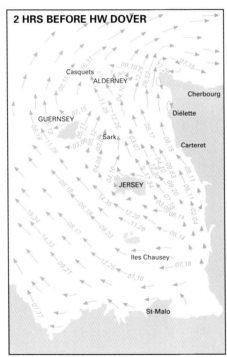

2 HRS BEFORE HW DOVER

HW St Helier +0300

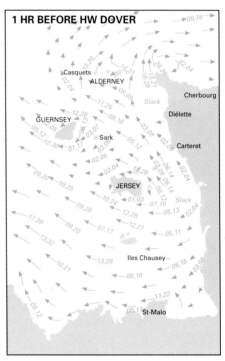

1 HR BEFORE HW DOVER

HW St Helier +0400

I. CHERBOURG TO CANCALE

The coast from Cap de la Hague to Mont St Michel

From the yachtsman's point of view the west coast of the Cotentin peninsula is pretty unpromising. It is shallow, there are a number of dangers well offshore and the harbours are all tidal limited. To the north are the fierce streams of the Alderney Race and to the south the largest range of tides in Europe. However, ashore it is a mellow and pleasant countryside largely untouched by foreign visitors and tourism with some of the best beaches in Normandy. It is well worthwhile hiring a car for a day or so to explore some of the hinterland and the following are possible diversions (From N to S).

A visit to CROSS Joburg.

A visit to the nuclear reprocessing plant at Flamanville (Open 0900–1800 April to September. 3 hour tour. ☎ 02 33 02 61 04.

The old town of Bricquebec 15km inland from Carteret with a well-preserved 12th-century castle.

The shallow estuary of Regnéville is only suitable for multihulls or bilge keelers but has the market town of Lessay at its head with a beautifully restored monastery. Charles Lindberg landed here at the end of the first transatlantic flight in 1927. Not far from Lessay is the ancient gem of Château de Pirou.

Granville is a popular resort but a dull comparison with St Malo except for the vicinity of Iles Chausey which are well worth a day trip.

Mont St Michel rates a day to itself. Only a bold navigator would do it by boat but a visit by car early in the day before the coaches arrive is rewarding.

Tidal streams

The Alderney Race attains its greatest rates 1M west of La Foraine beacon tower in the approaches to Goury, up to 10 knots N-going, 6½ knots S-going at springs. However these rates fall off appreciably as the harbour is approached and may be replaced by an opposite eddy close inshore.

The stream turns to the NNE 1M to the west of La Foraine at -0200 HW St Helier and to the S at +0430 HW St Helier.

La Haize du Raz passage inside Gros du Raz lighthouse is passable but only with SHOM chart 7133 and a suitable rise of tide.

See page 37 for transit of Alderney Race

DISTANCE TABLE

	Cherbourg	A de St-Martin	Goury	Alderney	Diélette	Guernsey	Carteret	Portbail	Jersey (St H)	Granville	Is Chausey	Cancale	St-Malo	St-Briac	St-Jacut	St-Cast	B de Fresnaie	Erquy	Dahouet	St-Brieuc	Binic	St-Q/Portrieux	Paimpol	Ile Bréhat	Lézardrieux	Pontrieux	Tréguier
Cherbourg		12	16	24	26	42	37	41	57	69	69	86	89	89	89	89	90	92	97	103	105	104	87	82	87	93	93
A de St-Martin	12		4	12	14	30	25	29	45	57	57	74	77	77	77	77	78	80	85	91	93	92	75	70	75	81	81
Goury	16	4		10	10	27	22	26	42	54	43	71	74	74	74	74	75	77	82	88	90	89	72	67	72	78	78
Alderney	24	12	10		17	22	28	32	40	60	58	71	72	72	73	73	73	76	80	85	81	79	67	64	69	75	75
Diélette	26	14	10	17		28	13	17	33	48	48	61	64	67	69	72	74	68	83	90	83	85	68	63	68	74	74
Guernsey	42	30	27	22	28		30	32	28	54	47	58	54	52	52	52	51	50	54	57	54	51	44	43	48	54	50
Carteret	37	25	22	28	13	30		4	22	35	35	47	44	46	48	51	53	63	68	73	73	72	63	62	67	73	73
Portbail	41	29	26	32	17	32	4		21	31	31	44	42	44	46	49	51	61	66	73	73	73	62	60	65	71	71
Jersey (St H)	57	45	42	40	33	28	22	21		30	25	34	35	35	35	35	35	37	43	48	48	45	44	42	47	53	60
Granville	69	73	70	62	48	54	35	31	30		10	13	22	26	28	31	33	43	48	55	65	65	74	77	82	88	91
Is Chausey	69	73	70	62	48	47	35	31	25	10		13	14	18	20	23	25	35	40	47	57	58	67	70	75	81	84
Cancale	86	74	71	71	61	58	43	39	34	13	13		17	21	23	26	28	38	43	50	60	61	70	70	75	81	84
St-Malo	89	77	74	72	64	54	44	42	35	22	14	17		7	9	12	14	24	29	36	36	37	46	46	51	57	60
St-Briac	89	77	74	72	67	52	46	44	35	26	18	21	7		2	5	7	17	22	29	29	29	39	39	44	50	53
St-Jacut	89	77	74	73	69	52	48	46	35	28	20	23	9	2		3	5	15	20	27	27	27	28	37	42	48	51
St-Cast	89	77	74	73	72	52	51	49	35	31	23	26	12	5	3		2	12	17	24	24	25	34	34	39	45	48
B de Fresnaie	90	78	75	73	74	51	53	51	35	33	25	28	14	7	5	2		10	15	22	22	23	32	32	37	43	46
Erquy	92	80	77	76	68	50	63	61	37	43	35	38	24	17	15	12	10		5	12	14	14	25	25	30	36	40
Dahouet	97	85	82	80	73	54	68	66	43	48	40	43	29	22	20	17	15	5		7	10	11	25	25	28	34	39
St-Brieuc	103	91	88	85	80	57	73	73	48	55	47	50	36	29	27	24	22	12	7		6	9	24	24	29	35	42
Binic	105	93	90	81	83	54	73	73	48	65	57	60	36	39	27	24	22	14	10	6		3	18	17	22	28	31
St-Q/Portrieux	104	92	89	79	85	51	72	73	45	65	58	61	37	30	28	25	23	14	11	9	3		15	14	19	25	28
Paimpol	87	75	72	67	68	44	63	62	44	74	67	70	46	39	37	34	32	25	25	24	18	15		8	13	19	22
Ile Bréhat	82	70	67	64	63	43	62	60	42	77	70	70	46	39	37	34	32	25	23	24	17	14	8		5	11	18
Lézardrieux	87	75	72	69	68	48	67	65	47	82	75	75	51	44	42	39	37	30	28	29	22	19	13	5		6	18
Pontrieux	93	81	78	75	74	54	73	71	53	88	81	81	57	50	48	45	43	36	34	35	28	25	19	11	6		24
Tréguier	93	81	78	75	74	50	73	71	60	91	84	84	60	53	51	48	46	40	39	42	31	28	22	18	18	24	

Distances are given over the shortest navigable route and are measured to and from inner harbour or anchorage

101 Cherbourg

A huge commercial and naval harbour with a large marina, Port Chantereyne, accessible at all time and in all weathers; 60 miles from the Solent it has everything for the yachtsman.

Location
N side of Cotentin peninsula between Cap Barfleur and Cap de la Hague

Shelter
First class

Warning
Strong cross streams on approach

Depth restrictions
Min. 5m in approaches; 3–4.5m in marina

Night entry
Leading lights and very well lit

Tidal information
A Standard Port

Mean height of tide (m)

HWS	HWN	LWN	LWS
6.4	5.0	2.5	1.1

Tidal streams
-0330 HW Cherb E-going starts
+0215 HW Cherb W-going starts

Berthing
On pontoons with fingers

Facilities
Those of a large city and major marina

Charts
BA 1106 (50), 2602 (10)
C 5604.3
Imray C32 (Plan), C33A

Weather
CROSS Joburg Ch 80 at 0715, 1545 and 1915 LT

Radio
Marina Ch 09 C/S Chantereyne

Telephone
☎ 33 (0)2 33 87 65 70
Email capitainerie.cherbourg@ville-cherbourg.fr

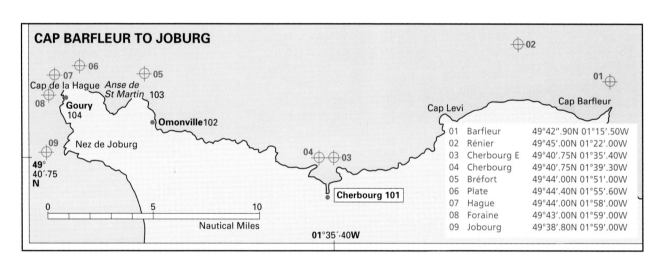

CAP BARFLEUR TO JOBURG

01	Barfleur	49°42".90N 01°15'.50W
02	Rénier	49°45'.00N 01°22'.00W
03	Cherbourg E	49°40'.75N 01°35'.40W
04	Cherbourg	49°40'.75N 01°39'.30W
05	Bréfort	49°44'.00N 01°51'.00W
06	Plate	49°44'.40N 01°55'.60W
07	Hague	49°44'.00N 01°58'.00W
08	Foraine	49°43'.00N 01°59'.00W
09	Jobourg	49°38'.80N 01°59'.00W

Cherbourg   *Patrick Roach*

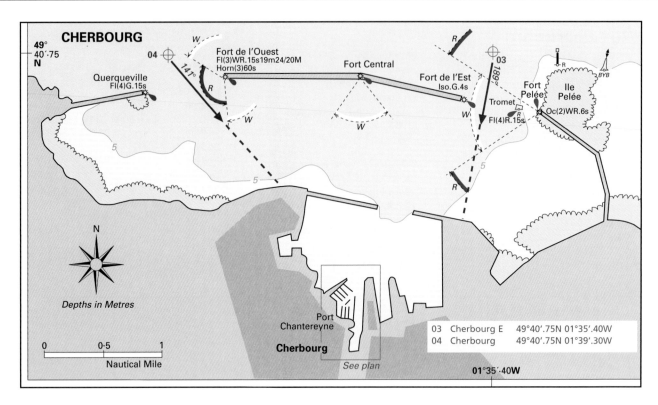

PILOTAGE

Approaches

From north

Navigate to ⊕03 off the E entrance or to ⊕04 off the West. There are no dangers or difficulties from this direction except to allow for the cross tidal streams.

By day

Various towers, TV masts and forts are conspicuous on the skyline above the town as is the breakwater with Fort Central in the middle of it.

By night

The E entrance is lit at Ile Pelée Oc(2)WR.6s on its E side and Fort de l'Est Iso.G.4s on its W side; Fort Central light is not visible from seaward; the W entrance has Fort de l'Ouest Fl(3)WR.15s on its E side and Querqueville Fl(4)WG.15s on its W side.

Both entrances also have conspicuous and well lit leading lines.

Commercial and naval shipping must not be impeded near the entrances.

From east

From ⊕01 off Barfleur to ⊕02 to ⊕03 off the E entrance. The banks and shoals extend up to 3M offshore between Cap Barfleur and Cap Levi. While sufficient water may be found further inshore up to 1M off, if the tide serves, the tidal streams run hard and overfalls are frequent over the uneven bottom inside Haut Fond des Equets (Fl.6s), Basse Nord Ouest Q. and the Tête Septentrionale Fl(2)6s buoys although the corner may be cut inside the latter to make the E entrance or ⊕03. Unlit E cardinal and red beacon towers mark the N extent of the rocks to the N and NE of Fort Pelée Oc(2)WR.6s; these

should all be left well to port before turning in to the entrance and leading line of 189° to leave the Tromet port buoy Fl(4)R.15s also to port.

From west

After rounding Cap de la Hague and passing the vicinity of ⊕06 and La Plate Beacon Tower Fl(2+1)WR.10s to starboard, leave Basse Bréfort buoy Q. and ⊕05 to starboard, Raz de Bannes N cardinal beacon tower ¾M to starboard and head for the W entrance or ⊕04. An additional precaution is to keep outside the 5m line.

Tidal streams

3M north of the breakwater the streams start as follows:
HW Cherbourg -0330 E-going
HW Cherbourg +0215 W-going

The maximum rates are 3 knots. The rate lessens as the coast is approached and a W-going eddy starts close to the coast and inside the breakwater at about HW −0130. This is particularly useful when proceeding W from Cherbourg as the W-going stream runs for 8 hours inshore.

Care must be taken when approaching from the N to allow for this cross-set especially at springs so as not to end up down-tide of the intended entrance.

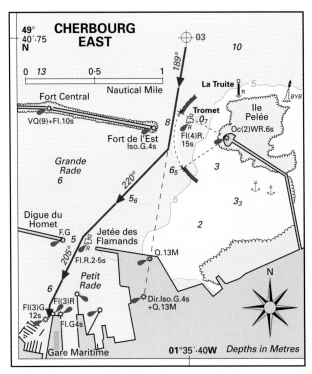

03 Cherbourg E 49°40'.75N 01°35'.40W

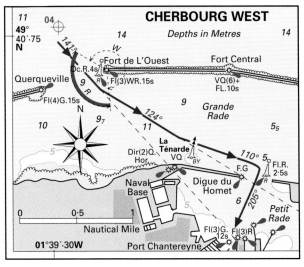

04 Cherbourg 49°40'.75N 01°39'.30W

Entrance

East entrance

From ⊕03 pick up and follow the leading line 189° (*Front,* white pylon, QW; *Rear,* white column, black stripes; IsoG.4s+Q) leaving Tromet red can buoy Fl(4)R.15s and Ile Pelée Oc(2)WR.6s to port, Fort de l'Est IsoG.4s to starboard. Ile Pelée light will change from red to white when it bears 120°. Once through the entrance turn on to a south westerly track for about 1M to pass through the inner entrance leaving Digue du Homet (White pylon, green top on top of blockhouse, F.G) to starboard and the red can buoy off Jetée des Flamands Fl.R.2.5s to port.
Note that the outer end of Jetée des Flamands covers at HW.

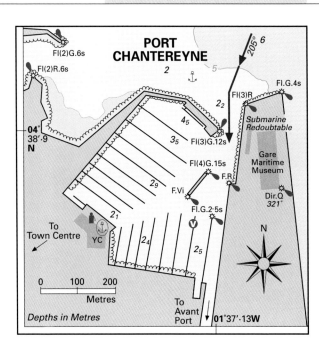

From the inner entrance Port Chantereyne will be seen just to the W of the conspicuous Gare Maritime bearing about 205°. The marina W mole head is marked by a green pylon Fl(3)G12s, the other side of the entrance is the corner of the quay with the Gare Maritime on it with a Q.R.

West entrance

From ⊕04 pick up the leading line 141° (*Front,* White triangle at root of Digue du Homet, Dir.2.Q(Hor), *Rear,* lattice structure on SE corner of Gare Maritime, Dir.Q). This line leaves Fort de l'Ouest Fl(3)WR.15s and offlying port hand buoy Oc.R.4s close to port and is about 2¼M from the inner harbour. Fort de l'Ouest light turns from white to red when it bears 122°. The end of the Querqueville mole Fl(4)G.15s will be well to starboard.

Once through the entrance pick up and turn to the next leading line 124° (*Front,* White pylon with green top on top of blockhouse on end of Digue du Homet, F.G; *Rear,* White pylon with black bands, Iso.G.4s+Q) to leave La Ténarde N cardinal buoy (unlit) to starboard. When this is abeam a turn to port to about 110° will be needed to clear the end of Digue du Homet. When the inner entrance is open turn to about 205° through it. (Starboard F.G, port red can buoy Fl.R.2.5s). Identify the marina entrance ahead, the W side is marked by a green pylon Fl(3)G12s and the other side of the entrance is the corner of the quay with the Gare Maritime on it marked by a Q.R.

Anchorage

Anchoring is prohibited in the vicinity of the two outer and inner entrances and discouraged in the Petite Rade.

Anchorage may be found in Baie de St Anne in 3m or more at the W end of the outer harbour but there is a prohibited area in the NW corner. In easterlies there is a less sheltered anchorage under the jetty running SE to the shore from Ile Pelée in 2–4m.

I. CHERBOURG TO CANCALE

Cherbourg. Port Chantereyne and Avant Port looking south   *SHOM*

The most usual anchorage for those not liking marina berths or wanting to make an early getaway is to the N of the marina N mole in 2–5m, mud.

Berthing

The W side of the entrance is marked by a green pylon (Oc(2)G.6s and the E corner of the Gare Maritime jetty by a Q.R). To the S of the entrance is a wave screen running NE/SW marked at the NE end by a white post (Fl.G.2.5s) and the SE end with a post (Fl.Vi). It may be passed on either hand to reach the visitors' berths to the S of it.

There are nearly 1300 berths in Port Chantereyne, 300 for visitors, maximum length 15m but up to 25m can be accommodated at the N end on moorings or pontoons where up to 4.5m depth may be found. Call on Ch 09 before entering if over 15m.

The Avant Port to the S now has no berths or facilities for visiting yachts.

Moorings

There are none for yachts except for larger ones in the N end of the marina.

Facilities

Water and electricity on pontoons; fuel from fuel berth by office 0800–1145, 1400–1645; 30-ton travel-lift; 600kg-crane; showers and heads by office; YC and chandler by office; shops and banks within 200m of marina entrance; large *supermarché* to the S of the Avant Port; market days Tuesdays and Thursdays; many restaurants and hotels of all qualities.

Ashore in Cherbourg

Travel

The railway station is 15 minutes walk from the marina near the town centre. There are regular and direct connections to Paris and the rest of France (☎ 08 92 35 35 35). The bus station is close by. The airport is to the E of the town at Maupertois; flights to Jersey, Guernsey, Alderney, Bournemouth, Bristol, Southampton and Exeter as well as French internal flights (☎ 02 33 88 57 60). Ferries run daily to Poole and Portsmouth (high speed) and a seasonable service to Guernsey. Taxis ☎ 02 33 53 36 38.

Leisure

There is much to see in the town with good markets, restaurants and shops.

The Gare Maritime has been converted into a major aquarium including a museum of deep underwater exploration and the decommissioned nuclear missile submarine *Le Redoutable*.

The theatre in the centre of the town and Trinity Church are worth a visit, as is the Thomas Henry Fine Art Museum with many of Millet's portraits. There is also a Natural History Museum and several fine parks and gardens.

Perhaps the best visit is to climb or take a bus up Montagne du Roule behind the town to visit the Liberation Museum in the old Fort du Roule whence there are splendid views over the town and harbour.

History

Napoleon inaugurated Cherbourg as a major port with the building of the massive breakwaters and the start of the fortifications. The defences around the harbour were extended in the middle of the 19th century to protect the growing naval base during a period of French maritime and colonial expansion.

During the American Civil War in 1864 the Confederate raider *Alabama* fought the Unionist ship *Kearsage* seven miles off the town in view of a large crowd ashore. The *Alabama* sank after nearly an hour's battle and many of the survivors were picked up by an English yacht *Deerhound* who was spectating. The wreck of the *Alabama* was not discovered until 1984 and recovery operations continue.

The town and base were surrendered to the Germans with little fight in 1940 but were defended vigorously by them before being retaken by the Allies in 1944 with the harbour blocked by wrecks and all the installations destroyed.

Before and after the second world war Cherbourg was the French terminal for major transatlantic liners – *Queen Mary*, *Queen Elizabeth*, *France*, *Liberté*, *Bremen*, *United States*, *America* – which berthed at the Gare Maritime.

Cherbourg developed as a major commercial and container port when the liner trade declined, to which has been added growing ferry traffic with England.

Napoleon pointing to England   *Martin Walker*

Cherbourg. Gare Maritime houses an excellent maritime museum   *Martin Walker*

Cherbourg fuel jetty   *Martin Walker*

102 Omonville-la-Rogue

A small harbour protected from the W, but not the E, with few facilities; suitable to wait a favourable stream round Cap de la Hague.

Location
10M west of Cherbourg

Shelter
From S through W to NW

Depth restrictions
From 2–7m in anchorage

Night entry
Possible with one directional light

Tidal information
HW and LW about 10 minutes before Cherbourg

Mean height of tide (m)

HWS	HWN	LWN	LWS
6.3	4.9	2.5	1.1

Tidal streams
HW Cherb +0215 E-going starts
HW Cherb -0220 W-going starts
Up to 4 and 5 knots respectively

Berthing
4 moorings otherwise anchor

Facilities
Shop, sailing school, restaurant

Charts
BA 1106 (50), SC 5604.3
SHOM 5636 (Plan)
Imray C32, C33A (Plan)

Weather
CROSS Joburg Ch 80 at 0715, 1545 and 1915 LT

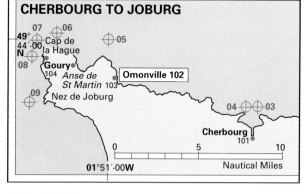

CHERBOURG TO JOBURG

05	Bréfort	49°44'.00N 01°51'.00W
06	Plate	49°44'.40N 01°55'.60W
07	Hague	49°44'.00N 01°58'.00W
08	Foraine	49°43'.00N 01°59'.00W
09	Jobourg	49°38'.80N 01°59'.00W

From E Leave Raz des Bannes N cardinal beacon tower ½M to the S and from a WNW track pick up the leading line/light as above.

PILOTAGE

Approaches and Entrance

From W and N The main danger is Les Tataquets rocks (drying 2.6m) which lie 800m N of the breakwater end. Give these a good berth before turning to the SE to pick up the leading line 257° (*Front*, White pylon, red top Iso.WRG.4s *Rear*, Church tower, unlit). At night the white sector is 10° wide with green to the N, red to the S. The white sector and the line leads clear S of L'Etonnard rocks and starboard beacon tower.

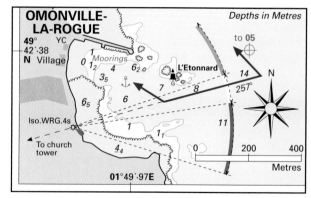

OMONVILLE-LA-ROGUE · Depths in Metres

⊕05 Bréfort   49°44'.00N 01°51'.00W

Omonville looking SW at half tide

Front leading mark & light (white with red top) · L'Etonnard beacon tower · Visitors' buoys

Moorings and Anchorage

With L'Etonnard well on the starboard quarter turn into the anchorage. There are 4 large white visitors' buoys at the E end of the moorings. If occupied, anchor in 5–7m to seaward of them in patchy sand.

Berthing

There is a clean sandy bottom at the inner end of the breakwater beyond a spur halfway along it where it dries 1m and where an alongside berth may be found. There are rocks alongside the breakwater to the E of the spur.

Facilities

There are two small cafés/restaurants and a sailing school where there are showers by the harbour, a small shop in the village and more in Beaumont Hague on the main road (5km).

103 Anse de St Martin (Port Racine)

An open, unlit bay just to the E of Cap de la Hague sheltered from W through S to ESE; safer as a tide-waiting anchorage in easterlies than Omonville.

Location
2M east of Cap de la Hague

Shelter
From W through S to SE

Depth restrictions
2.7m in anchorage

Night entry
Unlit

Tidal information
HW and LW about 20 minutes before Cherbourg with a greater range

Tidal streams
The stream inshore off the Anse sets to the W except for a brief period around HW Cherb +0200

Berthing
Anchoring only

Facilities
Small restaurant

Charts
SHOM 5636 is largest scale; BA 1106 shows details on small scale

Weather
CROSS Joburg Ch 80 at 0715, 1545 and 1915 LT

05 Bréfort	49°44′.00N 01°51′.00W
06 Plate	49°44′.40N 01°55′.60W

⊕05 Bréfort   49°44′.00N 01°51′.00W

PILOTAGE

Approaches, Entrance and Anchorage

Identify Pointe du Nez, a low bluff at the W end of the sandy beach at the head of the bay and approach this on a track of 187° making allowance for any cross stream in the offing which can be strong and variable. Pass 300m to the W of Parmentière, a shoal patch drying at CD and 400m to the E of Les Herbeuses rocks (drying 9m but with rocks awash at CD off them). Port Racine, a small drying harbour will soon appear in the SW corner of the bay off which there are a few small boat moorings. Anchor clear of them in 2–3m sand or tuck into the SE corner of the bay in easterly weather.

Facilities

None, except for a small restaurant up the hill from Port Racine. Port Racine claims, without much foundation to be the smallest port in France.

Anse de St Martin. Port Racine looking NW near HW. (Also see photo on page 21)

I. CHERBOURG TO CANCALE

104 Goury

A small drying harbour just south of Cap de la Hague; open to the SW with the strongest streams of the Race running outside it.

Location
¾M SSW of Cap de la Hague

Shelter
Only from the E

Warning
Strong surf in harbour in south westerlies

Depth restrictions
Harbour dries; 3m in anchorage.

Night entry
Ldg lts but not recommended

Tidal information
HW and LW at Goury are about 1 hour before Cherbourg

Mean height of tide (m)

HWS	HWN	LWN	LWS
8.1	6.6	3.5	1.4

Tidal streams
Fierce; see above

Berthing
Dry out alongside pier or anchor off

Charts
SHOM 7133 (10)
Imray C33A (Plan)
BA 1106 (50)

Weather
CROSS Joburg Ch 80 at 0715, 1345 and 1915 LT

Radio
None

Communication
☎ 33 (0) 2 33 52 85 92 *Fax* 33 (0) 2 33 52 39 27
Email marie-auderville@wanadoo.fr

Lifeboat
A lifeboat is based here

PILOTAGE

Approaches and Entrance

From ⊕08 make good a track of 140° to pick up the leading line well outside the 10m line and about 600m S of La Foraine beacon. It is 065° *Front*, Red square within a white square on end of breakwater, *Rear*, white pylon on a masonry hut, Q.R and Q.W respectively, to the S of the grey octagonal lifeboat building.

Keep exactly on the line and pass a 1.6m patch close to starboard, Diotret rock (4.8m) to starboard, Hervieu and Jet Aval beacons close to starboard, Jet d'Amont beacon to port and round the breakwater close to port.

Berthing

Alongside the wall if there is space and water but not if westerly weather threatens.

Anchorage

To the SW of Jet d'Amont beacon in 3m clear of the lifeboat slip, patchy sand but only in settled weather.

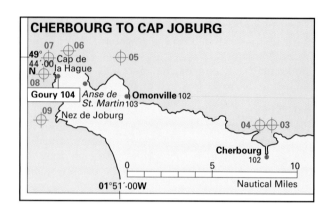

CHERBOURG TO CAP JOBURG

05	Bréfort	49°44'.00N 01°51'.00W
06	Plate	49°44'.40N 01°55'.60W
07	Hague	49°44'.00N 01°58'.00W
08	Foraine	49°43'.00N 01°59'.00W
09	Jobourg	49°38'.80N 01°59'.00W

Facilities

None, apart from a tourist information office, public toilets and a small restaurant. The latter has a good reputation and is often crowded at lunchtimes. The nearest shop is ¾M at Audeville. There is a memorial to a shipwreck in 1912 to the N of the car park.

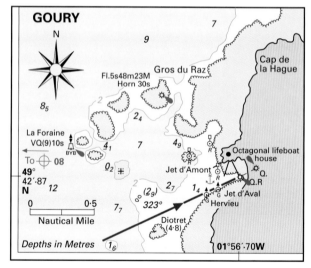

08	Foraine	49°43'.00N 01°59'.00W

Goury. Looking down the leading line   *Martin Walker*

Restaurant   Information   Lifeboat house   Rear ldg lt   Front ldg lt   Jet d'Aval   Lifeboat ramp

Goury looking ESE. The lifeboat may use the ramp inside the mole as well as that shown

Anse St Martin Anchorage beyond minute harbour   *Martin Walker*

I. CHERBOURG TO CANCALE

105 Diélette

A small fishing harbour that has been developed for yachts in the last decade. Shallow approaches and caution needed in strong westerlies. Sill to inner harbour.

Location
1M NNE of Cap de Flamanville nuclear power station

Shelter
Good in the marina; outer harbour exposed

Warning
Entry limited in strong westerlies

Depth restrictions
Least depth in approaches 0.5m

Night entry
Well-lit and directional light

Tidal information
HW and LW are about 40 minutes after St Malo

Mean height of tide (m)

HWS	HWN	LWN	LWS
9.7	7.4	3.5	1.2

Tidal streams
HW St Helier -0325 NE-going starts
HW St Helier +0220 SW-going starts

Berthing
On pontoons

Tidal streams
HW St Helier -0325 NE-going starts
HW St Helier +0220 SW-going starts

Berthing
On pontoons

Charts
BA 3653 (50)
SHOM 7133 (10)
Imray C33A (Plan)

Weather
CROSS Joburg Ch 80 0715,1345, 1915. From Harbour Office

Radio/Telephone
Ch 09 0800–2000 LT

Communications
☎ 33 (0) 233 53 68 78 Fax 33 (0) 233 53 68 79
Email port-dielette@wanadoo.fr

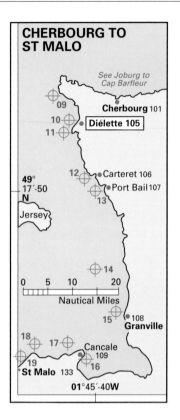

CHERBOURG TO ST MALO

PILOTAGE

Approaches

From ⊕10 identify the leading line 140° of a white tower with green top at head of W spur and a conspicuous white house above the port. At night this is in the white sector (10°) with the red to the NE and green to the SW. Cap de Flamanville W cardinal buoy Q(9) is just outside the green sector. There is reported to be 0.5m least depth on this line which shallows to drying 1m just to the NE of the outer entrance. A nuclear power station lies to the south- N of Cap de Flamanville.

09	Joburg	49°38'.80N 01°59'.00W
10	Diélette	49°33'.37N 01°52'.17W
11	Flamanville	49°32'.50N 01°55'.00W
12	Carteret	49°21'.20N 01°48'.06W
13	Portbail	49°17'.50N 01°45'.40W
14	Catheue	48°57'.80N 01°41'.50W
15	Granville	48°49'.50N 01°37'.70W
16	Cancale	48°40'.06N 01°49'.40W
17	Herpin	48°44'.50N 01°48'.00W
18	Rochefort	48°43'.50N 01°58'.40W
19	St-Malo	48°41'.50N 02°07'.25W

Diélette looking ESE

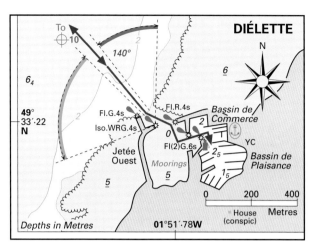

⊕10 Diélette   49°33′.37N 01°52′.17W

Diélette. The sill with depth gauge and signals above right
Martin Walker

Diélette. Outer waiting pontoons

Entrance

Once past the outer leading mark turn to port into the Bassin de Commerce. The arrival pontoon is by the harbour office and carries 2m. There may be room to stay here if a berth inside is not wanted.

Alternatively proceed straight to Bassin de Plaisance turning to starboard round the S mole. The entrance is at the W end of the submerged wall marked by a red post which must be left to port, with the fuel berth passed to starboard.

Berthing

On pontoons with fingers. Max 20m. The sill dries 5m and will be opened when there is 1.5m over it which is approximately HW±3 hrs 15 mins. Signal 3 vertical reds – Gate closed; 2 green over white – Gate open. There is 2.5m at the N end of the basin, 1.5m at the S end.

In the Avant Port the W wall can be dried out against but is exposed to NW winds and dries to 4–5m, hard sand.

Ashore in Diélette

Facilities

Water and electricity on pontoons; fuel at basin entrance; showers and heads in block by YC where also launderette; slip and 30-ton travel-lift; chandlery and mini market under YC; more shops in Flamanville a 15 minute walk; sailing school; restaurants in YC and at S side of harbour; café by harbour office.

Travel

Nearest railway station and airport at Cherbourg 15M. Local taxi ☎ 02 33 52 53 53.

106 Carteret

A drying estuary with a small marina between two seaside towns.

Location
Close to the SE of Cap de Carteret

Shelter
Good in the marina

Warning
Approach not recommended in strong westerlies

Depth restrictions
Least depth drying 3.3m in approach

Night entry
Lit but no ldg Lts

Tidal information
HW and LW are about 25 minutes after St Malo

Mean height of tide (m)

HWS	HWN	LWN	LWS
10.6	8.1	3.7	1.3

Tidal streams
HW St Helier -0325 NE-going starts
HW St Helier +0220 SW-going starts

Berthing
On pontoons in marina

Facilities
Usual small town

Charts
BA 3653 (50)
SHOM 7133 (10)
Imray C33A (Plan)

Weather
CROSS Joburg Ch 08 at 0715, 1345 and 1915 LT

Radio/Telephone
Ch 09 HW ±0230 hours
☎ 02 33 04 70 84 *Fax* 02 33 04 08 37
Email contact@port-des-isles.fr
www.mairie-barneville-carteret.fr

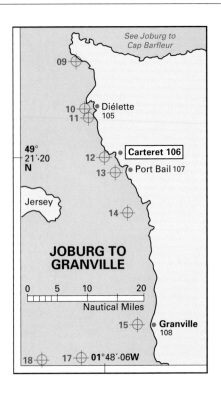

09	Joburg	49°38′.80N 01°59′.00W
10	Diélette	49°33′.37N 01°52′.17W
11	Flamanville	49°32′.50N 01°55′.00W
12	Carteret	49°21′.20N 01°48′.06W
13	Port Bail	49°17′.50N 01°45′.40W
14	Catheue	48°57′.80N 01°41′.50W
15	Granville	48°49′.50N 01°37′.70W
16	Cancale	48°40′.06N 01°49′.40W
17	Herpin	48°44′.50N 01°48′.00W
18	Rochefort	48°43′.50N 01°58′.40W
19	**St-Malo**	**48°41′.50N 02°07′.25W**

PILOTAGE

Approaches

The only danger in the approaches is Plateau des Trois Grunes 5M to the W with a least depth of drying 1.6m which is marked by a W cardinal buoy Q(9)15s. From ⊕12 make good a track of 040° with Cap de Carteret (grey tower, green top 81m, Fl(2+1)15s) on the port bow until the Jetée Ouest head (White column, red top Oc.R.4s) can be identified. Note that the outer part of this jetty submerges near HW. When approaching before HW the stream will be setting strongly to the NW outside. Just NW of the entrance on Cap de Carteret is a prominent marine national lookout station, lighthouse and communications mast.

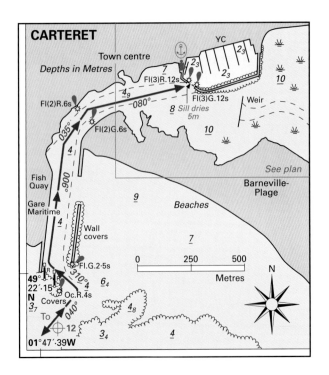

Entrance

Once the head of Jetée de l'Ouest has been rounded, the stream sets strongly up the channel until HW. Allow for this and leave the training wall head (White mast, green top, Fl.G.2.5s) 50m to starboard, regain the centre of the channel and proceed up harbour leaving the fishing quays 50m to port. The training wall will be submerged up to its N end near HW. Turn to starboard between the green and red metal columns Fl(2)G or R.6s and head for the marina gate marked by red and green pylons Fl(3)R or G.12s. There is a depth gauge by the port beacon. Traffic signals – 3 red, Gate closed; 2 green over white, Gate open.

Beware of strong set NW across the entrance before HW.

The sill dries 5m and opens or closes when there is 1.3m over it at about HW±2½ hours.

Berthing

There are over 300 berths in the marina, 60 for visitors. There appears to be no length limit but any vessel over 15m might have difficulty manoeuvring inside. The basin is dredged to 2.3m. The waiting pontoon is just inside the entrance below the office

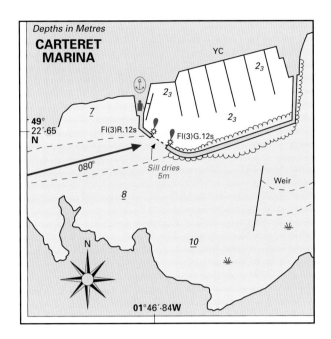

Carteret approach   *Peter Carnegie*

and the visitors' pontoon is the last one (F) at the end of the basin. There are plans to extend the marina to the eastward.

It would be possible to dry out in the estuary above the marina but it is crossed by a weir just above the entrance.

Fishing boats dry out alongside the fish quay in the entrance channel but the quay is high and a ladder would be needed unless a berth can be found by one.

Ashore in Carteret

Facilities

Water and electricity on the pontoons; no fuel but this may be restored; slip and 35-ton travel-lift in NE corner; the YC welcomes visitors where there are showers and heads; good quality shops and chandlery; a number of restaurants in town as well as in Barneville which is 30 minutes' walk.

Leisure

Walks and beaches, excellent restaurants.

Travel

The railway to Carteret no longer runs; nearest station Valognes (15km) or Cherbourg (25km) where there is also an airport and ferries to UK. There may be a bus but otherwise Taxi Côte des Iles ☎ 02 33 04 61 02. Tourist information office in the town ☎ 02 33 04 94 54. Vedettes to Jersey and Sark in season (tide dependent).

Looking NE at low water   *Peter Carnegie*

Carteret Marina looking SW at high water

107 Portbail

An all-drying yacht harbour and entrance with a small village

Location
4M SE of Cap de Carteret

Shelter
Adequate inside

Warning
Approach not recommended in strong westerlies

Depth restrictions
Approach channel dries 5.2m

Night entry
Ldg Lts but not recommended

Tidal information
HW and LW are about 30 minutes after St Malo

Mean height of tide (m)

HWS	HWN	LWN	LWS
11.4	8.7	4.0	1.4

Tidal streams
HW St Helier -0130 N-going starts
HW St Helier +0425 S-going starts

Berthing
In mud on pontoons; dried alongside pier.

Facilities
Minimal

Charts
BA 3653 (50)
SHOM 7133 (10)
Imray C33A (Plan)

Weather
CROSS Joburg Ch 80 at 0715, 1345, 1915 LT

Radio
Ch 9

Communication
☎ +33 (0)2 33 04 83 48

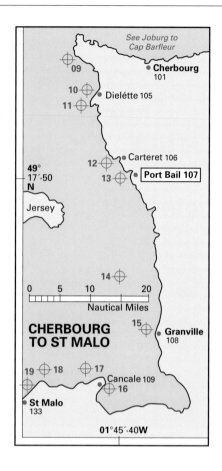

09	Joburg	49°38'.80N 01°59'.00W
10	Diélette	49°33'.37N 01°52'.17W
11	Flamanville	49°32'.50N 01°55'.00W
12	Carteret	49°21'.20N 01°48'.06W
13	Port Bail	49°17'.50N 01°45'.40W
14	Catheue	48°57'.80N 01°41'.50W
15	Granville	48°49'.50N 01°37'.70W
16	Cancale	48°40'.06N 01°49'.40W
17	Herpin	48°44'.50N 01°48'.00W
18	Rochefort	48°43'.50N 01°58'.40W
19	St Malo	48°41'.50N 02°07'.25W

PILOTAGE

Approaches

The start of the approach channel bears 042° from ⊕13 distance 2M. The fairway buoy is about half way, and to the NW of this line. There is a least depth of 0.7m close to the SW of this buoy and a prohibited anchorage to the SE where cables run. The best time to enter is HW -1.

Identify the leading line (*Front*, La Caillourie beacon white pylon, red top Q, *Rear*, Portbail church belfry (Oc.4s) 042°). A conspicuous water tower ½M to the W of the harbour assists identification. There is one set of port and starboard buoys before the outer end of the training wall (White beacon, red top Q(2)R.5s).

Thence the channel is bounded to the NW by the training wall marked by beacons with unlit buoys to the SE. It is dredged to drying 5.2m.

Entrance and Berthing

La Caillourie beacon lies just to the W of the pier/slip which form the W-side entrance to the drying harbour. Turn close to port round the end of the pier into the basin. The stream sets strongly across this entrance except at HW. The rest of the basin is occupied with head and stern moorings on a bottom of sand and mud which dries 7m. There is a drying pontoon along the NW side.

It is possible to dry out alongside the inner part of the jetty on the slip but ask at the Harbour Office as it is used by the vedettes and fishing boats. The outer part of the jetty has sloping piles.

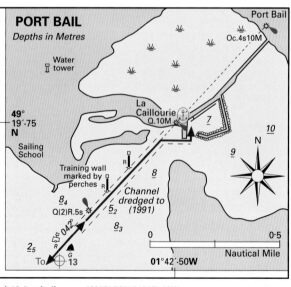

⊕13 Portbail   49°17'.50N 01°45'.40W

Portbail looking WSW at LW   *Peter Carnegie*

Portbail. Visitors' pontoon in the drying yacht basin   *Martin Walker*

Ashore in Portbail

Facilities

There are four water points, one by the harbour office; four showers and heads by the harbour office; slip in the NE corner of the basin; YC by the harbour office; sailing school operates from a slip on the W side of the peninsula to the W of the basin; modest shops across the bridge; market day Tuesday; a small hotel and two restaurants near end of bridge.

Leisure

The small Romanesque church of Notre Dame with its 6th-century baptistry is worth a visit; guided tours 1000–1130, 1500–1630.

109 Cancale

A drying port with open anchorages sheltered from the west, famous for its oysters.

Location
14M SW of Granville; 7M ENE of St Malo

Shelter
Only from the W at anchor

Warning
Exceptional tidal range

Depth restrictions
Harbour dries 6–7.5m

Night entry
Light on pier end

Tidal information
As for St Malo (Standard Port)

Mean height of tide (m)

HWS	HWN	LWN	LWS
12.2	9.3	4.2	1.5

Tidal streams
HW St Helier -0015 N-going starts
HW St Helier +0430 S-going starts
Maximum rate 2¼ knots

Berthing
Drying alongside berth may be possible; otherwise anchor

Facilities
Those of a fashionable fishing port

Charts
No large scale
BA 3659 (50)
Imray C33B

Radio/Telephone
None

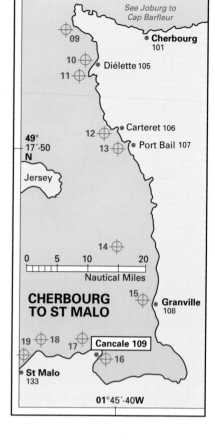

09	Jobourg	49°38'.80N 01°59'.00W
10	Diélette	49°33'.37N 01°52'.17W
11	Flamanville	49°32'.50N 01°55'.00W
12	Carteret	49°21'.20N 01°48'.06W
13	Port Bail	49°17'.50N 01°45'.40W
14	Catheue	48°57'.80N 01°41'.50W
15	Granville	48°49'.50N 01°37'.70W
16	Cancale	48°40'.06N 01°49'.40W
17	Herpin	48°44'.50N 01°48'.00W
18	Rochefort	48°43'.50N 01°58'.40W
19	St Malo	48°41'.50N 02°07'.25W

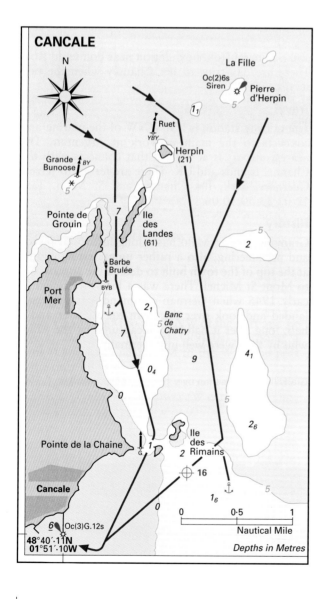

PILOTAGE

Approaches

From N and W

A night approach from these directions is not recommended unless the visibility is such as to be able to see the unlit buoys at a reasonable distance.

Identify Pointe de Grouin with its old semaphore building near the N end, Ile des Landes close to the E of it, Herpin Rock (21m) and Pierre de Herpin light tower. When the buoys Ruet W cardinal and Grande Bunoose N cardinal have been identified, pass between them and go through the narrow (150m) but deep (7m) channel between Pointe de Grouin and Ile des Landes to leave Barbe Brulée cardinal beacon tower to starboard. The stream runs fast but true through this channel.

If this passage does not appeal, leave Ruet buoy and Herpin Rock close to starboard before turning S towards Ile des Rimains.

Cancale looking W at half tide *Peter Carnegie*

Cancale. Port Mer, looking NW

Cancale may now be reached by passing through the narrow channel (least depth 0m) close to the E of the starboard beacon tower marking the extremity of the dangers off Pointe de la Chaine and the small island to the SW of Ile des Rimains. Otherwise pass to the E of Ile des Rimains with its fort before turning SW to close Cancale breakwater on a track of at least 230°.

From E and NE
There are no dangers on the approaches to ⊕16 from these directions provided Pierre d' Herpin and La Fille its NE outlyer and Ile des Rimains and its SW outlyer are all left to the W to approach Cancale breakwater or ⊕16 on a track of at least 230°.

History
Cancale is the most easterly Breton port of any substance and is steeped in the sea-going Breton traditions. During the 18th-century the Cancalese were famous all over the world as daring seamen and in the navy of Louis XIV entire ships' companies came from this port. Like so many ports along the coast they contributed to the corsair and privateer traditions of robbing the trade passing through the English Channel.

Three manifestations recall the past of Cancale:

The bisquines were the beautiful local design of fishing boat unique to this area with straight stems, overhanging counters, two masts setting lugsails with topsails above them and a huge jib set on a long bowsprit. Thankfully a few have been restored to their former glory and ply for pleasure between the port and Iles Chausey.

Strong Roman Catholic beliefs have been maintained, unlike further west in Brittany where communism between the Wars eroded the old faith. Their devotion to Notre Dame de Verger whose shrine stands above Pointe de Grouin remains steadfast.

The Fishery School founded in the 19th-century is nationally famous and did much to raise the standards and education of the fishermen.

Port Mer

Approaches
Port Mer and its anchorage on a track of 270° or less to avoid the shallow part of Banc de Chatry (0.4m).

Anchorage
Close SE of Ile des Rimains in 2m, sand and mud.

Off Port Mer as far W as moorings will allow to avoid the stream, on sand.

Other areas that may attract as anchorages should be treated with caution as there may only be a shallow layer of mud over rock which may not hold in the streams or in a blow.

Berthing
The inner side of the breakwater is much used by the vedettes at the outer end, and by fishing boats along the length of it. If seeking a berth on it, ask at the Harbour Office before settling down; a ladder may be needed to get ashore.

The bay and harbour are mostly flat sand and suitable for grounding with bilge keels or in a multi-hull in westerly weather.

Ashore in Cancale

Facilities at Cancale
There are few concessions to yachtsmen except for a water tap on the quay; there are many restaurants and cafés plus quite adequate shops and *supermarchés*.

Facilities at Port Mer
No shops in the vicinity but a restaurant, cafés and a sailing school by the beach.

Leisure
Consumption of oysters and shellfish.

Shellfish barge

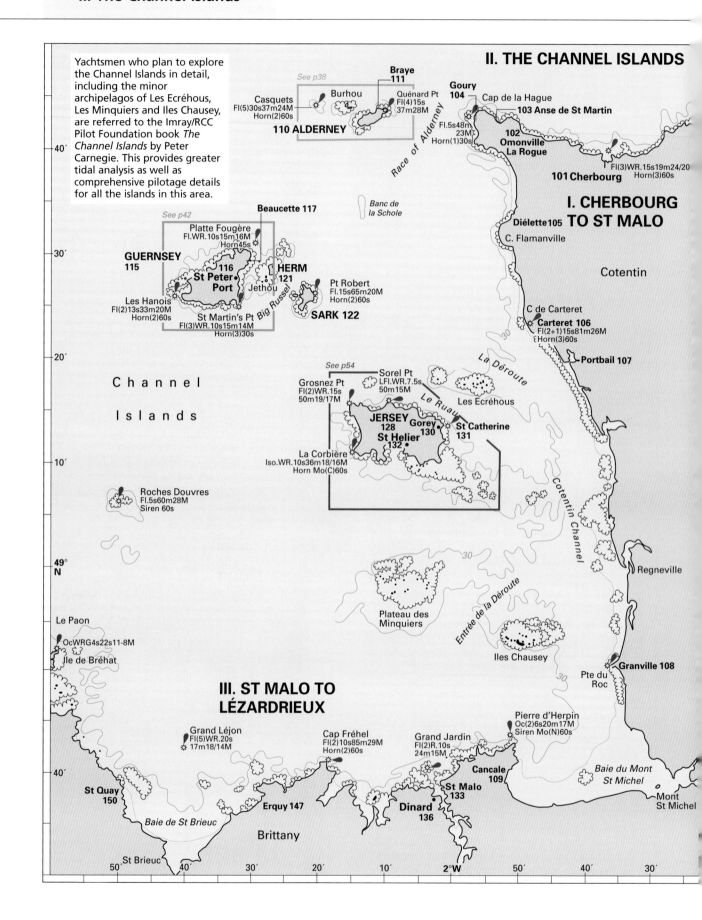

Yachtsmen who plan to explore the Channel Islands in detail, including the minor archipelagos of Les Ecréhous, Les Minquiers and Iles Chausey, are referred to the Imray/RCC Pilot Foundation book *The Channel Islands* by Peter Carnegie. This provides greater tidal analysis as well as comprehensive pilotage details for all the islands in this area.

II. THE CHANNEL ISLANDS

Braye 111

See p38

Burhou

Goury 104

Cap de la Hague

103 Anse de St Martin

Casquets
Fl(5)30s37m24M
Horn(2)60s

Quénard Pt
Fl(4)15s
37m28M

110 ALDERNEY

Fl.5s48m
23M
Horn(1)30s

102
Omonville
La Rogue

Race of Alderney

Fl(3)WR.15s19m24/20
Horn(3)60s

101 Cherbourg

I. CHERBOURG TO ST MALO

Diélette 105

C. Flamanville

Banc de la Schole

Cotentin

Beaucette 117

See p42

Platte Fougère
Fl.WR.10s15m16M
Horn45s

GUERNSEY
115

116
St Peter
Port

HERM
121

Jethou

Pt Robert
Fl.15s65m20M
Horn(2)60s

C de Carteret
Carteret 106
Fl(2+1)15s81m26M
Horn(3)60s

La Déroute

Portbail 107

Les Hanois
Fl(2)13s33m20M
Horn(2)60s

St Martin's Pt
Fl(3)WR.10s15m14M
Horn(3)30s

Big Russel

SARK 122

Channel

Islands

See p54

Sorel Pt
LFl.WR.7.5s
50m15M

Grosnez Pt
Fl(2)WR.15s
50m19/17M

Le Ruau

Les Ecréhous

JERSEY
128

Gorey
130

St Catherine
131

St Helier
132

La Corbière
Iso.WR.10s36m18/16M
Horn Mo(C)60s

30

Cotentin Channel

Roches Douvres
Fl.5s60m28M
Siren 60s

Regneville

49°
N

Plateau des
Minquiers

30

Entrée de la Déroute

Le Paon

OcWRG4s22s11-8M

Iles Chausey

Granville 108

Pte du
Roc

Ile de Bréhat

III. ST MALO TO LÉZARDRIEUX

Pierre d'Herpin
Oc(2)6s20m17M
Siren Mo(N)60s

Grand Léjon
Fl(5)WR.20s
17m18/14M

Cap Fréhel
Fl(2)10s85m29M
Horn(2)60s

Grand Jardin
Fl(2)R.10s
24m15M

Baie du Mont
St Michel

Cancale
109

Mont
St Michel

St Quay
150

Erquy 147

St Malo
133

Dinard
136

Baie de St Brieuc

Brittany

St Brieuc

II. The Channel Islands

⊕20	Alderney NE	49°45´.19N 02°09´.93W
⊕21	Alderney NW	49°44´.84N 02°12´.09W
⊕22	Swinge	49°42´.74N 02°15´.79W
⊕23	North Race	49°45´.80N 02°04´.30W
⊕24	South Race	49°41´.50N 02°06´.20W
⊕25	Schôle	49°36´.60N 02°16´.20W
⊕26	Fougère	49°31´.24N 02°27´.77W
⊕27	Jersey NW	49°14´.20N 02°18´.00W
⊕28	Jersey N	49°16´.55N 02°04´.90W
⊕29	Roustel NNE	49°29´.45N 02°28´.68W
⊕30	St Peter Port	49°27´.37N 02°31´.36W
⊕31	Musé	49°26´.24N 02°27´.53W
⊕32	Lower Heads	49°25´.74N 02°28´.53W
⊕33	St Martins SE	49°24´.72N 02°31´.37W
⊕34	Hanois SW	49°25´.69N 02°44´.08W
⊕35	Doyle N	49°31´.94N 02°31´.60W
⊕36	Beaucette	49°30´.25N 02°30´.08W
⊕37	Aligande (Herm)	49°27´.95N 02°28´.88W
⊕38	Percée (Herm)	49°27´.75N 02°27´.37W
⊕39	Forquies (Herm)	49°27´.38N 02°26´.45W
⊕40	Gouliot (Sark)	49°26´.15N 02°22´.88W
⊕41	Sark N	49°27´.48N 02°22´.00W
⊕42	Sark S	49°23´.79N 02°22´.48W
⊕43	Maseline (Sark E)	49°26´.14N 02°20´.48W
⊕44	Jersey SW	49°10´.24N 02°16´.08W
⊕45	St Helier	49°09´.94N 02°07´.33W
⊕46	Jersey SE	49°07´.80N 01°57´.16W
⊕47	Gorey	49°11´.94N 02°00´.78W
⊕48	Minquiers NW	49°00´.00N 02°23´.08W
⊕49	Minquiers SW	48°53´.50N 02°20´.00W
⊕50	Minquiers NE	49°01´.40N 01°54´.50W
⊕51	Minquiers SE	48°53´.00N 01°58´.61W

Cruising in the Channel Islands

The main ports and anchorages of Alderney, Guernsey, Herm, Sark and Jersey plus directions for transiting the Alderney Race are included in this Pilot for the benefit of those on passage to and from North Brittany.

Each island section contains advice on the optimum time to leave each port in any direction to make the best use of the tidal streams and there is also a Planning Guide below giving the distances between the islands and ports in France.

The Channel Islands have been part of Britain since 1066 with a brief interlude under German occupation during the Second World War. They have their own governments and Jersey and Guernsey both have Lieutenant Governors appointed by the Crown.

They are not part of the EU and VAT is not imposed. The main difference between UK/French coastal waters and the islands lies in the tides and tidal streams.

The streams run extremely fast round Alderney but the range is moderate. Perversely, this is reversed towards Jersey in the south where the range is large and the streams less swift. Throughout the islands and whatever the stage of the lunar cycle, the tidal streams are a force to be reckoned with.

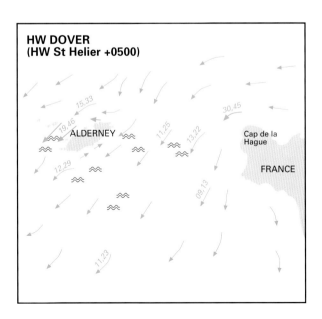

HW DOVER
(HW St Helier +0500)

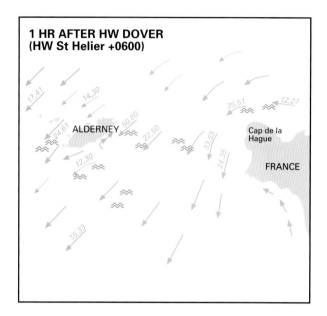

1 HR AFTER HW DOVER
(HW St Helier +0600)

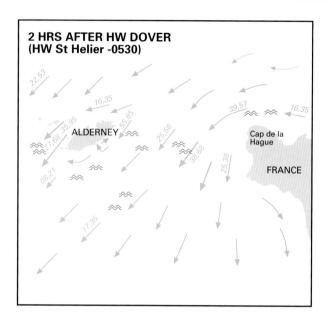

2 HRS AFTER HW DOVER
(HW St Helier -0530)

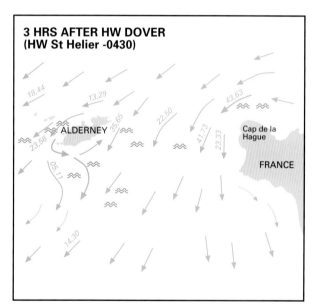

3 HRS AFTER HW DOVER
(HW St Helier -0430)

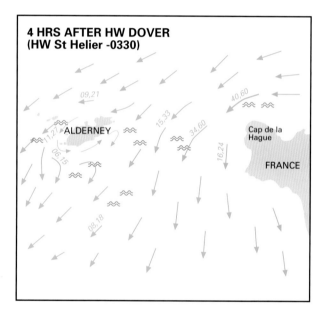

4 HRS AFTER HW DOVER
(HW St Helier -0330)

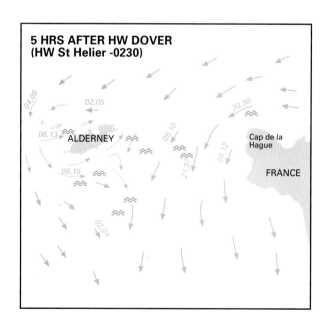

5 HRS AFTER HW DOVER
(HW St Helier -0230)

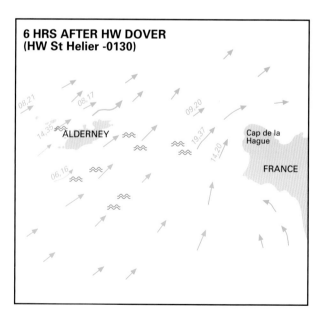

6 HRS AFTER HW DOVER
(HW St Helier -0130)

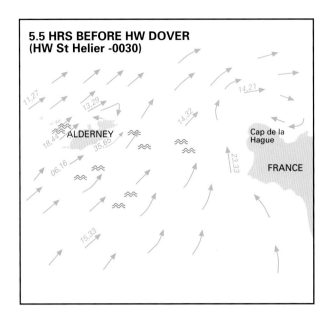

**5.5 HRS BEFORE HW DOVER
(HW St Helier -0030)**

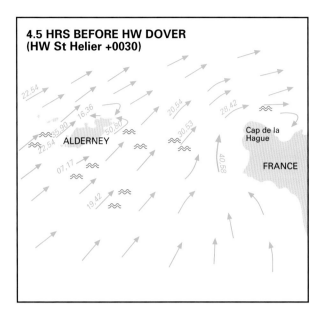

**4.5 HRS BEFORE HW DOVER
(HW St Helier +0030)**

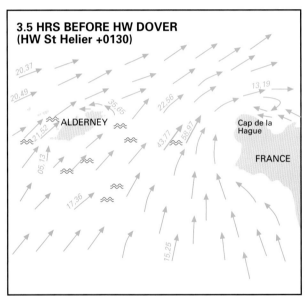

**3.5 HRS BEFORE HW DOVER
(HW St Helier +0130)**

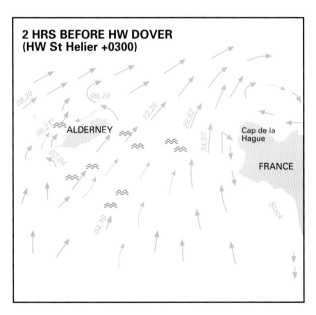

**2 HRS BEFORE HW DOVER
(HW St Helier +0300)**

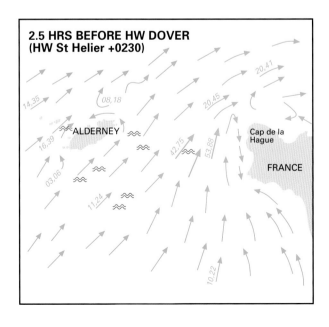

**2.5 HRS BEFORE HW DOVER
(HW St Helier +0230)**

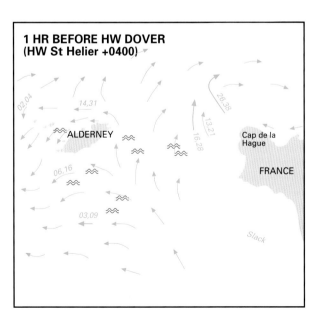

**1 HR BEFORE HW DOVER
(HW St Helier +0400)**

The Channel Islands ashore

Provisions and shopping

The advantages of a favourable tax regime are often negated by the cost of transport to the islands.

Fuel

Diesel prices are comparable to the UK and very much cheaper than French marina pump prices. Petrol is very much cheaper than in France and the UK. It pays to fill right up in the islands.

Money

The islands have their own currency in notes and coins. UK money is accepted readily, as are Euros but there may be difficulty getting Channel Islands money accepted in the UK outside banks.

Formalities

As the islands are not in the EU, a Customs and Immigration declaration must be made when stopping at any of the islands on the way from UK or France. Forms are usually supplied on arrival at Alderney, St Peter Port, Beaucette and St Helier.

Yacht Clubs

Visitors to the yachts clubs are welcome at Alderney, Guernsey and Jersey provided the usual courtesies are observed.

Laying up

Facilities are available at Alderney (limited), St Peter Port and St Helier but not usually at such advantageous rates as in France.

The tidal streams must always be reckoned with in the islands. Burhou in the Swinge   *Peter Carnegie*

Technical and navigational information

The data and information shown under *Cruising in Normandy and Brittany* on page 1 apply with the following exceptions:

Radio services

St Peter Port Radio and Jersey Coastguard offer a public service facility (link calls); the frequencies are shown under St Peter Port and St Helier.

Weather forecasts

Jersey Coastguard Synopsis and forecasts for Channel Islands area on Ch 25 and 82 at 0645, 0745, 0845 LT and 1245, 1845 and 2245 UTC.

BBC Radio Jersey Weather bulletins on 1026kHz and 88.8MHz at 0725, 0825, 1325, 1725 Monday–Friday, 0825 Saturday and Sunday, all LT. Jersey waters shipping forecasts on 1026kHz and 88.8MHz at 0625 and 1825 Monday–Friday, 0725 Saturday and Sunday, all LT.

St Peter Port Radio Weather bulletins for northern area on Ch 20 and 62 at 0133, 0533, 0933, 1333, 1733, 2133 UTC.

Alderney Island FM On 93.7MHz at every H+30 synopsis and forecast. See also page 5 for details of French forecasts in the area.

Search and Rescue

Coastguard facilities in the islands are provided by Jersey Coastguard and St Peter Port Radio who will respond to emergency calls on Ch 16 or the activation of Ch 70 on GMDSS. The islands are also in the area of responsibility of CROSS Joburg. There are all-weather lifeboats at Alderney, St Peter Port and St Helier. There are hospitals in Guernsey and Jersey.

Note that 'Jersey Radio' is now 'Jersey Coastguard'.

Alderney Race

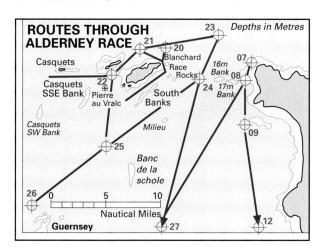

ROUTES THROUGH ALDERNEY RACE *Depths in Metres*

Transiting the Alderney Race

The Alderney Race derives its name from the great rates of tidal streams flowing through it which reach almost 10 knots at springs. It lies in the 9M strait between the E end of Alderney and Cap de la Hague. It has a clear fairway 2½M wide of water undisturbed by rocks or shoals between Race Rocks and the 16m rocky bank lying 4M WSW from Cap de la Hague.

Wind over tidal stream conditions in the Race always causes steep and breaking seas even in the fairway. These break heavily and dangerously over the eight shoal areas or rocks in the Race. These should be avoided except in the calmest conditions near slack water. These areas from S to N are:

1. **Banc de la Schôle** 8M S of Alderney. While clear of the strongest streams it has the least water (2.4m) over it and is constantly shifting. 1M N of its northern limit is a wreck with 3.2m over it marked by a N cardinal VQ buoy.

2. **Milieu** 3.75M SSE of Alderney with 14m over it.

3. **Alderney South Banks** running NE/SW 1M off the SE Alderney coast with 11m over them. (See pages 34 and 35 *Tidal streams* for the details of the flow inshore of them).

4. **Blanchard Rock** ¾M off the E end of Alderney with 3.7m over it.

5. **Race Rock** 1½M SE of Quenard Point with 5.5m over it.

6. **Inner Race Rock** ½M NW of Race Rock with 5.5m over it.

7. **16m Bank** 4M W by S of Cap de la Hague which has the most extensive overfalls.

8. **17m Bank** 2½M SW from Cap de la Hague which is the least dangerous.

The NE-going flood runs faster than the SW-going ebb but even the latter reaches 4 knots at neaps so timing the passage is all important in low-powered craft.

Transiting the Race

From N

Arrival in vicinity of ⊕23 should be timed for HW St Helier +0430 when the stream turn SW giving 5–6 hours fair to Guernsey or Jersey. A track in the main fairway via ⊕s 24 or 25 towards 26 or 27 should be maintained clear of the dangers south westerly to Guernsey or south south westerly to Jersey or St Malo.

From E

The inshore stream along the N side of the Cotentin peninsula starts at HW Cherbourg -0130 (HW St Helier +0100) and continues for 8 hours. The stream to the W of Cap de la Hague turns to the S at HW St Helier +0430 so there is plenty of time to carry a fair stream from Cherbourg 12M to the E, and thence S. An earlier arrival off Cap de la Hague at HW St Helier +0200 may be worth it to find the early S-going inshore eddy close W of La Foraine beacon off Goury. The penalty for not picking this eddy up, however is to face another 2½ hours at just past maximum flow, but easing off.

The Admiralty Tidal Stream Atlas for the Channel Islands NP 264 should be consulted for this passage and for all other passages through the Race.

From S and SW

Leaving Guernsey at HW St Helier -0230 will pick up the first of the N-going stream there and carry nearly 7 hours fair. Similarly a departure from St Helier at HW -0300 will carry a stream for 7 hours E and then N to clear the Race before it turns foul. In both cases a track must be maintained to clear Banc de la Schôle, Milieu, South Banks, the Race Rocks and the 16m Bank. The 17m bank should be avoided if possible if proceeding up the E coast of Jersey via ⊕s 14, 12, 9 and 8.

From W

The same timings and track apply if passing to the N of Guernsey from the W except an option to pass through the Swinge via ⊕22 will present itself. For this passage and for proceeding close along Alderney's SE shore see pages 39 and 40.

If passing through the Swinge from the SW or W beware Pierre au Vraic rock 2M to the WSW of ⊕22 which dries 1.2m.

The Casquet banks some 2M S of the Casquets with a least depth of 7.3m over them should also be avoided in strong wind and tidal conditions.

110 ALDERNEY

An attractive island beset by strong tidal streams and reefs. A harbour with yacht moorings at Braye which is open to the NE

Location
9M W of Cap de la Hague

Shelter
From SE through W to N

Warning
Many tidal dangers surround the island

Depth restrictions
3–13m at the moorings

Night entry
Well with leading lights

Berthing
On moorings or at anchor

Tidal information
HW St Helier +0045
LW St Helier +0045

Mean height of tide

HWS	HWN	LWN	LWS
6.2	4.7	2.5	0.9

Tidal streams
See below

Facilities
Usual supplies and repair support

Charts
BA 60 (25), 2845 (6), 3653 (50)
SC 5604.7, 5604.8
Imray C33A, Folio 2500

Weather
CROSS Joburg Ch 80 at 0715, 1545 and 1915 LT
Island FM on 93.7MHz every H+30
Daily weather map in harbour office

Radio
Ch 74 and 16 0800–2000
Water taxi Ch 37/80 ☎ 01481 822772

Telephone
Harbour Office ☎ 01481 822620
Email steve.shaw@gov.gg

20	Alderney NE	49°45′.19N 02°09′.93W
21	Alderney NW	49°44′.84N 02°12′.09W
22	Swinge	49°42′.74N 02°15′.79W
23	North Race	49°45′.80N 02°04′.30W

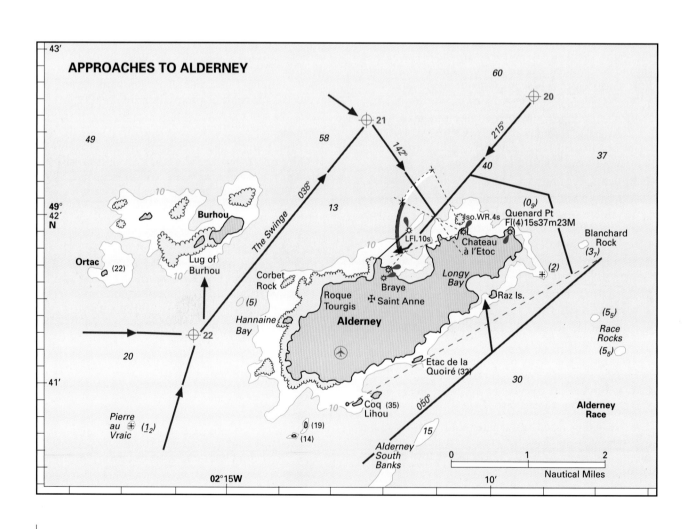

Warnings

The island is beset with the strongest tidal streams. The following areas should be given a wide berth in wind over tide conditions where the overfalls can be lethal – Swinge, Blanchard, Inner and Outer Race Rocks. The tidal flow can reverse in a short distance in some places near the shores.

Tidal streams

The tidal streams are shown in diagrams on BA chart 60, and also in *Admiralty Tidal Stream Atlas – Channel Islands* NP 264.

In the Swinge slack water is at HW St Helier –0230 and +0330. In the Race, about 1M to the E of the island the SW/NE going stream is slack at HW St Helier –0200 and +0330. It should be noted that the times of slack water do not coincide with times of HW and LW at Braye. Around the island the flood sets NE and the ebb SW but there are two inshore anomalies:

• Along the SE coast of the island the set is always to the NE except between HW St Helier +0500 to +0600 when it is slack. There little or no SW-going.

• Along the N corner of the island between Gros Nez Point at the root of the breakwater and the Grois Rocks off Chateau l'Etoc the inshore stream sets SW except between HW St Helier –0200 and HW. This counter-current runs at up to 4 knots at springs and is separated only by a narrow band of water from the main flood stream setting NE at the same rate. It must be noted that this sets strongly on to the submerged part of the breakwater when approaching Braye.

Both these anomalies can be made use of when approaching Braye from the S through the Race or entering harbour from the NE during the flood. They are of only limited use when coming through the Swinge.

PILOTAGE

Approaches

From N and E

From ⊕20 1½M N of the conspicuous Quenard Point lighthouse (Fl(4)15s) Braye harbour entrance will be open. Care must be taken on the ebb not to be set down into the Race off the E end of the island. From this position the leading lights (QW *Front* and *Rear*) will be visible at night but the beacons may be difficult to see by day particularly in the afternoon sun although mounted on day-glo orange triangles. If in doubt St Anne's church spire is conspicuous on the skyline; keep this bearing 215° until the leading marks can be identified and proceed into harbour taking care not to be set on to the submerged part of the breakwater in the latter stages.

Braye, Alderney looking SW   *Peter Carnegie*

II. THE CHANNEL ISLANDS

From N and W

Passing through the Swinge via ⊕22 is preferable at slack water which is at HW St Helier -0230 or when it is at its weakest NE-going from +0200 to +0330. The worst of the overfalls are between Corbet Rock and Burhou.

If passing N of Burhou to ⊕21 endeavour to pick out the two inconspicuous and spindly beacons which lead clear of the submerged breakwater. If they cannot be seen keep the lighthouses of Quenard Point and Chateau l'Etoc (Iso.WR.4s) well open or bearing more than 112° until St Anne's spire bears 215° and the leading line can be identified. At night keep in the white sector of Chateau l'Etoc until the leading lights are seen.

From S through the Swinge

The only off-lying danger is Pierre au Vraic which dries 1.2m and lies some 2M S of Ortac. Time arrival at ⊕22 either at slack water HW St Helier –0230 or between HW St Helier +0200 and +0330. See *Warning* above when using this passage.

From S passing SE and E of the island

Advantage may be taken of the almost permanent set NE along the SE coast. Aim to arrive off Raz Island between HW St Helier -0200 and -0400 to make the most of the favourable eddy round to Braye. There is a clearing transit of more than 240° of Etac de la Quoire and Coque Lihou which leads clear of the Brinchetais Ledge; otherwise keep outside the 20m line until Quenard Point bears 310° or less when course may be altered to the N to pass round Quenard Point with its offlyers of Sauquet Rock and The Grois Rocks. Keep outside the 15m line until St Anne's spire bears 215° and/or the leading line is identified.

Entrance to Braye Harbour

Once past the breakwater head, the straight channel clear of moorings is marked by red and green lit buoys and leads up to the pier and inner harbour.

Moorings

There are at least 80 visitors' moorings in rows parallel to the breakwater and more in the SE corner of Braye Bay. They have a small ring on top and unless a patent pick-up device is used may need to be lassoed initially in any wind. Yachts longer than about 15m may find some of the spaces between buoys too small.

Anchorage

There are many rocky patches in the bay that should be avoided if possible. In NE'ly winds some shelter may be found in the SE part of Braye Bay to the SW of Toulouse Rock clear of moorings. Anchoring is prohibited in the fairway.

Berthing

Berths alongside the pier are very unlikely to be available as it is used by the ferries. Ask the Harbour Office on Ch 74 before proceeding there

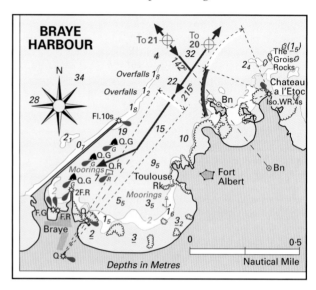

111 Braye

Facilities

Water and fuel from Mainbrayce Chandlers inside the inner harbour. There is a drying berth just to port inside the entrance and a tide gauge at this entrance shows the depth at the berth. Call on Ch 80. Water

Quenard Lighthouse looking W   *Peter Carnegie*

taxi call on Ch 37 or 80. Dinghy landing at the slip at all stages of the tide. Showers and heads by the Harbour Office. Yacht club on the quay welcomes visitors; shops and a small supermarket in Braye village; there is also a duty-free alcohol and tobacco outlet here which delivers on board. Restaurants, cafés and pubs in Braye Village and more ¾M up the hill in St Anne. Bicycle hire available in Braye. Post Office and banks in St Anne.

Leisure

An unspoilt and rural island with pleasant walks and rides.

Travel

A high-speed passenger service operates several times weekly from March to October from Portsmouth, Poole and Weymouth via Jersey and Guernsey. There is a direct ferry service from Southampton and local boats run to Cherbourg and Guernsey. Aurigny Air services (☎ 01481 822 886) have regular flights to Guernsey, Jersey and Southampton. Jersey and Guernsey have international airports.

Other anchorages

112 The Lug of Burhou

A bay opening to the S between Burhou and Little Burhou. It can be approached from the SW and ⊕22 avoiding the overfalls in the Swinge if they are active. A stern transit that leads in is Coupé Rock just open of the Garden Rocks on 154° (See BA chart 60). This anchorage has a very strong tidal flow through it near HW springs but is otherwise sheltered.

113 Hannaine Bay

At the W end of the island and suitable to wait for the stream in the Swinge if it is foul. The transit of the white pyramid beacon S of Roque Tourgis Fort open to the right of Fort Clonque on 055° should be carefully held as the passage is only 200m wide in the entrance (See BA chart 60). Anchor in 3m sand 100m or more from Fort Clonque.

114 Longy Bay

A bay on the SE shore S of Quenard Point and just W of Raz Island. Useful to wait the stream round the E end of the island. Enter leaving Queslingue (14m) 100m to port and the rock drying 0.6m clear to starboard (See BA chart 60). Well sheltered in NE-lies.

Departures

To N and E
HW St Helier –0230 will find slack water outside Braye, turning to the NE.

To N and W
HW St Helier +0400 will find the inshore stream starting to the SW and the best time to pass N of Burhou. If going through the Swinge HW St Helier +0300–0330 will find slack water there, turning to the SW.

To S
As above if going through the Swinge. If passing round Quenard Point before turning S, HW St Helier +0400 will find a counter-current against close inshore until Brinchetais Ledge when at HW St Helier +0500 the SW stream will be away.

History and local interest

To the Romans Alderney was known as Vecta Riduna and its inhabitants Ridunians, a title which is still heard today. The port then was in Longy Bay but it silted up in the Middle Ages. The French call the island Aurigny. The island was well placed for privateering on the trade through the English Channel in the 17th- and 18th-century but in the 19th-century respectability came with the building of the Admiralty Breakwater in 1864 with the intention of providing shelter for British warships; this never came to fruition and only 900m remains (plus the underwater rubble) as a continuing maintenance load on The Bailiwick of Guernsey's budget.

The island was evacuated during the Second World War and became a prison island for slave labour mainly from E Europe.

The island and area is famous for its bird life. Ortac is one of the principal gannetries in the British Isles, together with Garden Rocks (Les Etacs) off the W coast. Burhou, where landing is prohibited from March to July, is the nesting ground of puffins, storm petrels, Manx shearwaters and many gulls and is frequented by seals.

Longy Bay   *Peter Carnegie*

115 GUERNSEY

Guernsey is the western most of the Channel Islands; it is well developed and prosperous although not as commercialised as Jersey. It has two busy ports and five marinas, two for visitors who are well catered for and welcomed. Good access and shelter in most weathers.

Warnings

Tidal streams, while not so fierce as further north are strong and should always be considered. The tidal range is up to 10m. In thick weather and bad visibility navigation becomes difficult in the vicinity of the island even with radar and GPS.

26	Fougère	49°31'.24N 02°27'.77W
29	Roust el NNE	49°29'.45N 02°28'.68W
30	St Peter Port	49°27'.37N 02°31'.36W
31	Musé	49°26'.24N 02°27'.53W
32	Lower Heads	49°25'.74N 02°28'.53W
33	St Martins SE	49°24'.72N 02°31'.37W
34	Hanois SW	49°25'.69N 02°44'.08W
35	Doyle N	49°31'.94N 02°31'.60W
36	Beaucette	49°30'.25N 02°30'.08W
37	Aligande (Herm)	49°27'.95N 02°28'.88W
38	Percée (Herm)	49°27'.75N 02°27'.37'.W
39	Forquies (Herm)	49°27'.38N 02°26'.45W
40	Gouliot (Sark)	49°26'.15N 02°22'.88W
41	Sark N	49°27'.48N 02°22'.00W
42	Sark S	49°23'.79N 02°22'.48W
43	Maseline (Sark E)	49°26'.14N 02°20'.48W

116 St Peter Port

The main port and visitors' marina with all the facilities

Location
In the middle of the E side of Guernsey

Shelter
Uncomfortable in easterlies

Warning
See above under *Guernsey*

Depth restrictions
0.3m in harbour; 1.5–2m in marina

Night entry
Leading lights and well lit

Tidal information
Standard Port. Within 10 minutes of times at St Helier

Mean height of tide (m)

HWS	HWN	LWN	LWS
8.8	7.0	3.6	1.4

Tidal streams
HW St Helier -0245 N-going starts
HW St Helier +0300 S-going starts

Berthing
Alongside pontoons

Facilities
Comprehensive

Charts
BA 807 (25), 808 (25), 3140 (6)
SC 5604.9, 5604.11
Imray C33A, Folio 2500

Weather
St Peter Port Radio on Ch 20, 62 at 0133, 0533, 0933, 1333, 1733, 2133 UTC
CROSS Joburg Ch 80 at 0715, 1345 and 1915 LT
Weather map marina office

Radio
Port Control Ch 12
Victoria Marina Ch 37 and 80
Water taxi Ch 10
Telephone
Harbour authority ☎ 01481 720229
Signal station ☎ 01481 720085

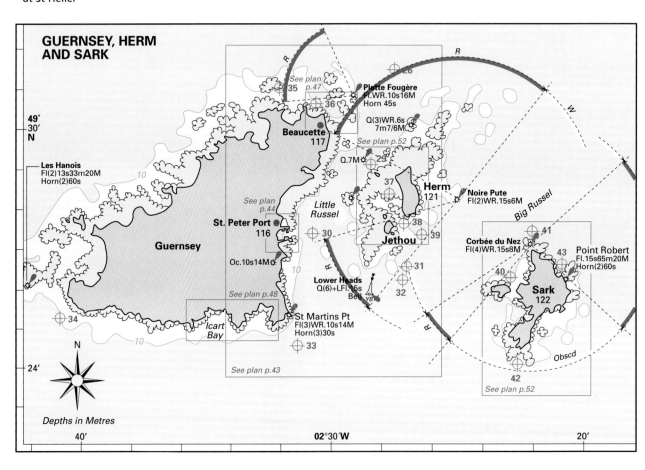

PILOTAGE

Approaches to St Peter Port

From NE via Big Russel

From the vicinities of ⊕24 or 25 pass to the E of Herm down the Big Russel to arrive at ⊕31 or 32 at HW St Helier -0330 with the last of the S-going stream. There will then be the minimum of overfalls in the area and the first of the N-going stream to carry across to St Peter Port. The corner may be cut here provided Victoria Tower and the right hand edge of Castle Cornet on 291° can be identified from ⊕31. This leads through the Musée Passage leaving the Musée Beacon (yellow with M topmark) 300m to the N. If this line cannot be seen, continue to ⊕32 and the Lower heads buoy (Q(6)+Fl.15s) and make good a track of 310° to St Peter Port.

From NE via Little Russel

The best time to arrive off the N end of the Little Russel is HW St Helier –0330 when only a weak N-going stream will be met for another hour and there will be water over the sills at Victoria marina (dries 4.2m) and Beaucette (dries 2.4m).

From ⊕26 1M NE of Platte Fougère

(Fl.WR.10s) pick up the first transit of Roustel (lattice structure with low black and white chequered base, Q) and Brehon (small beacon on squat round tower, Iso.4s) and continue down it leaving Tautenay (Black and white beacon, Q(3)WR.6s) well to port and Petite Canupe (S cardinal, Q(6)+LFl.15s) to starboard. 300m short of Roustel and ⊕29 alter to 220° on the main leading line of Castle Breakwater (White tower Alt.WR.10s) and Belvedere light (White square at rt hand end of Belvedere House near the skyline, Oc.W.10s). Leave Vale Mill Tower, the chimneys and tanks of St Sampson and Refée buoy (N cardinal, Q(6)+LFl 10s) all to starboard, to ⊕30 off the entrance.

From NW via Little Russel

Either pass N of the Grandes Brayes, Petites Brayes and Platte Fougère to reach ⊕26 and pick up the first transit 198° or use the Doyle Passage. Whichever is used HW St Helier –0300 is a good time as the stream will still be setting E along the N coast.

Doyle Passage

This is useful if going to Beaucette or as a short cut inside Platte Fougère. From ⊕35 pick up the transit Roustel (Lattice structure with black and white chequered base) in the centre of the gap between Herm and Jethou 149°; on this line the islet of Fondu may be just to the left of Roustel. Continue until Fort Doyle is abeam to starboard when track may be adjusted towards the waiting buoys outside Beaucette. Turn to port off the 149° line on to the Beaucette leading line 096°/276° and DO NOT overshoot it (*See inset on chart 807*). Continue exactly along this line (0.2m least depth) until Petite Canupe beacon (S cardinal) is left to port when course may be altered for ⊕29 or Roustel and the

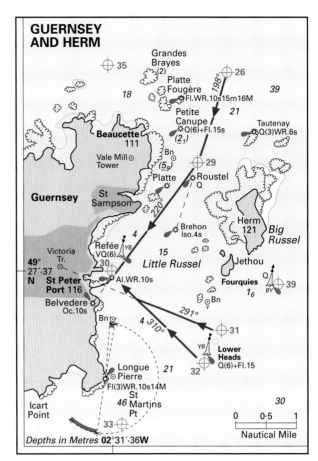

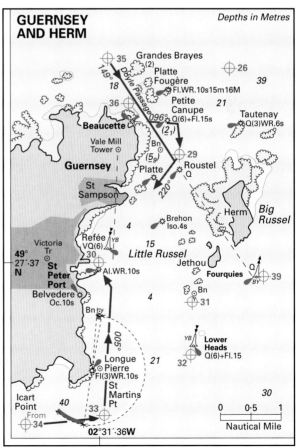

final leading line picked up. The 149° line may be held past Beaucette but it goes over drying 7.9m rocks and very close to Corbette d'Amont beacon. (*See chart 807*)

From NW via Les Hanois and St Martins Pt

There is more latitude tidewise in using this southern route and is probably just as quick approaching St Peter Port from the N as from HW St Helier −0500 the stream is fair along the S coast and up the Little Russel. It is preferable to the N entrance in poor visibility.

The best time to arrive at ⊕34 is HW St Helier −0500 to −0200. From here proceed along the S coast to ⊕33 keeping outside the 30m line. Identify Longue Pierre beacon (Black, top mark LP) just to the NE of St Martins Pt light (White concrete building, Fl.WR.10s); when Brehon Tower (squat and round, Iso.4s) is well open of Longue Pierre, course may be altered to the N towards ⊕30. The transit by day is Vale Mill Tower over the right hand green roofed shed at St Sampson on 005°. By night keep the Breakwater light (Alt.WR.10s) bearing less than 355°, and keep outside the 30m line.

From S

The stream sets N in the S part of the Little Russel from HW St Helier -0300 to +0300. The strongest flow is in the middle to E side. It reverses at HW St Helier +0030 on the Guernsey side while the N-going stream continues on the Herm side until HW St Helier +0300.

The Little Russel is clear of all dangers to yachts between Longue Pierre off St Martins Pt and Lower Heads S of Jethou provided the Breakwater Head light (Stone tower, Alt.WR.10s) is kept between 310° and 355°. The transit above of Vale Mill Tower/right hand green shed is useful if wanting to dodge a foul stream to St Peter Port and ⊕30.

Entrance to St Peter Port

Listen out on Ch 12 especially if a red light is exhibited on the pierhead which prohibits entry to all vessels except those under 15m and under power. The entrance is wide and clear except for other vessels entering or leaving. The Victoria marina leading lights will give a good indication of cross-stream outside. Contrary to usual convention keep to PORT (SOUTH) side on entering where the yacht approach channel marked by a green conical buoy Fl(2+1)G.10s and three red can buoys with Fl.R will be seen parallel to the Castle Cornet breakwater. When the last port hand buoy is reached just beyond the fuel berth, turn hard to starboard towards the waiting and visitors' pontoons and moorings. Visitors are usually met by the marina staff in a dory and directed but if not call on Ch 80.

Berthing

Alongside pontoons in Victoria Marina which is dredged to 2m (mostly with a soft bottom). Sill is

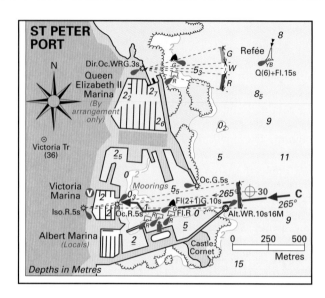

4.2m above CD. Limit 14m but longer can be accepted if there is room.

Moorings

There are several visitors' pontoons and moorings N of the marina entrance which provide an overflow for the marina and can become very crowded.

Anchorage

It would be unwise to anchor in the harbour except in an emergency. There are many old chains and blocks on the bottom. There is also very little room that would not encroach on fairways, manoeuvring areas and moorings. See page 48 for anchorage in Havelet Bay just to the S of St Peter Port.

Ashore and other marinas

Apart from Victoria Marina and Beaucette which are the two marinas for visitors, there are three others. Queen Elizabeth II Marina adjacent to St Peter Port may accept visitors by prior booking while Albert Marina in the S corner of St Peter Port is for locals as is the new marina at St Sampson, hitherto a commercial port.

There is a tourist information office by the marina and well worth visiting to find out what is on offer in this lively and bustling island if staying more than a day or so.

Facilities

Water and electricity on pontoons in marina; fuel from fuel berth on S side of harbour at duty-free prices; dinghy landing at steps outside marina entrance; both yacht clubs welcome visitors – the Guernsey Yacht Club is on the Castle Cornet peninsula; the Royal Channel Islands Yachts Club is close to the NE corner of the marina but has been due to move for some time; 75-ton travel-lift (the biggest in the islands); showers and heads on E pier of marina; many shops, restaurants, pubs, chandlers and hotels of all qualities, many within close walking distance; good maintenance and repair facilities; car and bicycle hire readily available.

Travel

There are daily passenger or Ro/Ro ferries to Portsmouth and fast ferries to Poole and Weymouth although the latter are more weather dependent. There are fast ferries to Herm, Sark, Jersey, St Malo and Cherbourg. There are daily or more frequent flights to Gatwick, Stansted, Manchester, Exeter, Southampton, Jersey and Dinard.

St Peter Port. Havelet Bay bottom right, then marinas; Albert (locals) Victoria (visitors) Queen Elizabeth II (by arrangement) and St Sampson (locals) at top of picture

St Peter Port towards low tide

II. THE CHANNEL ISLANDS

117 Beaucette Marina

A small intimate marina on the NE corner of the island; good marina facilities; small restaurant, only basic shops.

Location
NE corner of the island

Shelter
Good but uncomfortable in strong easterlies around HW

Warning
Entry should not be attempted in strong easterlies

Depth restrictions
0.2m patch on approach; sill dries 2.4m; deep inside

Night entry
Leading lights; pontoon lights inside

Tidal information
As for St Peter Port which is a Standard Port. Within 10 minutes of St Helier times

Mean height of tide (m)

HWS	HWN	LWN	LWS
8.8	7.0	3.6	1.4

Tidal streams
HW St Helier +0200 NW-going starts
HW St Helier –0600 SE-going starts

Berthing
On pontoons with fingers

Facilities
Good marina facilities; basic shops

Charts
BA 807 (25), 808 (25)
SC 5604.9, 5604.11
Imray C33A, Folio 2500

Weather
St Peter Port radio on Ch 20 and 62 at 0133, 0533, 0933, 1333, 1733, 2133 UTC
CROSS Joburg on Ch 80 at 0715, 1345, 1915 LT

Radio
Beaucette Marina on Ch 80
Marina ☎ 01481 245000
Email info@beaucettemarina.com

Ashore in Beaucette

The entrance in to this old quarry was made in the 1960s and it has been a marina since. The advantage over St Peter Port is that the sill dries 2.4m and entry is possible earlier than Victoria Marina.

Facilities

Water and electricity on the pontoons; fuel from the fuel barge at any time; showers, heads and launderette in office block; 16-ton travel-lift, 12-ton crane; basic shop in the marina, another 10 minutes walk outside; car and cycle hire through the office; restaurant by the office in season, otherwise many in St Sampson; possibility of laying up here but early booking needed.

Leisure

Beaucette is in a part of the island given over to glasshouse cultivation that used to be for tomatoes but is now more likely to be for the cut flower trade. There are attractive coastal walks towards Fort Doyle to the NW beyond which is the island's golf course. Hire of a car for a day or two to see the island's many other attractions is worthwhile.

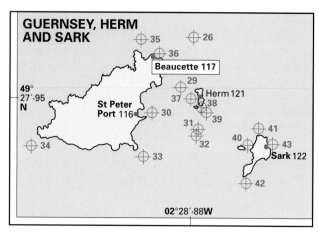

GUERNSEY, HERM AND SARK

26	Fougère	49°31'.24N 02°27'.77W
29	Roustel NNE	49°29'.45N 02°28'.68W
30	St Peter Port	49°27'.37N 02°31'.36W
31	Musé	49°26'.24N 02°27'.53W
32	Lower Heads	49°25'.74N 02°28'.53W
33	St Martins SE	49°24'.72N 02°31'.37W
34	Hanois SW	49°25'.69N 02°44'.08W
35	Doyle N	49°31'.94N 02°31'.60W
36	Beaucette	49°30'.25N 02°30'.08W
37	Alligande (Herm)	49°27'.95N 02°28'.88W
38	Percée (Herm)	49°27'.75N 02°27'.37W
39	Forquies (Herm)	49°27'.38N 02°26'.45W

Travel

An occasional bus, otherwise taxi. The airport is at the other end of the island and all the ferries run from St Peter Port

PILOTAGE

Approaches

From NW

The Doyle Passage is not recommended at night. From ⊕35 pick up the transit Roustel (lattice tower with square solid top) in the centre of the gap between Herm and Jethou 149°; the islet of Fondu may just be visible just to the left of Roustel. Continue until Fort Doyle is abeam to starboard when course may be altered for the waiting buoys outside Beaucette and the entrance.

Beaucette Marina   *Peter Carnegie*

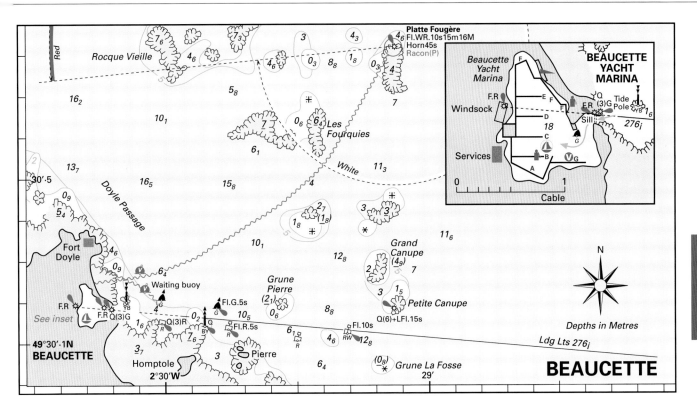

From E and Little Russel

A night passage is dependent on picking up the leading lights (both F.R) before Petite Canupe is reached Q(6)+LFl15s.

Leave Petite Canupe S cardinal beacon to starboard and fairway marked to port on the leading line 276° (*Front*, White patch on N side of entrance, *Rear*, mast on top of office building); this may be difficult to see in the afternoon sun. The channel is buoyed by 2 red and 1 green buoy, all lit.

Note that there is a 0.2m patch in the later stages. Leave a S cardinal beacon to starboard just before the entrance.

Entrance

The rocks are painted white on either side and there is a depth gauge showing depth over the sill on the N side. Boats LEAVING have priority.

When through the entrance turn hard to port before the first wall and G pontoon will be seen ahead with its yellow hauling off buoys; if not allocated a berth here, turn hard back to starboard round a starboard hand buoy for the rest of the marina. The fuel berth will be seen ahead at this stage.

Berthing

Either on fingers or alongside pontoons

Moorings and Anchorages

There are 8 yellow waiting buoys to the N of the entrance if there is not enough water over the sill. There is space to anchor in about 5m off Fort Doyle to the N of these moorings.

Apart from the four hauling-off buoys just inside the entrance which are there in the event of strong easterlies, there are no moorings inside nor is there room to anchor in the deep (mostly 18m+) and rocky marina.

S Martins looking N   *Peter Carnegie*

Guernsey. Les Hanois lighthouse looking NW

118 Havelet Bay

Lies on the S side of Castle Cornet and is a convenient anchorage for those not caring for the hurly-burly of St Peter Port. Enter between Oyster Beacon (Yellow spindle with O topmark) and Moulinet beacon (Yellow spindle with M topmark) and anchor as convenient in between 1.1m and 7m avoiding the rocky patches towards the edges. The entrance is also marked by port and starboard buoys (Fl.R and G). The moorings on the N side are private. A landing slip just to the W of Castle Cornet is convenient for the Guernsey Yacht Club. This bay is subject to swell near HW on the N-going stream.

119 Icart Bay

On the S side of the island, it is over ½M wide with Fourquie de la Moye (drying 3.3m) in its middle. Locate the Martello Tower at the head of Petit Bôt Bay and approach it on a track of between 350° and 005° or with the tower just over the point to the SW of it. Anchorage in 3m may be found 100m S of the points in relative shelter from W through N to E.

120 Moulin Huet Bay

There are three small bays here – Saints Bay, Moulin Huet and Petit Port. Avoiding Moulière (dries 8.5m) anchor in a suitable depth between Moulin Huet and Petit Port. Saints Bay has a fibre optic cable running through it which is marked by a beacon.

Departures

To N and W southabout

The optimum time to leave St Peter Port is HW St Helier +0300 which carries the first of the S-going stream to St Martins, a fair stream along the S coast and a further 1 or 2 hours W-going stream to clear the island. This means leaving Victoria Marina early to clear the sill. Leaving at HW St Helier +0200 will find a foul stream to St Martins Pt but turning fair along the S coast.

To N and W northabout

Leave HW St Helier +0200 to carry the last of the N-going stream up the Little Russel and benefit from 6 hours of W and SW-going stream in the Channel.

To NE

Leaving HW St Helier –0230 or as soon as the sill can be cleared to take the first of the N-going up the Little Russel and then carry nearly 7 hours fair to Alderney and the Race.

To SW

Leave at HW St Helier +0300 to catch the first of the S-going stream and carry 3 hours of fair stream thereafter.

To SE

Bound for St Helier the tide is fair from HW St Helier –0500 to HW +0100.

For Granville or St Malo leave earlier in order to make the half tide sill at Granville or HW at St Malo.

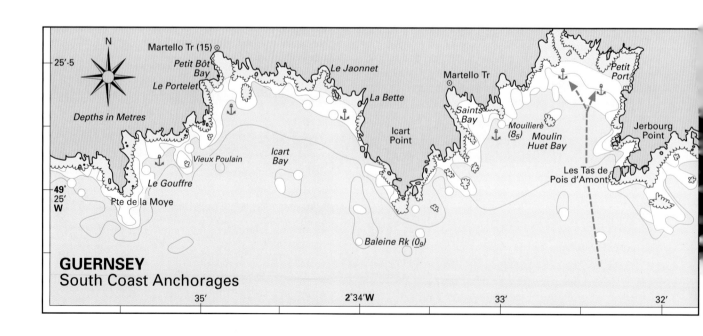

GUERNSEY
South Coast Anchorages

121 HERM (AND JETHOU)

Herm has many delightful anchorages where permission is needed to stay overnight; minimal facilities. Jethou is private and landing prohibited.

Location
3M east of Guernsey

Shelter
Depending on wind direction

Depth restrictions
Drying 3.3m at quay; 2.5m in Alligande Passage

Night entry
Not recommended although there are some lights

Tidal information
As for St Peter Port which is a Standard Port; within 10 minutes of St Helier times

Mean height of tide

HWS	HWN	LWN	LWS
8.8	7.0	3.6	1.4

Tidal streams
Complex round the islands; see *Admiralty Tidal Atlas* NP 264

Berthing
Various anchorages

Facilities
Water and a basic shop

Charts
BA 808 and 807 (25), Imray Folio 2500

Weather
St Peter Port Radio on Ch 20 and 62 at 0133 0533, 0933, 1333, 1733, 2133 UTC.
CROSS Joburg on Ch 80 at 0715, 1545, 1945 LT

Radio
None except for St Peter Port
Telephone near the quay

See previous page for positions of neighbouring waypoints

PILOTAGE

Approaches

Alligande Passage This is the most direct route from St Peter Port ⊕30 to ⊕37.

It is usable drawing 2m from half tide onwards as far as the Vermerette beacon. When the Vermerette's rock (drying 4.3m) is covered there will be 1m at the end of Herm Quay.

Leave Alligande Beacon (green with A topmark and lit) 200m to the S and identify Vermerette Beacon (yellow with V topmark and lit). Align this with the white patch on Herm Quay on 074°. This will lead in to the Percée Passage. When 200m short of Vermerette Beacon, turn to port and align the two white pillars to the left of Herm Quay on 078°. This leads in to the anchorage and quay.

The drying area to the NE of Vermerette is sand and stones and not rocky as shown on the BA charts. Also the drying 4.3m should be bracketed as it refers to the Vermerette Rock and not the surrounds that dry approximately 2m.

Ashore in Herm

Facilities

Water tap on the quay; heads and showers near the quay; basic shop near the quay; café and a good restaurant and hotel.

Travel

Frequent ferries run from St Peter Port and this may be a preferable way to visit the island if in a deep draught boat.

Percée Passage While proceeding along the first transit 074° for the Alligande Passage (see above), identify the Corbette Beacon to the N (yellow with red disc topmark) and Vale Mille Tower on Guernsey. Turn to 128° when Vale Mill is open by two of its widths to the LEFT of Corbette Beacon and hold this alignment to leave Epec Beacon (Green with E topmark and lit) to starboard, Percée Beacon (W cardinal and lit) to port and continue through the gap until the 20m line is reached when all the dangers will be passed except for the Forquies whose N cardinal buoy should be left to starboard.

Anchorage

It may just be possible to lie afloat to the E of Vermerette Beacon if drawing 2m over the slackest of neaps. Otherwise bilge keels or legs will be needed.

37 Alligande (Herm) 49°27'.95N 02°28'.88W
38 Percée (Herm) 49°27'.75N 02°27'.37'.W
39 Fourquies (Herm) 49°27'.38N 02°26'.45W

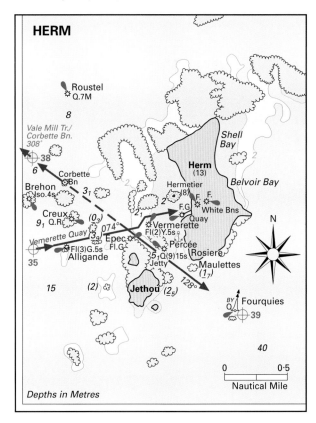

II. THE CHANNEL ISLANDS

The Quay *Peter Carnegie*

The deepwater anchorage is off Rosière Steps just to the S. This may be approached from the Percée Passage by keeping Hermetière well open of Rosière Steps to avoid the Meulettes and anchoring as the depth dictates to the E of Mouette. The stream runs strongly to the S through this anchorage until half tide when the sands to the N start to uncover, and dinghy work can be dangerous especially in south westerlies. The ferries use Rosière Steps when Herm Quay dries at the bottom half of the tide.

On the E side of the island there are good beaches and pleasant anchorages sheltered from the W at Shell Bay and Belvoir Bay. See previous plan.

History

The States of Guernsey bought the island in 1949 from the Crown and it has been maintained in an excellent state by the Wood family since then with a permanent community of about 40. In the centre is the Manor house with a 12th-century Chapel of St Tugual. Ask at the Administrative Office near the quay for permission to stay overnight (☎ 01481 722377).

Percée Channel *Peter Carnegie*

122 SARK AND BRECQHOU

A high, rugged island independent since 1565 with its own parliament. There are no cars, two small harbours and a number of anchorages. Brecqhou is private and landing is prohibited.

Location
3M SE of Herm, 6M E of Guernsey

Shelter
Wind dependent

Warning
Complex tidal streams round island

Depth restrictions
Creux harbour dries

Night entry
Lights are inadequate for navigation round Sark at night.

Tidal information
HW and LW St Helier +0010

Mean height of tide (m)

HWS	HWN	LWN	LWS
9.0	6.6	3.5	1.0

Tidal streams
See *Admiralty Tidal Atlas* NP264

Berthing
Generally at anchor

Facilities
Basic needs from village

Charts
BA 808 (25), Imray Folio 2500

Weather
St Peter Port radio on Ch 20, 62 at 0133, 0533, 0933, 1333, 2133 UTC
CROSS Joburg Ch 80 at 0715, 1545, 1915 LT

Radio
Ch 12 (when manned)

Communications
Harbourmaster ☎ 01481 832332

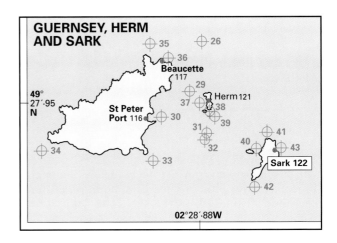

GUERNSEY, HERM AND SARK

49°27′.95 N

02°28′.88W

Beaucette 117
St Peter Port 116
Herm 121
Sark 122

Ashore in Sark

Facilities

Water from taps on the quays in both harbours; diesel may be available from the power station in cans in an emergency; bank, shops and post office in the village; several hotels, pubs and restaurants round the island.

Leisure

Bicycles and rides in horse-drawn carriages may be hired. Transport by tractor and trailer is available up and down the hill for the less energetic; otherwise a walk or ride to the dramatic La Coupée between Sark and Little Sark is worthwhile.

II. THE CHANNEL ISLANDS

Maseline *Peter Carnegie*

Creux *Peter Carnegie*

PILOTAGE

Tidal streams The flood flows SW and the ebb NE at up to 6–7 knots at springs. There are many eddies and reversals inshore at full ebb or flood which are not shown on the *Tidal Atlas* or in *The Channel Islands*. The least streams are at half tide.

123 La Maseline

Approaching from the NE, Point Robert lighthouse is easily identified. Round the Petite Moie and the Grande Moie outside the 20m line until La Maseline jetty is seen and approach it on a bearing of 220° between Grande Moie and Grune du Nord over which the stream runs strongly. Leave Founiais beacon (yellow with F topmark) to port and anchor clear and to the NW of the jetty. This jetty is for commercial and ferry use only, has 4m alongside most of it and may be used briefly to land or take off crew provided it is clear.

124 Creux Harbour

This small drying harbour to the S of Maseline also offers access via a tunnel to the track up to the village. The only approach is from the SSE with Point Robert lighthouse in transit with the white arched entrance to the Creux tunnel over the centre of the harbour wall bearing 344°. Proceed up this transit until a convenient depth for anchoring is found clear of any mooring buoys. It is possible to dry out alongside the wall (dries approximately 3m) in the harbour but permission should be sought and a recce carried out beforehand.

It is prohibited to pass S between Les Burons (16) and Creux harbour.

125 Derrible and Dixcart Bays

These two bays on the SE coast are popular with visiting yachts. They are separated by Point Chateau and although sheltered to some extent from the SW are sometimes subject to swell. Both give access to the village but the climb is easier from Dixcart through the valley.

The approach transit of 337° shown on chart 808 is no longer visible but the approach is wide and danger free provided the Balmée, Baleine and La Conchée rocks are avoided. Anchor as close-in in either bay as depth, and other yachts, allow, on sand.

126 Gouliot Pass

This passage between Sark and Brecqhou is 80m wide with clean sides and a least depth of 2.6m. The tidal stream through it generally follows the direction of that in the Big Russel but it tends to turn earlier in the Passage. Slack water is at half tide. Spring rates can reach 7 knots.

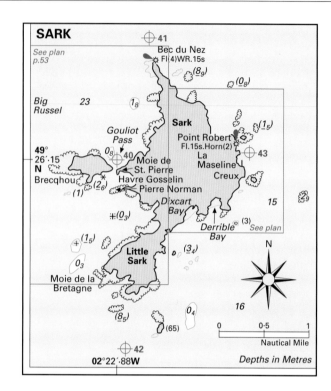

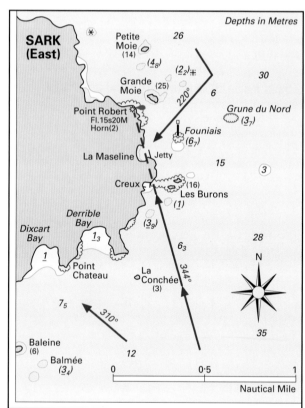

Passage N Keep the Bec du Nez bearing 022° well open of Moie St Pierre to clear Pierre Norman and a rock drying 2.6m to the S of Brecqhou. When through continue on the stern transit of 186°/006° of Moie de la Bretagne open of Moie de St Pierre and in the centre of the Passage to clear Grune Gouliot to the W and the Episseresses to the E.

Passage S Pick up the transit of Moie de la Bretagne open of Moie St Pierre and in the centre of the Passage 186°, when to the W of Bec du Nez. Turn to port in to Havre Gosselin when clear of Moie St Pierre and its off-lyer, or to the SW when abeam of Pierre Norman to clear the drying 2.6m rock to the S of Brechou.

127 Havre Gosselin

Another popular anchorage sheltered all round except from the SW. A swell can build up at certain states of the tide. Sark Mill is no longer visible and the approach transit on chart 808 is invalid. Leave Les Dents (1m) S of Brecqhou 200m to port on a track of 070° and identify Pierre Norman (dries 8.8m) and leave it to starboard. A conspicuous fissure on the N inner side of the Havre may help to lead in. A number of moorings put down by the Sark YC now take up nearly all the space to anchor and are available to visitors at a fee. Otherwise anchor where depths and space allow, mostly sand. There is a good dinghy landing and 299 steps up the cliff to the top of the island.

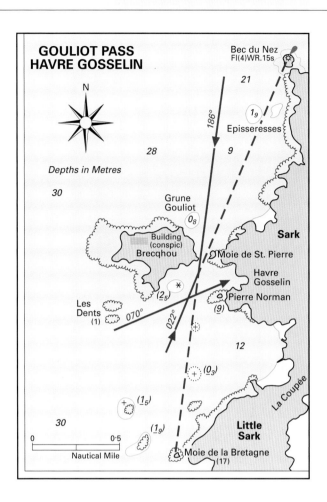

Gouliot pass and Havre Grasselin   *Peter Carnegie*

128 JERSEY

The largest, most commercial and populated of the Channel Islands with a greater influx of visitors in the season than all the other islands. There are three Marinas in St Helier (two for visitors), a drying port at Gorey and many anchorages round the coast.

129 St Helier

The capital of the island and principal port

Location
20M SE of Guernsey, 30M NW of Granville.

Shelter
First class in marinas

Warning
Tidal range over 10m

Depth restrictions
1.8m in Collette entrance; sill dries 3.3m in St Helier

Night entry
Well lit, good leading lights

Tidal information
St Helier is a Standard Port

Mean height of tide (m)

HWS	HWN	LWN	LWS
11.0	8.1	4.1	1.4

Tidal streams
Up to 5 knots off E end of island

Berthing
On pontoons in marinas

Facilities
Everything that is needed

Charts
BA 1135 (25), 1137 (25), 1138 (25), 3278 (6)
SC 5604, 5604.15, 5604.16
Imray C33A, C33B

Weather
Jersey Coastguard Ch 25, 82 at 0645, 0745, 0845 LT and 1245, 1845 and 2245 UTC.

Radio
Harbour Control Ch 14
Ch 18 wind speed and direction at St Helier every 2 minutes
Telephone
Harbour Office ☎ 01534 885599
St Helier Marina ☎ 01534 885508
La Collette Marina ☎ 01534 885529

27	Jersey NW	49°14'.20N 02°18'.00W
28	Jersey N	49°16'.55N 02°04'.90W
44	Jersey SW	49°10'.24N 02°16'.08W
45	St Helier	49°09'.94N 02°07'.33W
46	Jersey SE	49°07'.80N 01°57'.16W
47	Gorey	49°11'.94N 02°00'.78W

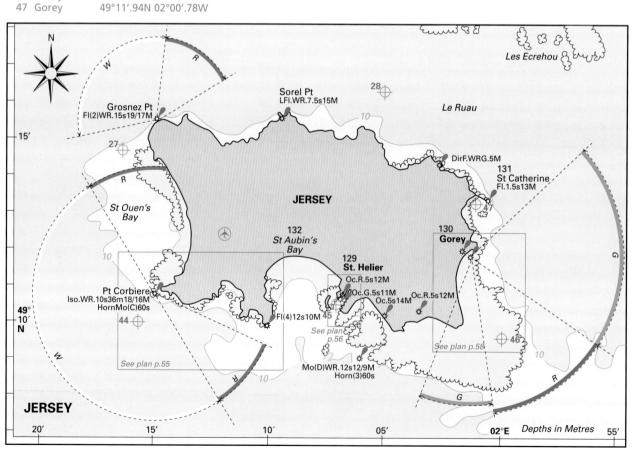

PILOTAGE

Approaches to St Helier

From N and W

The S-going stream along the W coast runs from HW St Helier +0400 to –0300; the E-going stream along the S coast starts at HW St Helier +0600 and continues until HW. An arrival off Grosnez Point at the NW corner of the island at HW St Helier –0400 will carry a fair stream for 3 hours plus to find plenty of water over the sill at St Helier or to enter La Collette basin.

From N

The Swashway Channel can be used in daylight provided the Great Rock on the Paternosters can be identified to keep open of Grosnez point on a back bearing of 045° to keep clear of Moulière Rock (dries 0.6m). *See chart 1136.* Otherwise proceed from ⊕27 to ⊕44.

At night and coming from SW

Keep in the white sector of La Corbière light to ⊕44 remaining outside the 20m line. From here Noirmont Point and light (Fl(4)12s) will be visible. Keep the lighthouse well open of Le Fret Point and at night the light bearing 095° or less to close Noirmont Point. Shortly before Passage Rock buoy (VQ N cardinal) comes abeam, alter course to 110° on the stern transit of La Corbière lighthouse just open to the left of the white patch on La Jument Rock, or at night the junction of the red and white sectors of La Corbière is on the same bearing. If neither are visible, keep Noirmont Point bearing less than 095°and pass to the N of Les Fours buoy (Q N cardinal) until the Western Passage leading line 082° is picked up.

By day only

The Dog's Nest beacon on this line is conspicuous and the leading lights at night (*Front*, Oc.5s, *Rear*, Oc.R.5s) are easily identifiable. Leave Ruaudière Rock buoy (Starboard Fl.G.3s) to starboard and turn short of East Rock buoy (Starboard Q.G) at ⊕45 on to the Red and Green Passage line 023° which leads in to the harbour. (*See Plan on next page for Entrance*)

If joining Western Passage transit further to the W, note that Passage Rock buoy is to the N of the transit and that Passage Rock to the S carries 4m. The least depth in the area on the transit is 2.7m but shallower dangers exist further to the S both here and in the vicinity of Les Fours.

From SW and S

There are three alternative approaches:

- Join the Western Passage transit in the vicinity of Passage Rock and proceed as above.

- Use the Red and Green Passage by day or night. This passes over a 1.2m patch and within 200m of rocks drying 1.5m so there must be enough water and/or the transit held exactly. Approaching from the SSW in deep water

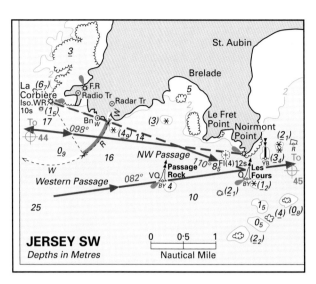

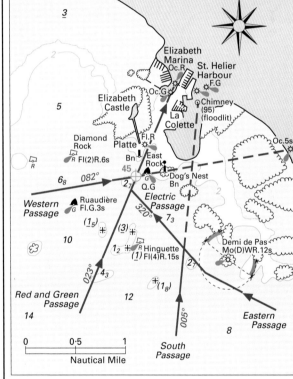

navigate to identify the marks well inside the harbour entrance bearing 023°. They are two thin metal columns, the rear on land and the front on a white painted caisson with a vertical red stripe. The lights are synchronised (*Front*, Oc.G.5s *Rear*, Oc.R.5s). This line leads right up to the inner harbour entrances (*See plan above*).

If this line cannot be picked out by the time the 20m line is crossed, consider using the South, Eastern or Electric Passage instead (*See plan above*).

II. THE CHANNEL ISLANDS

- The South, Eastern and Electric Passages are all approaches using the same stretch of hazard-free water with a least depth of 2.7m between Demi de Pas light (Mo(D)WR.12s) and Hinguette buoy. A day or night passage with the illuminated power station chimney (95m, conspicuous) bearing 350° will clear Demi de Pas; otherwise approach Demi de Pas between 330° and 050° until 400m from it when turn to the NW to leave Hinguette buoy (Port hand Fl(4)R.15s) to port. Then pick up the Red and Green Passage line 023° to proceed into harbour via ⊕45.

From SE

Identify Demi de Pas and approach on a bearing of 315°or more to pass S of Plateau de la Frouquie buoy (S cardinal Q(6)+LFl.15s) and then proceed via the South, Electric or Eastern Passages. The tidal stream off the SE corner sets N from 1½ hours before to 3 hours after HW then S from 4 hours after to 3½ hours before HW.

Port Control Signals

Exhibited on the Control Tower:

3 F.R.(vert) or Oc.	Stop
3 F.G.(vert) or Oc	Proceed, one way traffic
2 F.G.(vert) 1F.W. or Oc.	Proceed, two way traffic.
1 Oc.Y	Vessels less than 25m may enter or leave contrary to the signals.

St Helier Marina entrance

G outside	Clear for entry
G inside	Clear for exit
G & W	2-way traffic
R	No entry or exit or gate closed.

The R and G lights will be on at the same time. Collision avoidance is the skipper's responsibility.

Entrance and Berthing

Keep watch on Ch 14 when entering or leaving but there is no need to call Port control before proceeding. Yachts must keep clear of commercial shipping. The Red and Green Passage line leads right up to the inner entrances. When the Port Control Tower is abeam turn hard to starboard into La Collette or St Helier harbour.

La Collette

Two red buoys mark the shallow water in the entrance on the E side. Keep well to the W side on entry. Visitors' berths are on the first pontoon inside on the port hand. Dredged to 1.8m in entrance and basin.

St Helier marina

There is a pontoon outside for waiting; otherwise use La Collette. The sill depth is 3.5m above CD. A bottom-hinged gate rises 1.4m above this sill to retain 2.4m inside although this is not uniform and

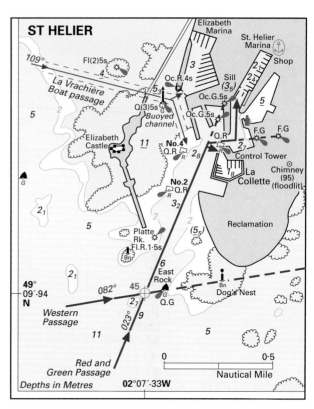

45   St Helier 49°09'.94N 02°07'.33W

there are shallow patches particularly on the N and W sides. The gate is automatic and entry is possible about 3 hours either side of HW. There is a tide gauge by the entrance showing depth of water over the sill.

Elizabeth Marina

Not for visitors without prior arrangement. It is reached by a buoyed channel running N by W from a red buoy to the N of No.4 port-hand buoy. Access is about 3 hours either side of HW. There are yellow waiting buoys outside and the light control is same as for Port Control. Access also via La Vrachière.

La Vrachière Boat Passage

This runs N of Elizabeth Castle to Elizabeth Marina and the main harbour. It dries 5.3m across the causeway to the Castle and there is rarely reason for visitors to use it but it is shown on the Plan.

Moorings and Anchorage

There are no moorings in St Helier harbour nor is anchoring allowed or advisable.

Ashore in St Helier

Facilities

Water and electricity on pontoons at St Helier and La Collette. Fuel (both diesel and petrol) from the fuel berth in St Helier on the South Pier opposite the entrance, depth alongside limited – about HW ±3 hours. Also from fuel barge off end of South Pier and fuel pontoon at entrance to La Collette. Both at all states of tide. Showers and heads at St Helier and La

Collette; chandlers, engineers and boat-builders all nearby; travel-lifts and cranes at St Helier and La Collette; launderette at St Helier; St Helier Yacht Club is on South Pier and welcomes visitors as does Royal Channel Islands Yacht Club at St Aubin; shop open long hours at St Helier Marina; this is the nearest to La Collette; a multitude of shops, supermarkets, markets and restaurants in the town.

Leisure

A visit to the Tourist Office near to St Helier Marina is well worthwhile if staying more than a day to find out what the island offers. The diversions are considerable as would be expected in a major holiday island and a car hired to view the sights would add to the scope.

Travel

There are daily passenger and Ro/Ro ferries to Portsmouth and fast ferries to Poole and Weymouth, although the latter are more weather dependent. There are fast ferries to Carteret, Granville, St Malo, and Guernsey. There are daily or more frequent flights to Gatwick, Stansted, Manchester, Exeter, Southampton, Guernsey and Dinard.

History

The Bailiwick of Jersey includes Les Ecréhous and Les Minquiers the latter being the southernmost territory of the British Isles. The Norman and French influence is perhaps the strongest here in all the islands and the patois still survives.

The islands seafarers and boat-builders were renowned from the 16th- to 19th-centuries and their exploits are well recorded in the Maritime Museum

St Helier Approaches to marinas *Peter Carnegie*

near St Helier Marina. Elizabeth Castle, besides being the major defence of the port was the Governor's residence until the late 18th-century. Hermitage Rock which is part of the Castle breakwater is reputed to be the past home of St Helier, hermit, missionary and patron saint.

Departures

Times are related to HW St Helier.

To NW

The stream turns to the N on the W side of the island 3 hours before HW but only turns fair on the S side at HW. The later the departure after HW, the greater the likelihood of overfalls in the vicinity of La Corbière. If passing Guernsey to the W, a departure 2 hours before HW would be favourable to carry the W-going stream along the S side of the island. A later departure at HW if going to St Peter Port should carry the last of the N-going stream up the Little Russel.

To N

Departure 3 hours before HW and proceeding eastabout through the Violet Channel will give nearly 7 hours fair stream along the S coast and then N to reach Alderney or clear the Race before it turns foul.

To W and SW

Departure 1 hour after HW will give the most favourable tidal conditions for 6 hours.

To S and SE

Departure time will depend on whether Les Minquiers are passed to the W or E. If passing to the W, departure at 3 hours after HW will give at least 3 hours of W-going stream to clear Les Minquiers followed by 5 hours generally favourable to reach St Malo in time for the locks or sill.

II. THE CHANNEL ISLANDS

Unless bound for Granville the streams do not serve so well going E of Les Minquiers but a departure at 1 hour after LW will carry 3 hours of generally favourable stream to arrive in time to cross the sill.

130 Gorey, Jersey

A drying harbour on the NE corner of the island with anchorages sheltered from the W.

The data for Gorey is the same as for St Helier except for:

Tidal streams

The N-going stream starts off Gorey at HW St Helier −0200 and attains 3.2 knots at springs; the S-going starts at HW St Helier +0500 and attains 5 knots at springs.

Night entry

Lit but not recommended

Charts

The largest scale chart is 1138 (25)

Radio

Ch 74 during ferry operations

Telephone

Harbourmaster ☎ 01543 885573 (Jersey Harbours)

PILOTAGE

Approaches

From N and E

Provided Banc du Chateau has sufficient water over it (least depth 0.4m) navigate to the vicinity of Inner Road buoy (starboard hand) and pick up the leading line 298° on the pierhead. If coming from the N and with insufficient water over Banc du Chateau, consult chart 1138 which shows two transits to lead in to the Outer Road (one shown on the Plan) and thence to the leading line.

From E

Navigate to pick up the leading line 298° outside the 15m line and follow it closely to leave the Inner Road buoy and Ecureuil Beacon (Green, triangle topmark) close to starboard. After passing Ecureuil borrow a little to starboard to avoid Azicot rock (drying 0.9m) close to the SW.

From S

From ⊕46 or close to the Violet Buoy (RW, ball topmark, Fl.10s) navigate northwards and either pick up the transit 332° shown on chart 1138 and go up the Outer Road, or follow the 327° transit shown on the Plan to leave the unlit Le Cochon port buoy to port, La Noire E cardinal beacon and Horn Rock Beacon (Red, can topmark) to port to pick up the 298° leading line just beyond Horn Rock.

Entrance and Berthing

The outer part of the pier is used by ferries from Carteret but some alongside drying space is kept for visitors.

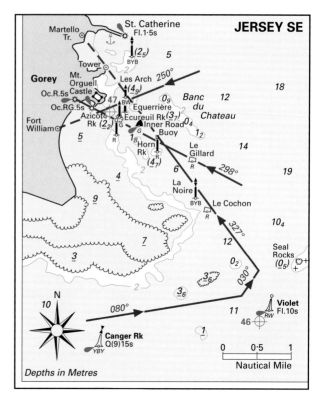

| 46 | Jersey SE | 49°07′.80N 01°57′.16W |
| 47 | Gorey | 49°11′.94N 02°00′.78W |

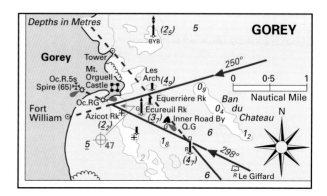

Gorey with St Catherine beyond   *Peter Carnegie*

Moorings and Anchorages

There are two orange visitors' mooring 200m E of the pier in about 2m. There are 12 yellow drying visitors' moorings in the harbour, otherwise anchor clear of them as depths permit.

Facilities

Water and some electricity on pier; fuel at pierhead; showers and heads on pier; good selection of shops, restaurants, cafés in Gorey.

Leisure

A visit to Mont Orgueil Castle is a must.

Other Anchorages

There are a number of partially sheltered anchorages around the coast that are described in The RCC Pilotage Foundations *The Channel Islands* by Peter Carnegie, or from study of charts *1136*, *1137* and *1138*. Ones that may be useful are:

131 St Catherine Bay

Lies 1½M to the N of Gorey. Sheltered from the N and W by a long breakwater and useful to await a favourable stream round the SE or NE corner. The approaches from the N and E are clear of immediate off-lying dangers. Anchor as far in as depth and moorings allow to the S of the breakwater, mostly sand but with rock patches. There are rocks all along the breakwater. There is a landing slip, an inshore lifeboat, a sailing club and café but otherwise no facilities.

132 St Aubin Bay

A wide bay close to the W of St Helier which provides shelter from the SW through N to E . Turn off the Western Passage in the vicinity of Ruaudière buoy towards Diamond Rock buoy and select an anchorage where wind and depths dictate. St Aubin harbour dries but there are sometimes drying berths alongside the E quay. Landing may be made in the harbour or through La Vrachière boat passage to the N of Elizabeth Castle (dries 5.3m). The Royal Channel Islands Yacht Club house is on the other side of the road to the harbour and welcomes visitors.

North coast

There are a number of small harbours and fair weather anchorages on the N coast that has dramatic scenery at the west end. From E to W these are Rozel, Bouley Bay, Bonne Nuit Harbour and Grève de Lecq. Chart *1136* and *The Channel Islands* are needed to explore them.

Brelade Bay

On the S coast has two pretty anchorages but the bay is rock strewn and chart *1137* and *The Channel Islands* are needed to find them in safety.

St Catherine   *Peter Carnegie*

St Aubin   *Peter Carnegie*

Rozel   *Peter Carnegie*

II. THE CHANNEL ISLANDS

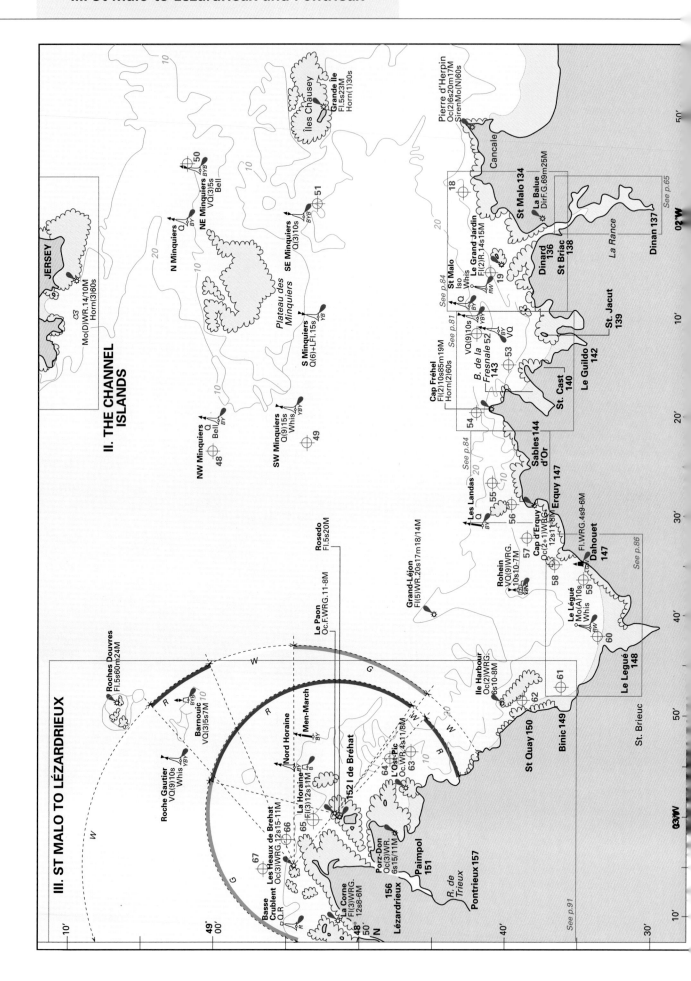

II. THE CHANNEL ISLANDS

JERSEY
cs
Mo(D)WR.14/10M
Horn(3)60s

Grande Île
Fl.5s23M
Horn(1)30s
Îles Chausey

Pierre d'Herpin
Oc(2)6s20m17M
SirenMo(N)60s
Cancale

18

St Malo 134
La Balue
DirF.G.69m25M

50
BYB

N Minquiers
Q
BY

NE Minquiers
VQ(3)5s
Bell

51
BYB

St Malo
Q
Iso
Whis
RW

Le Grand Jardin
Fl(2)R.14s15M

19

Dinard
136
St Briac
138

Dinan 137

See p.65

La Rance

See p.84

SE Minquiers
Q(3)10s

S Minquiers
Ql(6)+LFl.15s
YB

See p.81

VQ(9)10s
52
BY

53
VQ

St. Jacut
139

B. de la
Fresnale 143

Le Guildo
142

NW Minquiers
Q
Bell
BY

48

SW Minquiers
Q(9)15s
Whis
YB

49

Cap Fréhel
Fl(2)10s85m19M
Horn(2)60s

54

St. Cast
140

Sables 144
d'Or

See p.84

Les Landas
Q
BY

55

56

Cap d'Erquy
Oc(2+1)WRG.
12s11-8M

Erquy 147

Plateau des
Minquiers

Grand-Léjon
Fl(5)WR.20s17m18/14M

Rohein
VQ(9)WRG.
10s10-7M

57

58

Fl.WRG.4s9-6M
Dahouet
147

Rosedo
Fl.5s20M

Le Léguė
Mol(A)10s
Whis

59
RW

60

Ile Harbour
Oc(2)WRG.
6s10-8M

Le Léguė
148

Le Paon
Oc.F.WRG.11-8M

III. ST MALO TO LÉZARDRIEUX

Roches Douvres
Fl.5s60m24M

W

G

Barnouic
VQ(3)5s7M
BYB

10

R

Men-Marc'h
BY

Nord Horaine
B

Roche Gautier
VQ(9)10s
Whis
YBY

R

La Horaine
Fl(3)12s11M

52 I de Bréhat

W
W

61

62

Binic 149

St Quay 150

See p.86

Les Heaux de Bréhat
Oc(3)WRG.12s15-11M

66

65

W
G

64
L'Ost-Pic
Oc.WR.4s11/8M

63

10
R

67

Basse
Crublent
Q.R
R

La Corne
Fl(3)WRG.
12s8-6M
R

Porz-Don
Oc(3)WR.
6s15/11M

Paimpol
151

156
Lézardrieux

R. de
Trieux

Pontrieux 157

See p.91

49° 00'
48° 50'
N

St. Brieuc

Pontrieux 157

III. St Malo to Lézardrieux and Pontrieux

⊕18 Rochefort	48°43′.50N	01°58′.40W
⊕19 St Malo	48°41′.50N	02°07′.25W
⊕48 Minquiers NW	49°00′.00N	02°23′.08W
⊕49 Minquiers SW	48°53′.50N	02°20′.00W
⊕50 Minquiers NE	49°01′.40N	01°54′.50W
⊕51 Minquiers SE	48°53′.00N	01°58′.61W
⊕52 Banchenou (for St Briac, St Jacut and St Cast)	48°42′.00N	02°11′.42W
⊕54 Fréhel	48°42′.00N	02°18′.80W
⊕55 Les Justières	48°40′.20N	02°26′.50W
⊕56 Chenal d'Erquy	48°39′.15N	02°29′.00W
⊕57 Erquy	48°38′.24N	02°30′.05W
⊕58 Plateau des Jaunes	48°37′.16N	02°36′.10W
⊕59 Dahouet	48°35′.40N	02°34′.90W
⊕60 Légué (St. Brieuc)	48°34′.20N	02°41′.10W
⊕61 Binic	48°36′.30N	02°46′.15W
⊕62 St Quay-Portrieux	48°38′.90N	02°48′.45W
⊕63 L'Ost-Pic	48°47′.10N	02°53′.80W
⊕64 Paimpol	48°47′.90N	02°53′.80W
⊕65 Lézardrieux	48°53′.30N	02°58′.60W
⊕66 La Gaine NW	48°55′.50N	03°01′.50W
⊕67 Jument	48°55′.48N	03°07′.20W
⊕68 Tréguier	48°54′.34N	03°11′.61W

This part of the coast, embracing the wide and sandy bay of St Brieuc with its scattered rocks lying well offshore, has major ports at its W and E ends and several attractive anchorages and minor harbours in between. Because it is off the direct track between St Malo and Jersey or Lézardrieux, it is less frequented by yachtsmen although an excellent area for bilge-keelers or shallow draught yachts. The deeper keeled are well catered for in Dahouet to the westward although with the exception of St Quay-Portrieux all harbours are tidal limited until Lézardrieux is reached. The tidal stream slacken off appreciably in this large, wide bay.

Warnings

The bays of St Briac, Fresnaie and Lancieux still carry warnings of the risk from second world war mines. The risk must now be very small but is something to be considered if anchoring in remote areas in these bays.

St Malo. Le Grand Jardin lighthouse with St Malo spire right centre bearing 118°

Mont St Michel   *Martin Walker*

DISTANCE TABLE

	Cherbourg	A de St-Martin	Goury	Alderney	Diélette	Guernsey	Carteret	Port Bail	Jersey (St H)	Granville	Is Chausey	Cancale	St-Malo	St-Briac	St-Jacut	St-Cast	B de Fresnaie	Erquy	Dahouet	St-Brieuc	Binic	St-Q/Portrieux	Paimpol	Ile Bréhat	Lézardrieux	Pontrieux	Tréguier
Cherbourg		12	16	24	26	42	37	41	57	69	69	86	89	89	89	89	90	92	97	103	105	104	87	82	87	93	93
A de St-Martin	12		4	12	14	30	25	29	45	57	57	74	77	77	77	77	78	80	85	91	93	92	75	70	75	81	81
Goury	16	4		10	10	27	22	26	42	54	43	71	74	74	74	74	75	77	82	88	90	89	72	67	72	78	78
Alderney	24	12	10		17	22	28	32	40	60	58	71	72	72	73	73	73	76	80	85	81	79	67	64	69	75	75
Diélette	26	14	10	17		28	13	17	33	48	48	61	64	67	69	72	74	68	83	90	83	85	68	63	68	74	74
Guernsey	42	30	27	22	28		30	32	28	54	47	58	54	52	52	52	51	50	54	57	54	51	44	43	48	54	50
Carteret	37	25	22	28	13	30		4	22	35	35	47	44	46	48	51	53	63	68	73	73	72	63	62	67	73	73
Port Bail	41	29	26	32	17	32	4		21	31	31	44	42	44	46	49	51	61	66	73	73	73	62	60	65	71	71
Jersey (St H)	57	45	42	40	33	28	22	21		30	25	34	35	35	35	35	35	37	43	48	48	45	44	42	47	53	60
Granville	69	73	70	62	48	54	35	31	30		10	13	22	26	28	31	33	43	48	55	65	65	74	77	82	88	91
Is Chausey	69	73	70	62	48	47	35	31	25	10		13	14	18	20	23	25	35	40	47	57	58	67	70	75	81	84
Cancale	86	74	71	71	61	58	43	39	34	13	13		17	21	23	26	28	38	43	50	60	61	70	70	75	81	84
St-Malo	89	77	74	72	64	54	44	42	35	22	14	17		7	9	12	14	24	29	36	36	37	46	46	51	57	60
St-Briac	89	77	74	72	67	52	46	44	35	26	18	21	7		2	5	7	17	22	29	29	29	39	39	44	50	53
St-Jacut	89	77	74	73	69	52	48	46	35	28	20	23	9	2		3	5	15	20	27	27	27	28	37	42	48	51
St-Cast	89	77	74	73	72	52	51	49	35	31	23	26	12	5	3		2	12	17	24	24	25	34	34	39	45	48
B de Fresnaie	90	78	75	73	74	51	53	51	35	33	25	28	14	7	5	2		10	15	22	22	23	32	32	37	43	46
Erquy	92	80	77	76	68	50	63	61	37	43	35	38	24	17	15	12	10		5	12	14	14	25	25	30	36	40
Dahouet	97	85	82	80	73	54	68	66	43	48	40	43	29	22	20	17	15	5		7	10	11	25	25	28	34	39
St-Brieuc	103	91	88	85	80	57	73	73	48	55	47	50	36	29	27	24	22	12	7		6	9	24	24	29	35	42
Binic	105	93	90	81	83	54	73	73	48	65	57	60	36	39	27	24	22	14	10	6		3	18	17	22	28	31
St-Q/Portrieux	104	92	89	79	85	51	72	73	45	65	58	61	37	30	28	25	23	14	11	9	3		15	14	19	25	28
Paimpol	87	75	72	67	68	44	63	62	44	74	67	70	46	39	37	34	32	25	25	24	18	15		8	13	19	22
Ile Bréhat	82	70	67	64	63	43	62	60	42	77	70	70	46	39	37	34	32	25	23	24	17	14	8		5	11	18
Lézardrieux	87	75	72	69	68	48	67	65	47	82	75	75	51	44	42	39	37	30	28	29	22	19	13	5		6	18
Pontrieux	93	81	78	75	74	54	73	71	53	88	81	81	57	50	48	45	43	36	34	35	28	25	19	11	6		24
Tréguier	93	81	78	75	74	50	73	71	60	91	84	84	60	53	51	48	46	40	39	42	31	28	22	18	18	24	

Distances are given over the shortest navigable route and are measured to and from inner harbour or anchorage

133 St Malo, Dinard and La Rance to Dinan

St Malo is a major ferry, commercial and yachting port with access in all weathers to two marinas. There is a small yacht basin at Dinard but not for visitors. Above the Barrage, La Rance is dammed for 8M and the water level is subject to the power station requirements. Above another lock the river is canalised for 3M to Dinan where masted navigation ceases. There are two small marinas between the Barrage and Dinan.

Location
38M S of Jersey, 22M SW of Granville

Shelter
Complete inside

Warning Strong cross streams in approach

Depth restrictions
St Servan sill dries 2m; depths above Barrage subject to sluice openings

Night entry
Clear, well lit leading lights

Tidal information St Malo is a Standard Port and has it's own predictions.

Mean height of tide (m)

HWS	HWN	LWN	LWS
12.2	9.3	4.2	1.5

Tidal streams (Across entrance)
HW St Helier – W-going starts
LW St Helier – E-going starts

Berthing
Alongside pontoons in all marinas

Facilities
All those of a major city and yachting centre.

Charts
BA 3659 (50), 2700 (15)
SHOM 4233 (15), 7130 (15)
Imray C33B (Plan)
BA 2700 or SHOM 7130 are essential if using any approach other than the main one from the NW. SHOM 4233 essential above the Barrage.

Weather
From Granville Ch 80 at 0703, 1533 and 1903
From Cap Fréhel Ch 79 at 0545, 0803, 1203, 1633 and 2003

Radio
Ecluse du Naye Ch 12 – 2½ hrs either side HW
Les Bas Sablons Marina Ch 09
Telephone
Harbourmaster ☎ (0)2 99 202 501
L.B Sablons ☎ (0)2 99 817 134
Hon. British Consul
Mme.Véronique Rondel, C/o Brittany Ferries, Gare Maritime du Naye, 35400, St Malo ☎ (0)2 23 18 30 30

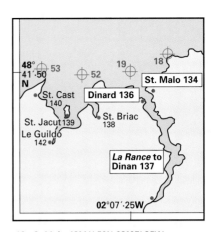

19 St Malo 48°41'.50N 02°07'.25W

St-Malo looking N

III. ST MALO TO LEZARDRIEUX AND PONTRIEUX

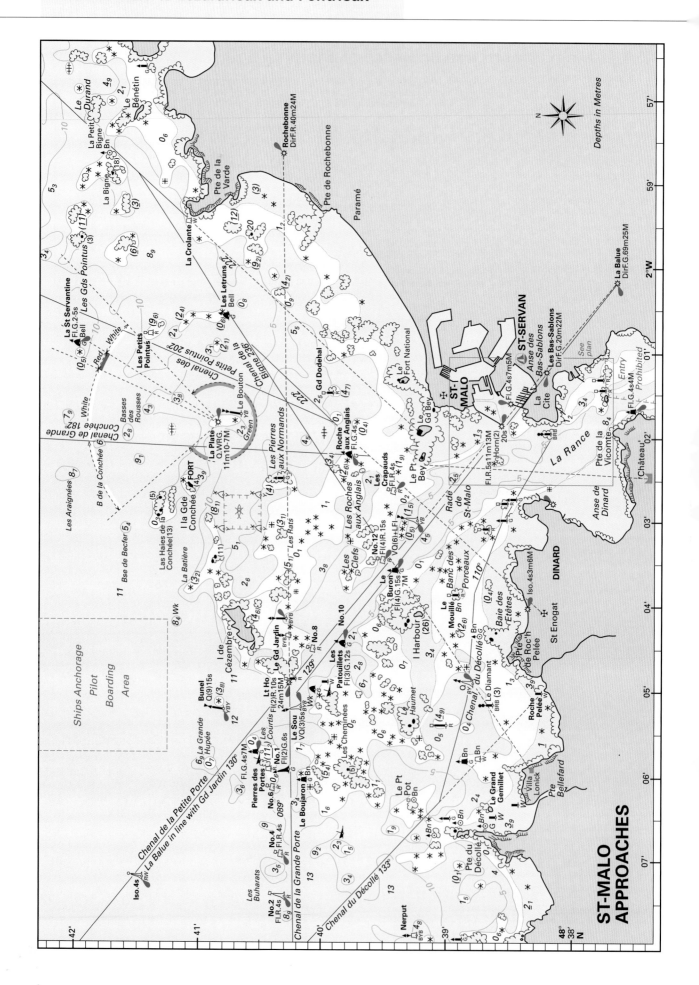

ST-MALO
APPROACHES

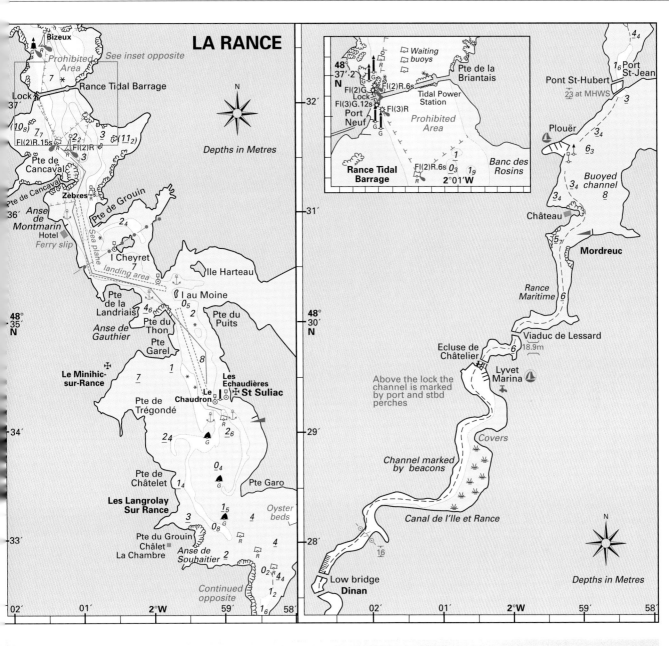

LA RANCE

Depths in Metres

Bizeux

Prohibited Area   See inset opposite

Rance Tidal Barrage

Lock

10_8 7
Fl(2)R.15s 2_2 3 (11_2)
Pte de Cancaval
Fl(2)R 3

Pte de Cancaval
Zébres Pte de Grouin

Anse de Montmarin 2_4
Hotel
Ferry slip Sea plane landing area

I Cheyret 7 Ile Harteau

Pte de la Landriais 4_6 I au Moine
Anse de Gauthier Pte du Thon 0_5 2 Pte du Puits

Pte Garel

Le Minihic-sur-Rance 7 1 8 **Les Echaudières**
Le Chaudron **St Suliac**

Pte de Trégondé 2_4 2_6

0_4

Pte de Châtelet 1_4 Pte Garo

Les Langrolay Sur Rance 3 0_8 1_5 4 *Oyster beds*

Pte du Grouin
Châlet La Chambre *Anse de Souhaitier* 2 4
0_2 4_4
1_2
Continued opposite 1_6

Inset

See inset opposite

Waiting buoys **Pte de la Briantais**
Fl(2)G
Fl(2)R.6s
Lock
Fl(3)G.12s Tidal Power Station
Port Neuf Fl(3)R *Prohibited Area*

Banc des Rosins
Fl(2)R.6s 0_3 1_9
Rance Tidal Barrage 1
2°01'W

Right panel

4_4
Pont St-Hubert 1_6 **Port St-Jean**
2_3 at MHWS 3

Plouër 3_4
6_3
Buoyed channel 8
3_4
3_4
Château
5_7 **Mordreuc**

Rance Maritime 6

Ecluse de Châtelier *Viaduc de Lessard* 18.9m
6 **Lyvet Marina**

Above the lock the channel is marked by port and stbd perches

Covers

Channel marked by beacons

Canal de l'Ile et Rance

Low bridge
Dinan 16

Depths in Metres

St Malo La Rance. Looking up-river to the two road bridges across Port St Hubert narrows (see page 75)

III. ST MALO TO LEZARDRIEUX AND PONTRIEUX

PILOTAGE ST MALO

Approaches

Apart from the extensive Minquiers to the N there are few off-lying dangers to bother a yacht in the approaches. The extensive shallows and rocks to the N and NE of the entrance are all clearly shown on chart 2700 and this is not an area to be navigating in poor visibility.

There are six entrances that can be used, three by day and night and three by day only. They are:

From NW – Chenal de la Petite Porte

The main channel and the most used but subject to strong cross streams. A possibility if the leading marks cannot be seen but a minimum of 1M visibility needed for safety, or radar.

From W – Chenal de la Grande Porte

The deepest but not the main channel. The best to use if visibility precludes seeing the leading marks, as buoys and beacons are close together.

From N – Chenal de la Grande Conchée

The channel used by the fast ferries from the Channel Islands. A radar or minimum of 1M visibility needed for safety.

From E and NE by day only – Chenal des Petits Pointus and Chenal de la Bigne

Both need 1M + visibility for safety.

Both these channels have a least depth of 0.5m – nearly 5m at MLWN – but have shallower dangers close to the lines.

From W – Chenal de la Décollé

By day only. An interesting navigation exercise otherwise of no advantage over Chenal de la Petite Porte.

Chenal de la Petite Porte (Lines S and T)

Approach ⊕19 and the landfall buoy (RW, ball topmark. Fl.15s on a track of 130°) and align the first leading line of Le Grand Jardin (granite tower, red top, F(2)R.10s) and La Balue lighhouse (grey square tower on skyline behind town, F.G) on 130° - Line S. Follow this line to leave:

Grande Hupée rock 0.7m 200m to port.
Bunel (W cardinal buoy, Q(9)15s) 600m to port.
Le Courtis lighthouse (Green, Fl(3)G.15s) 300m to starboard.

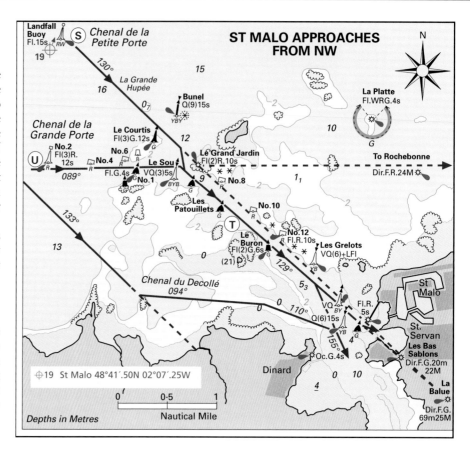

At some stage La Balue will become hidden behind Le Grand Jardin when borrow to starboard to keep it just open.

When Le Courtis bears 280° leave this line and make 160° for 400m to pick up Line T which is Les Bas Sablons lighthouse (white square tower with black top, Dir.F.G 20m) in line with La Balue on the skyline bearing 129°. This line leaves:

Le Grand Jardin lighthouse 180m to port. A port beacon stands 100m SW of the lighhouse and must also be left to port.
Le Sou E cardinal spar buoy VQ(3)15s 300m to starboard.
Basse du Nord starboard buoy (unlit) 250m to starboard.
No 8 port buoy (unlit) 250m to port.
Les Patouillets starboard buoy (unlit) 190m to starboard.
No 10 port buoy (unlit) **300m to port.**
Le Buron (Green tower, Fl(4)G.15s) 120m to starboard.
No 12 port buoy (Fl.R.10s) 100m to port.
Les Grelots S cardinal buoy (VQ(6)+LFl) to port.
The channel now approaches Plateau de la Rance, a shoal containing rocks drying 0.5m and marked by lit N and S cardinal buoys which may be left on either hand.

For St Malo or Les Bas Sablons Marina

Continue on Line T to leave the shoal to starboard and either turn to port round the end of Mole des Noires Fl.R.5s on to 070° on the line of Ecluse du

Naye with 3 F.R leading lights (*See page 69 for lock signals*), or continue for the Marina entrance (Fl.G.4s) behind the ferry terminal berthing extension (F.G). (*See also page 71 for details*).

For Dinard, or the Barrage and La Rance

After passing Les Grelots S cardinal buoy make good a track of 155° to leave Plateau de la Rance well to port to enter the Rade de Dinard or proceed up to the Barrage (*See page 73*).

Chenal de la Grande Porte (Line U)

This channel cuts a small corner if coming from Cap Fréhel or Banchenou buoy, passing inside Le Courtis. It is also a safer channel in poor visibility than any of the others.

From ⊕19 navigate to a position ¼M to the W of No.2 light buoy (port hand, Fl.R.12s). From here Le Grand Jardin lighthouse (granite tower, red top Fl(2)R.10s) will be in line with Rochebonne lighthouse (white faced, square tower Dir.F.R 40m) bearing 089°. Le Grand Jardin will shortly obscure the latter so borrow a bit to the S to just open it. Leave the following marks:

No.2 pillar buoy (port, Fl.R.12s) 50m to port.
No.4 buoy (unlit) 50m to port.
No.6 buoy (unlit) to port.
Le Boujaron starboard beacon tower 300m to starboard.
No.1 pillar buoy (Fl.G.4s) close to starboard.
Pierres des Portes port beacon tower 200m to port.
Le Courtis green lighthouse (Fl.G.4s) 300m to port.
Le Sou E cardinal buoy (VQ(3).5s) 100m to starboard.

When Le Sou is abeam turn on to Line T – Les Bas Sablons lighthouse (white square tower with black top Dir.F.G) and La Balue (square tower on skyline Dir.F.G) on 129°. Proceed then as above for La Petite Porte.

Chenal de la Grande Conchée. By day only (Lines Z and X)

There are no leading lights for this channel but it is wide and lends itself to the use of parallel index on radar. Navigate to a position 1M N of La Platte

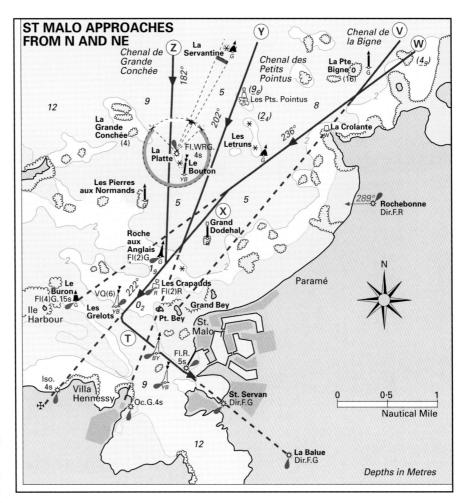

lighthouse (Green tower, Fl.WRG.4s) in its white sector, and by day identify Ile Cézembre and La Grande Conchée which has a small fort on it. The exact line is 182° on Le Petit Bey which has a more conspicuous fort on it, or a parallel index on the same line to leave La Platte 400m to the E.
Proceed down this line leaving:
La Grande Conchée (4m high) 400m to starboard.
La Platte green beacon tower (FlW becoming Fl.G.6s) 400m to port.
Le Bouton S cardinal (VQ(6)+LFl) buoy 450m to port.

From here the Roche aux Anglais starboard buoy (Fl(2)G.6s) should be visible ahead at 1M.
Les Pierres Normands unlit starboard beacon 350m to starboard.
Les Roches aux Anglais (Fl(2)G.6s) close to starboard, 200m past Les Roches aux Anglais buoy turn to make good 222° to leave **Les Crapauds** port buoy (Fl.R) to port with **Les Grelots** W cardinal buoy (VQ(6)+LFl) fine on the starboard bow. When Les Grelots buoy is abeam turn on to Line T 129° - Les Bas Sablons lighthouse, (white square tower, black top Dir.F.G) and La Balue lighthouse (square tower on skyline, Dir.F.G) to pass between Plateau de la Rance and Mole des Noires and so to the locks or the Marina.

Chenal des Petits Pointus. By day (Lines Y and X)

A wide and easy channel with only one danger (Les Petits Pointus) close to the line. Like La Grande Conchée it lends itself to the use of parallel index with radar.

Navigate to a position ¼M E of La Servantine starboard buoy whence the line is 202° on Le Petit Bey with its conspicuous fort, and Villa Hennessy, a prominent villa in the NE part of Dinard. Make good this track to leave Les Petits Pointus port beacon 150m to port or set up a parallel index on La Platte of 650m on a track of 202°. Once Les Petits Pointus is passed leave:

La Platte green lighthouse 650m to starboard.
Le Bouton S cardinal buoy 400m to starboard.
Grand Dodehal port beacon 400m to port.

Shortly after passing the latter alter to make good 222° to leave Les Rochers Anglais starboard buoy 200m to starboard and Les Crapauds port buoy close to port. Course may be altered when well clear of Les Crapauds to leave Le Petit Bey to port, Plateau de la Rance to starboard and Mole des Noires to port and so to the locks or Marina.

Chenal de la Bigne. By day (Lines V, W and X)

This is the most direct channel from the E. There is a narrow part at the E end but once past this there are no particular dangers or difficulties.

Navigate to a position where Rochefort cardinal beacon tower bears 260° 0.7M. This is on the first leading line of Le Crolante white beacon tower in transit with the NW edge of Le Grand Bey bearing 222°. The latter is the larger of the two islets with forts on them just to the NW of St Malo town. Keep close to this line to leave:

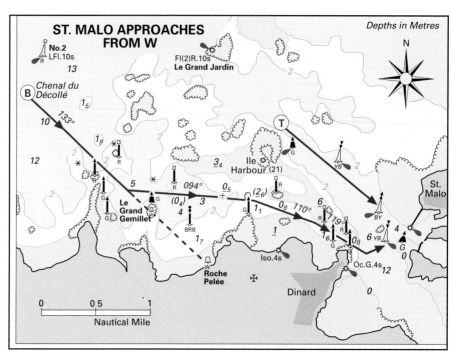

Basse aux Chiens E cardinal buoy 100m to starboard.
Basse du Durand shoal with a least depth of 0.7m 200m to port.
La Petite Bigne starboard beacon 80m to starboard.

Chenal de Décollé. By day. (Line B)

This is an interesting navigational exercise but it saves no time or distance if coming from the W to St Malo, over using Chenal de la Grande Porte and is not recommended.

It should not be attempted. Chart 2700 and SHOM 7130 show the lines and tracks to be followed. There are no difficulties initially provided the first leading line of Le Grand Genillet white beacon tower (*Front*) and Roche Pelée white beacon tower (*Rear*) on 133° can be positively identified before commitment. The difficulties occur at the E end to the N of Pointe de Dinard where the channel is narrow, there is no established leading line and the channel constantly changes.

It would be prudent to reckon on a least depth of drying 1m and to make the passage on a rising tide with aid of either of the large-scale charts.

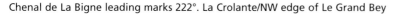

Chenal de La Bigne leading marks 222°. La Crolante/NW edge of Le Grand Bey

134 St Malo Port

Entrance

The line of the lock is 071° and is shown by two
F.R lights.

Entry procedure

The locks are worked 2½ hours either side of HW.
The gates are sometimes left open from 1½ hours
before to HW and this is the best time to pass
through. Take note of the traffic signals and
beware of a strong N set outside the gates before
and just past HW, and if the Barrage is
discharging seawards. Unless the lock is very
crowded a yacht should secure on the side on
which an attendant is standing. There are ladders
on the sides; the attendants will sometimes pass
down a line to take up warps.

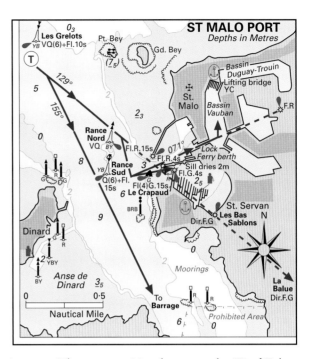

ST MALO PORT
Depths in Metres

Entry signals

Normal lock working

No entry until authorised

Vessels may enter

No entry. Keep 200m+ clear of gates

Both gates open

No entry until authorised

Vessels may pass through

No entry until authorised

Berthing

There are four interconnected basins with a
common access through Ecluse du Naye. They
are maintained to a depth of 5.4m and shown on
the plan above. Yachts use Bassin Vauban,
berthing alongside pontoons at the N end where
yachts double or treble up provided a passage is
left between the pontoons. Overflow, or for
yachts over 12m use the W wall under the city
walls which usually attracts no charge. Further
overflow into Bassin Duguay-Trouin through the
lifting bridge during special events.

Anchorages and Moorings

Anchoring is prohibited anywhere in the main
channels out to the outer entrance. The only
exception is in a narrow strip outside the
moorings off Dinard where the streams run
strongly and the bank from drying to deep water

is steep. There are waiting buoys to the W of Ecluse
du Naye, outside the Les Bas Sablons Marina and to
the N of the lock to the Barrage. To avoid any of
these alternatives, plan to time arrival between HW
−2 and HW +2 and proceed in to either lock or over
the sill in to the Marina.

Ashore in St Malo

Facilities

Water and electricity on the pontoons; occasional
taps on the quay; fuel only from fuel berth in Les Bas
Sablons marina; showers and heads next to the
Harbourmaster at the N end of the basin; Yacht
Club Societé de la Baie de St Malo (SNBSM) is by
the pontoons, welcomes visitors and hosts a number
of races to and from the UK; chart agent Libraire
Maritime, 5 rue Broussais; also another in Les Bas
Sablons Marina; slips, cranes, travel-lift, engineers,
electricians and repairs all at Les Bas Sablons
Marina; Bureau du Port and Tourist Office are close
together at the N end of the Basin and are mines of
information. The former on port information and
particularly the details of intended water levels
above the Barrage and times of sluice openings; the
latter on the myriads of leisure activities in the area;
shops are of many varieties and all qualities, mostly
in the old town (Intra Muros); restaurants and hotels
an infinite variety from the Duchesse Anne just
inside Porte St Vincent, to those to satisfy very much
more modest tastes and pockets. They are mostly
Intra Muros and although a large number are
situated near Porte St Vincent a further exploration
is worthwhile; Hotel Univers in Place Chateaubriand
is a traditional yachtsmen's watering hole.

Travel

Train to Rennes whence there is a high-speed link to
Paris; the station is ½M E along the road across the
lifting bridge. Bus timetables and details from the
Tourist Office; the bus station is just beside it.

St Malo. Drying moorings at Dinard which is out of picture to the right. On the skyline, water tower conspic from seaward and to the left château-like building with twin towers which is a leading mark for Chenal de la Grande Conchée

Airport at Dinard-Pleurtuit has flights to the Channel Islands and Exeter and connections to Paris. Ferries daily to Jersey, Poole, Portsmouth and less frequently to Plymouth; the ferry terminal is to the SW of Ecluse du Naye; *vedettes* to Dinard and elsewhere run from the quays to the N.

Leisure

A visit to the Tourist Office to find the wide variety of entertainment on offer is worthwhile and should satisfy the most fractious family or crew. If only here for a day, the least that should be tried is a walk round the walls (¾ hour easy stroll) from which a lot can be gleaned of the town's history, together with a visit to the museum in Hotel de Ville in the E corner of Intra Muros near which there is a small aquarium.

A longer stay should include the magnificent new Grand Aquarium (on the outskirts, bus or taxi) which is world class and a visit to Chateaubriand's tomb on Le Grand Bey – but don't get caught there by the tide or you will stay there. There are splendid beaches close by on the W and N sides of the town.

If hiring a car, visit Mont St Michel to the east and enjoy lunch in Cancale or at Pointe de Grauin (See page 62).

History

The town itself started when it was an isolated rock with a monastery founded in the 6th-century by a monk called Aaron. He was succeeded by a Celt of Welsh origin St Maclou or St Malo who was the Bishop of what is now St Servan. St Servan declined as the powerful walled town grew on the isolated rock and the inhabitants, known as Malouins became famous seamen, corsairs and explorers. In the 16th-century and later they forced all shipping coming up the Channel to pay tribute and also brought wealth from further afield. Jacques Cartier who started the colonisation of Canada lived in and sailed from here. They were the first colonists of the Falklands – hence the Argentine name of Las Malvinas. They declared St Malo an independent republic in 1590 – *Ni francais, ni Breton, Malouin suis* – a state of affairs that did not survive.

As the centuries passed the walled town took its present form with massive fortifications and fine granite mansions for the wealthy merchants and sea captains, and the causeway Le Sillon was built to join it to Paramé.

The town resisted four attempts by the English to take it, one in 1758 when the Duke of Marlborough landed with 15,000 men near Cancale. In the 19th-century the docks were developed to the SW of Le Sillon and the Malouins took up more peaceful pursuits such as fishing where they were one of the leaders in the cod fishery off Newfoundland.

In 1944 80% of the old town was destroyed by General Patten and the USAAF before the Germans surrendered. The subsequent restoration has been remarkable in the detail of its faithfulness to the original state.

St Malo Tour Solidor   *Robin Rundle*

135 Les Bas Sablons Marina at St Servan

Contact
☎ 02 9981 71 34 *Fax* 02 9981 91 81
Email portplaisance@ville-saint-malo.fr

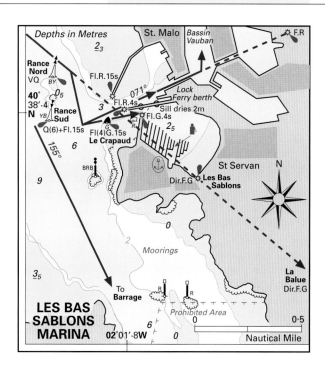

PILOTAGE

Approaches

See pages 66 and 67 for approaches to the Marina along lines S and T. Leave Line T when Rance Nord N cardinal has been passed and head for Le Crapaud starboard buoy Fl(4)G.15s. Turn short of this to port to about 080° to head for the Marina entrance.

Entrance

The entrance is to the S of the ferry berthing extension that is marked by a Fl.R.4s. The S side of the Marina entrance is marked by a Fl.G.4s and there are large illuminated screens showing the depth over the sill which dries 2m. A 2m draught should be able to enter from about LW + 1½ to HW +4.

Three red lights displayed on a mast by the sill prohibit movement in and out of the Marina while a ferry is (un)berthing at the adjacent pier.

Berthing

There are 1220 places in the Marina, maximum 12m. There are 86 visitors' berths on pontoons A and B the first inside the entrance. The Marina is dredged to 2.5m but there is less at the inner end. The visitors' berths on pontoon A are from 36–66 and 43–75, on pontoon B from 92–102 and 91–101. Modernisation of pontoons and facilities is underway 2006–2008. At busy periods Marina staff may visit yachts waiting outside to allocate berths other than at these pontoons.

The Marina is sheltered in all weathers although some movement may be felt around HW in strong NW-lies.

Harbour radio

Channel 12 should be watched while underway in the harbour. The Marina guards Ch 09 but there is no need to call them before entry.

Moorings

There are some waiting buoys off the Marina entrance with 2m under them but there is shallower water close to the SW of them.

Ashore in St Servan

Facilities

Water and electricity on the pontoons; fuel at the root of pontoon K; credit card, or cash at the office; showers and heads at roots of pontoons A, B, E and F; 30-ton travel-lift and cranes to cope with masts or engines; slip for trailed craft and also to dry out against on hard bottom; engineers, electricians, shipwrights, chandlers and chart agent all on site; laundrette just outside Marina; shops within short walking distance, marketdays Tuesdays and Fridays; restaurants, cafés and bars of all qualities and prices nearby.

Travel

See under St Malo on the previous page for details. The ferry terminal is within walking distance from the Marina.

Leisure

See also under St Malo on the previous page. A visit to the Tourist Office at the N end of Bassin Vauban is worthwhile if staying for a few days. There is an Olympic swimming pool open all the year round nearby and the Tour Solidor, a short walk to the S, has a museum of Cape Horners; it is open in French working hours except on Mondays. Nearby in the old Fort d'Aleth is a Second World War Museum. The striking Grand Aquarium is on the hill above St Servan and well worth a taxi ride.

History

St Servan is more ancient than St Malo and is near the site of the Gallo Roman town of Aleth. The quarter immediately to the S of the Marina still bears this name. Aleth remained the bishopric and the dominant of the two towns until the 12th-century when it declined in relation to St Malo with its powerful defences and ambitious inhabitants.

The Tour Solidor, of three towers arranged in plan like an ace of clubs, was built in 1392 to guard La Rance.

136 Dinard

Approaches

See page 67 Chenal de la Petite Pointus for the approach to Dinard, and the Plan opposite.

Entrance

Visitors are not catered for here unless a previous arrangement has been made.

A marked channel dredged to 1m runs in to the yacht club almost parallel to the shore on the N side of the bay. This culminates in a pool or wet basin of between 1m and 2m depth. The channel is used by the vedettes and the area is covered with moorings. There have been plans to expand these facilities for some time.

Anchorages and Moorings

There are no visitors' moorings but many private ones in the bay.

At neaps it is possible to work into the bay and find enough water at anchor to stay afloat at LW out of the stream and clear of moorings. At springs the bank drops down steeply from drying to 7m and although the holding is good the streams here can be strong when the Barrage sluices are opened.

Ashore in Dinard

Facilities

Water from the yacht club or slip in cans; fuel from pumps in the wet basin; landing at the YC or *vedette* slips; the slip on the E side never dries; the large Yacht Club de Dinard is well known for its hospitality to British yachts and can provide showers; it is rather more formal than many French yacht clubs. There are restaurants of all qualities, sizes and prices (hotels, cafés and bars) nearby in the town.

Travel

See page 69 under St Malo. There is no bus to the airport and a taxi must be taken.

History

Dinard became a holiday resort much patronised by the English and Americans in the Victorian age and the architecture and the ambience in the town still reflect these prosperous times. Picasso painted here in the 1920s and a strange statue of Alfred Hitchcock commemorates the town's annual festival of English language films.

There are a number of British graves in the cemetery near the top of the town, many from the loss of HM Ships *Charybdis* and *Limbourne* in 1943.

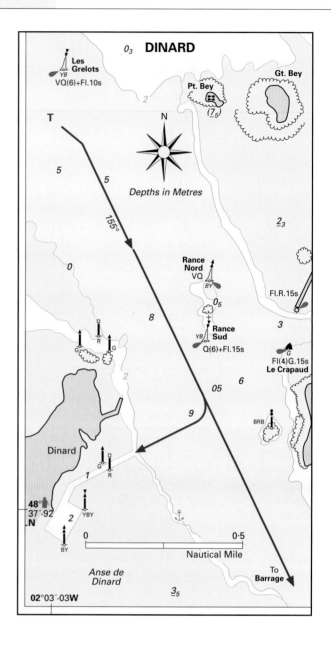

137 La Rance to Dinan

See plan on page 73.

The Barrage was built in 1966 to harness the power of the high tides and it continues to supply electricity to the national grid. As a further benefit a large area of navigable water was created and navigation to Dinan improved.

Before passing through the Barrage, the annual pamphlet showing the Regulations and times and heights of HW between June and September should be obtained from the Bureaux des Ports at Vauban, Les Bas Sablons Marina or the lock at the Barrage. This shows the times that the water level above the Barrage will be 4m, or 8.5m above CD. The rate of rise or fall is variable but does not normally exceed

4m per hour. This can be exceeded in exceptional circumstances when fierce currents can be generated both above and below the Barrage. It is therefore difficult to calculate the depth needed when anchoring and a good margin for safety should be added.

Warnings

The prohibited areas above and below the Barrage marked by buoys and in some cases joined by ropes and shown on the charts and plan on the next page, must not be entered due to the currents from the sluices.

Chart

SHOM 4233 is essential

Radio

Ch 13 with the Barrage and Plouër Marina

Approaches to Barrage

From Rade de Dinard pass between Ile Biseux and La Jument starboard beacon tower leaving the latter 50m to starboard. Continue down the increasingly narrowing channel between the prohibited area and the shore. If early for the lock an anchorage may be found close to the shore just S of La Jument but the waiting buoys outside the lock where there is 1.5m may be more convenient. To avoid waiting try to arrive 15 minutes before the hour.

Lock working

The locks work between 0430 and 2030 and when the depth of water outside exceeds 4m. The gates open for incomers on the hour and for outgoers on the half hour. ☎ 02 99 16 37 37 may get them to open outside these times. Be prepared to pass your draught and mast height to the lockkeeper on demand.

Fishing boats and vedettes take precedence over yachts at the locks.

Yachts with masts coming from seaward should precede those without; those with masts going seaward should let those without enter first. This is because the lifting bridge at the N end of the lock clears mastless boats and can then be lowered sooner. (But the bridges do not open between 1200 and 1400, 1700–1900, only the locks for motor boats).

Ropes hang down from the sides of the lock and it is not necessary to make fast securely as there is little turbulence.

Lock signals
Signals at the lock

3 G	Vessels may pass
3 R	No entrance
2 G and 1 Wh	No movement

Signals on the Barrage

2 cones point up, white above black	Sluices open inwards
2 cones point down, black above white	Sluices open seawards

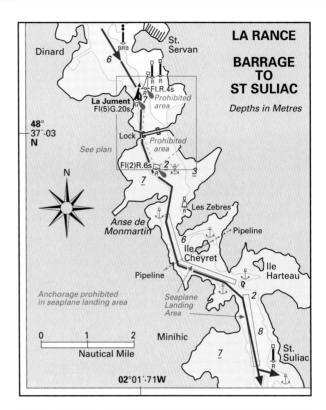

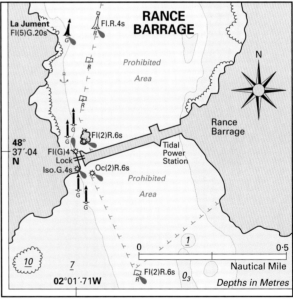

From the Barrage to St Suliac

A yacht passing through the lock from seaward between 2 and 1½ hours before HW should have plenty of time to reach the lock at Chatelier before the level starts to fall.

On leaving the Barrage lock, leave three port hand buoys and the prohibited area close to port, starboard beacons to starboard. The last port hand buoy Fl(2)R.6s is the only navigational light above the Barrage. The channel to St Suliac carries a least depth of 2m above CD. There is a certain amount of vedette traffic on the river.

SHOM 4233 is now essential for further navigation although there is plenty of water as far as St Suliac.

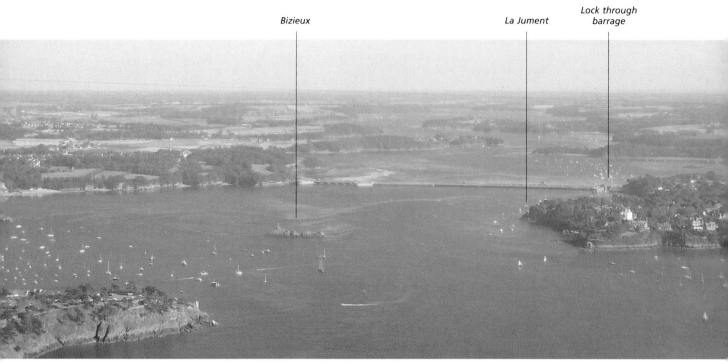

Bizieux   La Jument   Lock through barrage

St Malo looking S to barrage and La Rance

St Jacut looking NE. The tiny harbour has partly filled with sand over the winter gales. Moorings and anchorage to the right

St Malo. La Rance. Plouër marina entrance bearing 284°

Note that anchorage is prohibited N of Les Zebres port beacon tower except for a small area indicated on 4233, that there is a prohibited area on either side of a pipeline which crosses by Ile Cheyret, and which is marked by beacons, and that there are three seaplane landing areas in which anchoring is prohibited.

Anchorages and Moorings

With the prohibitions above in mind, it is possible to anchor almost anywhere outside the channel where depth allows. However it is advisable to get as close to shore as possible and to avoid the headlands where the currents are strong. The bays are often filled with local boats at moorings but there are sometimes white mooring buoys with no names or numbers on them that are available for visitors. The following are possible anchorages:

1. Anse de Monmartin at the S end of the bay in 4m or closer in. Good landing slip near the hotel.

2. In the pool N of Ile Cheyret in 2m+.

3. In the bay to the S of Ile Harteau.

4. In the bay opposite St Suliac between Pointe de Lonrogley and Pointe du Ton. There are many moorings here and it is difficult to get out of the strong current. Slip and yacht yard. Restaurant at Minihic up the hill.

5. S of Les Echaudières off St Suliac in 1m+. There are three visitors' moorings in 2m off the slip at St Suliac.

Ashore in St Suliac

St Suliac is a small, sleepy country town with a post office and a shop or two; also a restaurant and a *créperie*. There is a good dinghy landing at the slip but it dries to soft mud at LW. There is a water tap by the slip.

On Saturday in mid-August the Pardon of St Suliac takes place with a candle-lit procession up to the pagoda shrine of Our Lady of La Rance on the point N of the village.

St Suliac to Le Chatelier lock

SHOM 4233 shows the run of the steadily decreasing channel. The buoys, however show the direct route in shallower water, least depth drying 0.8m which should present no problems with a 4m+ rise. This leads to the power line and the two bridges crossing the narrowest part of the river between Port St Hubert and Port St Jean. The lowest clearance is 20m below the S bridge. The pool below the bridges is the last one possible to anchor in and stay afloat but the current runs fiercely through it and an anchorage as close as possible to the side should be sought. There are landing slips on either side.

Above here a least depth in the channel of drying 6m should be assumed. The channel is narrow and winding and close attention should be paid to the buoys and beacons.

Plouër-sur-Rance

This marina in the old millpond is 1M above the bridges and maintains 2m inside the sill. The gate

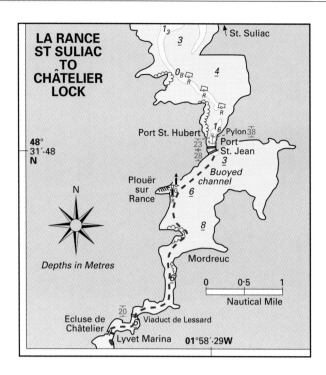

opens when there is 8.2m depth, with 1.5m over the sill. The entrance is between Nos 50 and 52 port hand buoys on the line of Plouër church bearing 284° between the entrance beacons. Red and green lights indicate the state of the gate. There are waiting buoys outside the entrance. Bureau du Port watches Ch 09 during working hours. There are 10 places for visitors on pontoon B, the first inside the gate.

There is water and electricity on the pontoons, showers and heads, a bar/restaurant nearby and another in the village where there are shops, banks and a post office.

Mordreuc

A small village on the E bank above Plouër with a landing slip and a small bar/restaurant. Red warning lights are shown here if exceptional currents are expected.

Le Chatelier and lock

The Lessard viaduct with a clearance of 20m crosses the river ¼M below the lock and opening bridge at Le Chatelier. The channel is marked by port and starboard poles between the viaduct and the lock. The sill is 6.43m above datum but there has been some silting and the lock and bridge are usually operated when the level reaches 10m at St Suliac. Mooring lines are provided which should be kept taut until the turbulence, which can be considerable has subsided. The lock is 39m long, 7.9m wide. Ch 14 is watched when the lock is working. ☎ 96 39 55 66 for lock opening times or further details.

Le Chatelier to Dinan

It is as well to check on the depth of water above the lock before proceeding. The stretch is dredged from time to time but expect some 1.5m patches, and dry spells lower the water level appreciably.

La Rance. Châtelier looking ESE. The swing bridge is
opening to let the yacht in the lock through

Lyvet Marina is above the lock on the E bank
where there is a water tap and a small food store.
There are pontoons here with 2m under them and
ten places for visitors on Pontoon B.

When leaving the lock, turn slowly to port to pass
between the pair of red and black posts on the first
bend, thereafter between the red posts and the
towpath. See plan on page 77. The clearance under
the power line just below Dinan is 16m.

At Dinan there are quays and a pontoon with
short (6m) fingers on the W bank. All are crowded
in the summer and there is a steady stream of
vedettes when the lock is open.

Ashore in Dinan

Facilities

Water and electricity on the pontoons, water taps on
the quays; showers, heads and launderette at the
bureau du port; crane for masts up to 400kg;
restaurants and shops, some on the quay otherwise
it is a steep climb up the hill through cobbled streets
and medieval houses to the main town where there
is an abundance.

La Rance looking WSW up final reach to Dinan

St Malo. La Rance. Château opposite Mordreuc looking
downstream to the two bridges

Travel

Buses and railway to Rennes. Nearest airports
Rennes and Dinard.

History

Dinan has a far longer and important history than its
almost-namesake Dinard. The centre of the town
has many ancient houses and the ramparts date back
to the 13th-century. The church of St Saveur is well
worth a visit for its Gothic extravagance and there
are many other medieval gems to be seen. The
ubiquitous Duchesse Anne, twice Queen of France
to different kings, had connections with the town.

Further travel by canal

Masted navigation ceases at Dinan. The depth in the canal to Rennes (Canal de l'Ile et Rance) is stated as 1.3m but may well be less after a scarcity of rain. There is little point in continuing to Nantes as the Vilaine River can be navigated from there to Redon and thence to the sea.

No inland waterway documentation is required to reach Dinan but will be if proceeding further and rules and regulations for French waterways will apply. The minimum requirement for any vessel of less than 15m is that the helmsman must possess a RYA Helmsman's Overseas Certificate of Competence and that a current tax disc (*vignette*) is held. Details of the latter may be obtained from Voies Navigable de France, rue Ludovic Boutleux, 62400 Béthune, France. The French Government Tourist Office. 178 Picadilly, London W1V 0AL and can supply details of any closures (*chomages*). The following references may be of further help:

Cruising Association's Introduction to the French Inland Waterways

Cartes Guides Fluviacartes No 12 Canaux Bretons which has strip maps of the canals; available from Imray Laurie Norie and Wilson Ltd.

RYA Book of Euroregs for Inland Waterways Marian Martin Adlard Coles Nautical.

Inland Waterways of France David Edwards-May Imray Laurie Norie and Wilson Ltd.

Waterway Routes through France Jane Cumberlidge Imray Laurie Norie and Wilson Ltd.

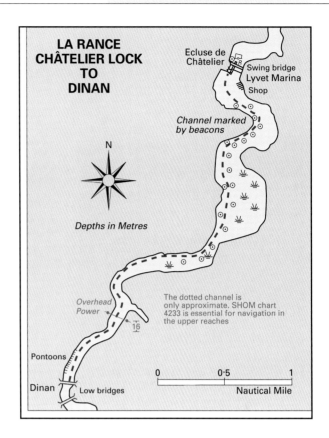

La Rance. Early morning at Dinan

III. ST MALO TO LEZARDRIEUX AND PONTRIEUX

138 St Briac

A small, drying bay with a sectored light leading in to it and a pleasant village spread out around it.

Location
7M W of St Malo

Shelter
Open to the NW

Depth restrictions
Much of the harbour dries

Night entry
Sectored leading light

Tidal information
Within 5 minutes and 0.2m of those at St Malo

Mean height of tide (m)

HWS	HWN	LWN	LWS
12.0	9.1	4.1	1.4

Berthing
Anchor and/or dry out

Facilities
Those of a small village

Charts
BA 3659 (50)
SHOM 7155 (49)
Imray C33B

Weather
From Cap Fréhel on Ch 79 at 0545, 0803, 1203, 1633 and 2003

Radio/Telephone
None

PILOTAGE

Approaches and Entrance

From ⊕52 and the Banchenou N cardinal buoy (V.Q) identify Ile des Hébihens and Ile Agot and navigate to a position 0.3M N of Porte des Hébihens rocks. From here make good a track of 125° between Les Herplux port beacon and La Moulière starboard beacon in the white sector of the Dir Iso WRG.4s light (R to N, G to S); this is on a white pillar on the shore line at the end of a wall which leads round to the bridge; the latter is not visible until the final corner is rounded. Port and starboard beacons define the channel from Ile du Perron inwards but the inner bay is full of moorings.

Anchorages

Deep draught yachts may find an anchorage in fine weather in 1m or more to the SW of Ile du Perron. Bilge keelers may find shelter further in clear of the many moorings.

St Briac looking NW *Peter Carnegie*

Ashore in St Briac

Facilities

An unspoilt holiday village with some small hotels, a restaurant and modest shops all rather scattered through the village. Toilets, showers and water are provided on the Westside Anse de St Briac beach.

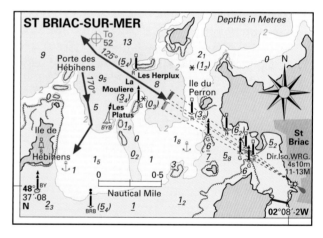

139 St Jacut – Baie de Lancieux

A wide, shallow and sandy bay sheltered from the W

See *Warning* on page 61

Location
2M W of St Briac

Shelter
Open to the N and NE

Depth restrictions
S part of bay dries

Night entry
Unlit

Tidal information
Within 5 minutes and 0.2m of St Malo

Mean height of tide

HWS	HWN	LWN	LWS
12.0	9.1	4.1	1.4

Berthing
At anchor or dried out on sand

Facilities
Small scattered village

Charts
BA 3659 (50)
SHOM 7155 (49)
Imray C33B

Weather
From Cap Fréhel on Ch 79 at 0545, 0803, 1203, 1633 and 2003

Radio/Telephone
None

52 Banchenou 48°42'.00N 02°11'.42W

PILOTAGE

Approaches and Anchorages

From ⊕52 or the Banchenou N cardinal buoy identify Portes des Hébihens rocks and from a position 100m E of them make good a track of 170° leaving Les Platus W cardinal buoy 400m to port. From here an anchorage in 1–2m off the E side of Ile des Hébihens can be found, or 1½M further S on drying sand off St Jacut clear of the moorings.

Ile des Hébihens is private but landing is allowed.

Facilities

Above the harbour at St Jacut is the yacht club in a small wooden shack. From here it is about 1M up hill to the scattered village with a few cafés and shops. Not much for adults but fun for children.

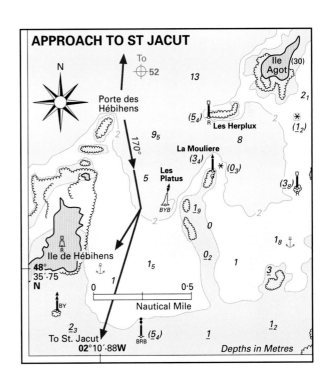

APPROACH TO ST JACUT

St Jacut Harbour   *Robin Rundle*

St Jacut anchorage looking SW.
The small harbour and slip are right centre

140 St Cast

A sheltered harbour except from the SE, with yacht moorings and some facilities. Expansion into a marina has been approved and work expected to start in 2005. Berthing arrangements uncertain until completed.

Location
4M SE of Cap Fréhel

Shelter
Good except from SE

Depth restrictions
Mooring area dredged to 1.5m+

Night entry
Partially lit; no ldg Lts

Tidal information
Within 5 minutes and 0.2m of St Malo

Mean heights of tide (m)

HWS	HWN	LWN	LWS
12.0	9.1	4.1	1.4

An inshore lifeboat is maintained here

Berthing
Head and stern visitors' moorings in area next to fishing boats.

Facilities
Basic by the harbour; more in St Cast village 1M

Charts
BA 3659 (50)
SHOM 7155 (49) (No Plan)
Imray C33B

Weather
From Cap Fréhel on Ch 79 at 0545, 0803, 1203, 1633 and 2003

Radio
Ch 09 during working hours

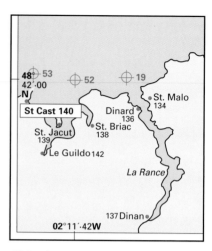

52 Banchenou 48°42'.00N 02°11'.42W

Ashore in St Cast

The port is a mile from the town but has enough facilities to satisfy most needs.

Facilities

Water and fuel at the root of the breakwater; showers and heads at the SW end of the block of flats/shops by the harbour; 10-ton slip; 12-ton crane; launderette in town; chandler and basic provision shops by the harbour; *supermarché* in town.

Travel

Nearest station Lamballe with bus connection. Nearest airport Dinard. Taxi ☎ 02 96 41 86 16

St Cast looking WNW

PILOTAGE

Approaches

Coming from ⊕52 and the Banchenou buoy to the NE, avoid the Bourdinots Rocks drying 2m and marked by an E cardinal spar buoy. At night identify the Iso.WG.4s on the breakwater end and approach in one of the white sectors, between 204° and 217°, or 233° and 245°. The green sector between covers the Bourdinots Rocks and the buoy there is unlit. Le Bec Rond beacon at the harbour entrance is also unlit.

Moorings

There are 10 moorings for visitors, maximum 13m. Arrivals should pick up a buoy or anchor to seaward of the fishing boat moorings and go in by dinghy to the office to arrange a mooring, or do this on Ch 09.

Bec Ronde

Visitors' mooring area

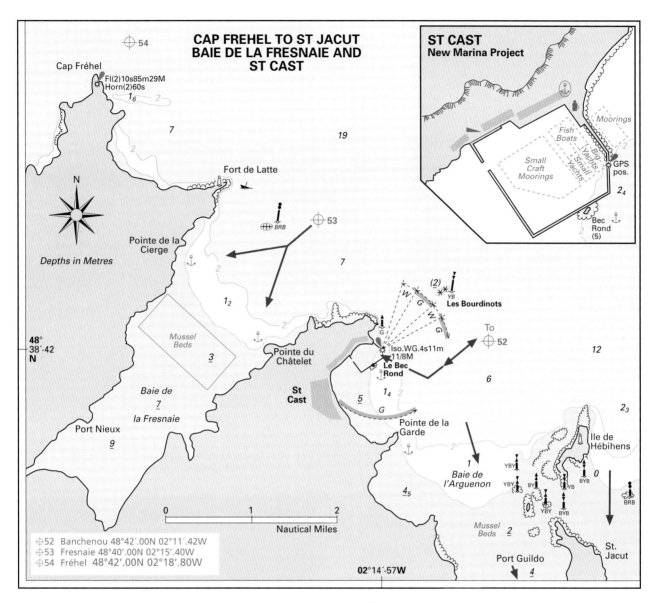

CAP FREHEL TO ST JACUT BAIE DE LA FRESNAIE AND ST CAST

ST CAST
New Marina Project

Cap Fréhel
Fl(2)10s85m29M
Horn(2)60s

Fort de Latte

Pointe de la Cierge

Depths in Metres

48° 38'·42 N

Mussel Beds

Pointe du Châtelet

Baie de la Fresnaie

St Cast

Port Nieux

Les Bourdinots

Iso.WG.4s11m 11/8M
Le Bec Rond

Pointe de la Garde

Baie de l'Arguenon

Ile de Hébihens

St. Jacut

Mussel Beds

Port Guildo

Nautical Miles

⊕52 Banchenou 48°42'.00N 02°11'.42W
⊕53 Fresnaie 48°40'.00N 02°15'.40W
⊕54 Fréhel 48°42'.00N 02°18'.80W

02°14'·57W

III. ST MALO TO LEZARDRIEUX AND PONTRIEUX

St Cast Harbour   *Robin Rundle*

The first two and NE-most of the rows of buoys parallel to the breakwater are for fishing boats. This and the yacht section immediately to the SW are dredged to 1.6m so there is access at all stages of the tide.

Warnings

A new marina is being built with parts expected to be available in 2008.

Anchorage

- To the SE of Bec Rond in 2m clear of moorings
- 1M to the S, to the SSE of Pointe de la Garde, sheltered from the S through W to NW. Slip and YC nearby.

See *Warning* on page 61.

141/142 Baie de l'Arguenon and Port Le Guildo

Baie de l'Arguenon dries from 2m to the S of St Cast and leads via the channel of the Rivière d'Arguenon in the sands to the Port of Le Guildo where there is a quay drying 7.6m used by coasters drawing up to 4.5m.

There is no reason why yachts which can take the ground should not find their way up there but the quay is grubbily commercial and right on the main road.

A wide bay with a large inner part drying but offering shelter from the W in deep water.

See *Warning* on page 61.

143 Baie de la Fresnaie

PILOTAGE

Approaches

The approaches from ⊕53 to two possible anchorages are shown on the plan opposite and for which BA chart 3659 and SHOM 7155 are of just large enough scale. Avoid the two dangerous wrecks off Fort de la Latte, the easternmost marked by an unlit BRB buoy with a two black ball topmark.

Anchorage

- There is a good anchorage in sand and mud and good holding off Pointe de la Cierge with Fort de la Latte bearing 010° 0.6M.

- 1M to the SW is a small landing slip with some moorings off it where it dries 3.5m (*See photograph*)

- A further 1½M up the bay is Port Nieux which has a quay and small jetty where alongside berths dry 7.8m

- On the SE side of the bay an anchorage can be found in 2m to the NW of Pointe du Châtelet. To the S of the point is a beach, some moorings off it and a caravan site.

- It is possible to tuck into the bay immediately S of Fort de la Latte to visit the Fort.

Ashore in Baie de la Fresnaie

There is a road from just to the S of Pointe du Châtelet over the hill to St Cast village if desperate for supplies.

Fort de la Latte is worth the climb up from the sea. The tower, which contains a cannon-ball factory, can only be reached over a couple of drawbridges and is a favourite with filmmakers. Guided tours only.

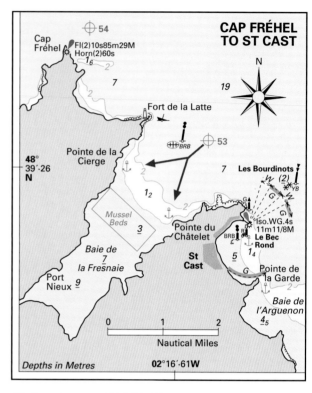

53	Fresnaie	48°40'.00N 02°15'.40W
54	Fréhel	48°42'.00N 02°18'.80W

Baie de la Fresnaie. Anchorage 1M S of Fort de la Latte. Note shellfish farm grids on drying sand

Baie de la Fresnaie. Fort de la Latte from NW

144 Sables d'Or-les-Pins (Grève de Minieu)

A wide sandy bay open to the N with some shelter from the W but little from the E; a lively little resort but no facilities for yachts.

Location
4M W of Cap Fréhel; 3M E of Erquy

Tidal information
Within 10 minutes and 0.5m of St Malo

Mean height of tide

HWS	HWN	LWN	LWS
12.0	9.1	4.1	1.4

Berthing
Anchoring or drying out on sand

Charts
BA 3674 (50)
SHOM 7155 (49)
Imray C33B

Weather
From Cap Fréhel on Ch 70 at 0545, 0803, 1203, 1633 and 2033

PILOTAGE

Approaches

From the 077°/257° track between ⊕54 and 55 identify Ile St Michel with a diminutive chapel on its summit. Bring Pleurien spire and a conspicuous water tower beyond into transit 177°; this line is well open of the large hotel on the plage. Follow this line in to a suitable depth to anchor. Do not stray to the E of it where a dangerous rock near the middle of the beach awaits, 600m W of Rocher Bénard.

Anchorage

There is an anchorage to the SE of Rocher Bénard in 2–4m, sand but beware of Rocher Fournel drying 11m further to the SE at the end of a spit from the shore; otherwise anywhere in the bay clear of rocks.

Berthing

Port Barrier has a substantial jetty built for the export of stone from the quarries but has silted considerably. It would be possible to dry out alongside but a previous recce would be advisable as the bottom alongside has become uneven. It is also a good walk to the village.

A small river flows into the W end of the bay at Pointe du Champ du Port where there is a short sloping breakwater with some moorings off it.

Ashore in Sables d'Or-les-Pins

There is no slip except at Pointe du Champ du Port which is cut off from the village by the river; land anywhere on the sands in the bay. The village sprawls along the beach and up the road inland; the Harbourmaster is in the Sailing School at the W end where there is a water tap. Two garages, chandler and a *supermarché* lie up the road. There is a casino and several restaurants plus a large hotel on the beach.

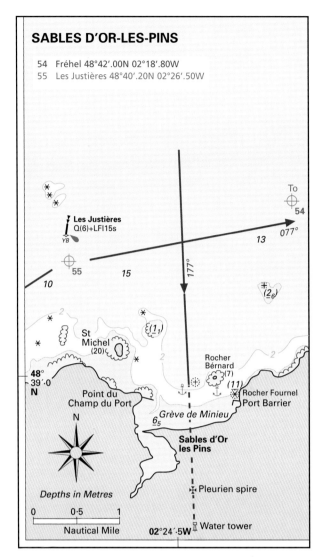

SABLES D'OR-LES-PINS

54 Fréhel 48°42'.00N 02°18'.80W
55 Les Justières 48°40'.20N 02°26'.50W

Sables d'Or-les-Pins. Pointe du Champ du Port from NW at LW. The small breakwater, slip and moorings at W end of the bay

Sables d'Or-les-Pins. Port Barrier from the N at LW. The drying jetty is just visible behind the breakwater

III. ST MALO TO LEZARDRIEUX AND PONTRIEUX

145 Chenal d'Erquy

A well marked short cut between Cap Fréhel and Cap d'Erquy

Tidal information
    HW St Malo -0010
    LW St Malo -0020

Mean height of tide (m)

HWS	HWN	LWN	LWS
11.4	8.8	4.2	1.5

Tidal streams Max 2¼ knots
HW St Helier -0540 ENE-going starts

PILOTAGE

6M from Cap Fréhel to Cap Erquy

Approaches

From E and ⊕54

Close the coast to the W of Cap Fréhel until the S edge of Amas du Cap, a large rock to the W of the Cap, is touching the end of Cap Fréhel bearing 077° (Line J). At night keep Cap Fréhel Fl(2)10s bearing 075° and make good a track of 257° to ⊕55. On reaching the latter with Les Justières S cardinal spar buoy Q.(6)+LFl.15s just abaft the beam, alter to make good 240° on Line K towards ⊕56. From here Basses du Courant N cardinal spar buoy VQ(6)+LFl10s and Cap d'Erquy (unlit) should be visible to pass between.

Cap Fréhel   *Peter Carnegie*

If radar is available a parallel index of 650m from Cap d'Erquy on a track of 240° will lead through.

Line K will be in the green sector of Rohein light ahead VQ(9)WRG.10s. From ⊕56 with Basses du Courant well abaft the beam, make good 235° towards ⊕57 passing through the coloured sectors of Erquy Breakwater light. From ⊕57 make good 255° towards ⊕58 passing S of Plateau des Portes d'Erquy and N of Plateau des Jaunes.

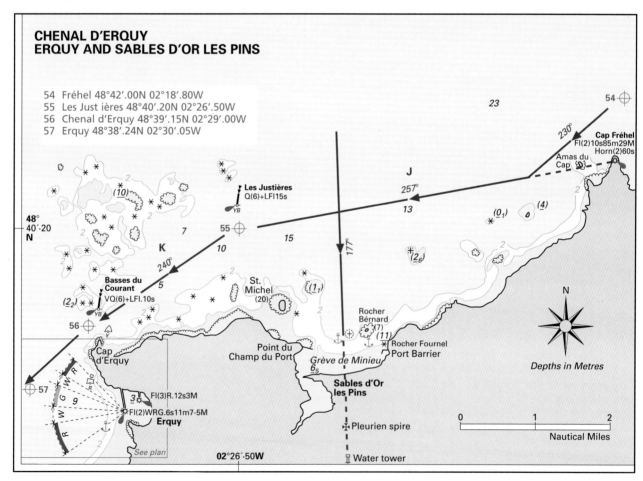

CHENAL D'ERQUY
ERQUY AND SABLES D'OR LES PINS

54 Fréhel 48°42'.00N 02°18'.80W
55 Les Just ières 48°40'.20N 02°26'.50W
56 Chenal d'Erquy 48°39'.15N 02°29'.00W
57 Erquy 48°38'.24N 02°30'.05W

146 Erquy

A drying fishing port barely protected from the W by two short jetties. No facilities for yachts which must dry out on sand or anchor well out; the shops are some way from the port.

Location
8M W of Cap Fréhel, 6M E of Dahouet

Shelter
Only from the E

Depth restrictions
Harbour dries well out

Night entry
One sectored light

Tidal information
HW St Malo -0010
LW St Malo -0020

Mean height of tide (m)

HWS	HWN	LWN	LWS
11.4	8.8	4.2	1.5

Tidal streams
HW St Helier -0540 ENE-going
HW St Helier 0000 WSW-going

Berthing
Alongside berth unlikely; anchor only

Faclities
Those of a small town ½M from port

Charts
BA 3674 (50), 3672 (20)
SHOM 7155 (40)
Imray C33B

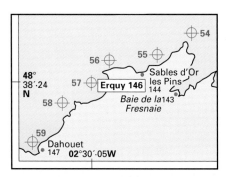

57 Erquy 48°38'.24N 02°30'.05W

Weather
From Cap Fréhel on Ch 79 at 0545, 0803, 1203, 1633 and 2033

PILOTAGE

Approaches

From E

See page 84 for directions to ⊕56 and Cap Erquy whence follow the coast round at about 0.3M leaving Trois Pierres unlit port hand can buoy to port and so to an anchorage.

From W

Pass 1½M S of Rohein (white tower, black top VQ(9)WRG.10s13m) and make good 085° in the S white sector of Erquy breakwater lighthouse (White tower, red top Oc(2+1)WRG.12s), passing S of ⊕57.

Anchorage

Yachts must not anchor in the white sectors of Erquy light by day or night. At night an anchor light must be shown.

56 Chenal d'Erquy 48°39'.15N 02°29'.00W
57 Erquy 48°38'.24N 02°30'.05W
58 Plateau des Jaunes 48°37'.16N 02°36'.10W

The recommended anchorage is with the breakwater lighthouse bearing less than 080° and Cap D'Erquy bearing 350°. The bottom is gently shelving and flat so that one can get further inshore with safety at neaps. The part of the harbour inside the inner breakwater mostly dries 3m and is covered with mooring chains.

It would be possible to anchor off the inner breakwater end (but buoy the anchor) and to go ashore to the shops or for a meal over HW.

Erquy   *Peter Carnegie*

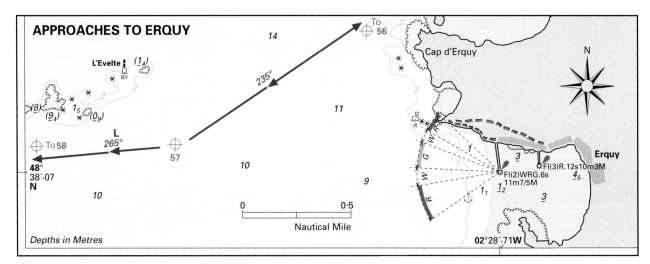

APPROACHES TO ERQUY

Depths in Metres

III. ST MALO TO LEZARDRIEUX AND PONTRIEUX

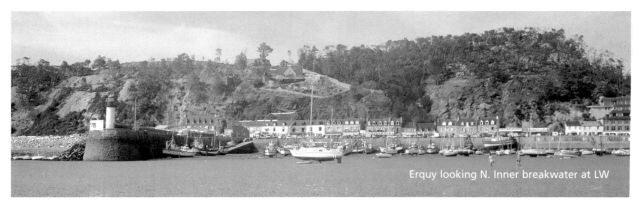
Erquy looking N. Inner breakwater at LW

Ashore in Erquy

The shops are a good ½M from the port but there are some cafés and restaurants by the harbour which may be worth a long dinghy ride ashore.

Facilities

Water tap by the root of the inner breakwater where there is also a sailing club; fuel from garage in town; slip at the sailing club

History

Erquy was the scene of action by Sir Sydney Smith in 1796 in the frigate Diamond with a brig and a lugger in support. A French convoy of a corvette, two sloops and three luggers were seen in Erquy under the protection of the shore batteries. A landing party of seamen from Diamond stormed the batteries and the whole convoy was burnt. The British lost 3 killed and 5 wounded.

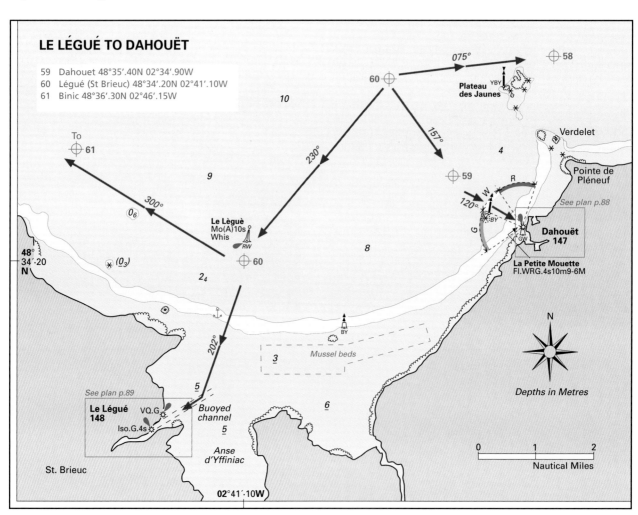

LE LÉGUÉ TO DAHOUËT

59 Dahouet 48°35′.40N 02°34′.90W
60 Légué (St Brieuc) 48°34′.20N 02°41′.10W
61 Binic 48°36′.30N 02°46′.15W

Baie de St Brieuc

It is 20M across the mouth of this shallow, rock encumbered bay from Erquy in the E to Ile de Bréhat in the NW. The dangers are well separated so although precise navigation is not required, care must be taken and the tidal range is still 10m at springs.

Only St Quay (Port 150) offers a marina at all states of tide and all weathers; Dahouët, Le Légué, Binic and Paimpol have locked marinas or harbours with sills mostly drying about 5m, and Erquy is an open anchorage.

147 Dahouët

An unusual drying harbour with a small marina and some facilities. Dangerous to enter in any weather from the N and NW.

Location
8M W of Erquy, 6M E of Le Légué

Shelter
Good inside
Warning
Shallow approach dangerous in strong W-lies or N-lies

Depth restrictions
Dries 4.5m in entrance; sill 5.5m

Night entry Possible but no leading lights

Tidal information
HW St Malo -0010
LW St Malo -0025

Mean height of tide (m)

HWS	HWN	LWN	LWS
11.3	8.6	4.0	1.3

Tidal streams
HW St Helier -0430 ESE-going
HW St Helier +0010 W-going starts

Berthing
On pontoons in marina

Facilities
Modest but adequate

Charts
BA 3674 (50)
SHOM 7154 (48)
Imray C33B

Weather
From Cap Fréhel on Ch 79 at 0545, 0803, 1203, 1633 and 2003

Radio/Telephone
Ch 16 (Working hours)
Harbourmaster ☎ (0)2 96 72 82 85

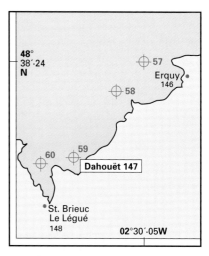

59   Dahouët 48°35'.40N 02°34'.90W

PILOTAGE

Approaches

From ⊕58 make 155° and from ⊕60 make 075° to ⊕59 ½M off the entrance. On both approaches avoid Le Dahouët rock (1.3m) to the S of an unlit N cardinal pillar buoy. Approach La Petite Mouette lighthouse (Green and white, Fl.WRG.4s) on a track of 120° in the white sector, leave it 50m to starboard and pass between it and an unlit red beacon.

Entrance

After rounding La Petite Muette align on 160° on two white posts on the outer edge of the slip below the pagoda shrine; at night continue slowly round to 185° on the Fl(2)G.6s light to leave it to starboard. There is a tide gauge showing the depth over the sill to starboard. Once past the slip keep over to the N side until the marina entrance opens up; this is marked by red and green posts. There are no navigational lights beyond the Fl(2)G.6s but sufficient street and house lights to see the channel.

Dahouët looking SE at half-tide

III. ST MALO TO LEZARDRIEUX AND PONTRIEUX

Berthing

There are 20 visitors' berths (max 12m) alongside the E side of the pontoon to starboard inside the entrance and it is usual to double up. Do not attempt to go on the other side between pontoon and wall.

In the outer harbour, fishing boats berth two or three abreast on the quay but it may be possible to find a drying berth here or further up the drying inner harbour; the latter is packed with drying moorings. Ask at the Port Office before going here.

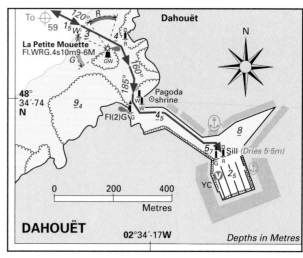

59   Dahouët 48°35'.40N 02°34'.90W

Dahouët Marina Entrance   *Peter Taylor*

Ashore in Dahouët

Facilities

Water and electricity on the pontoons; fuel from a long hose from garage at head of inner drying harbour; showers and heads by harbour office (card needed); basic shops, fish from cold store otherwise 1km walk to Val André to the NE; cafés and small restaurants by harbour, otherwise several in Val André.

Travel

Nearest railway station at Lamballe (13 km); nearest airport at St Brieuc (35 km). Taxi ☎ 02 96 72 25 04

Leisure

Not much, but the local Tourist Office by the harbour may be able to help. Val André is an active holiday resort with a good beach. There are vedette trips every 4 or 5 days to Ile de Bréhat when the tide serves.

148 St Brieuc – Port Le Légué

Le Légué is the port of St Brieuc the major city of the district. St Brieuc sprawls over the hills 300 feet above and about a mile from Le Légué. The latter is a commercial port with some concessions to yachts; it has a drying entrance to a lock with a sill drying 5.1m. Approach not recommended in strong northerlies.

Location
6M WSW of Dahouët, 6M SE of Binic

Shelter
Good inside the locks

Warning
Long shallow approach open to the N sector

Depth restrictions
Dries 5.7m in approach channel

Night entry
Partially lit but no ldg Lts

Tidal information
HW St Malo -0010
LW St Malo -0020

Mean height of tide (m)

HWS	HWN	LWN	LWS
11.4	8.8	4.0	1.4

Tidal streams
HW St Helier –0430 S-going start
HW St Helier 0000 N-going starts

Berthing
Alongside in basin

Facilities
Boatyard and basic shops in Le Légué

Charts
BA 3674 (50) (Plan)
SHOM 7154 (48)
Imray C33B

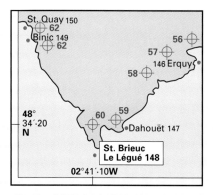

60 Légué (St Brieuc) 48°34'.20N 02°41'.10W

Weather
Cap Fréhel on Ch 79 at 0540, 0803, 1203, 1633 and 2003

Radio/Telephone
Ch 12, 16 (±1½ hours HW)
☎ 02 96 33 35 41

PILOTAGE

Approaches

See page 87. From ⊕60 or Le Légué landfall buoy (RW pillar, Mo(A).12s) make 202° with sufficient rise of tide to allow for it drying 5.7m in the channel and proceed down the buoyed channel. As not all the buoys are lit, a first-off night entry would be unwise. No.1 starboard buoy (Fl.G.2.5s), No.2 port buoy (Fl.R.2.5s), Pointe d'Aigle jetty head (White tower, green top VQ.G) and Custom House jetty (White column, green top Iso.G.4s) will assist. Proceed up the channel, crossing to the S shore after passing Tour de Cesson, to the lock gates. The sill dries 5.1m and the locks work HW ±1–2 hours. Vessels may secure to the S wall immediately outside to wait.

Entrance and Berthing

The lock is 85m long and 14m wide.

The tide gauge on the N side of the entrance indicates depth over the sill, the one on the S side depth above CD.

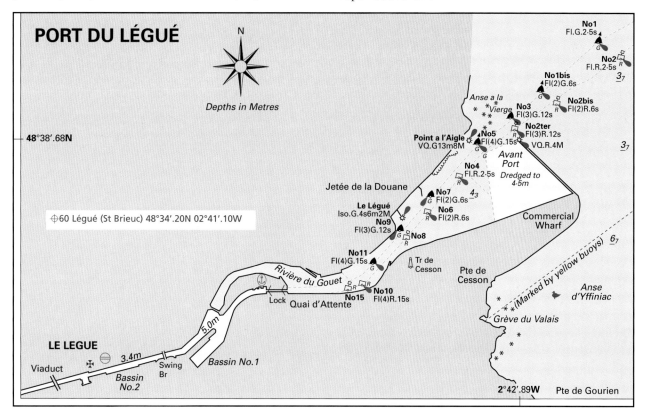

Entrance to Le Légué   *Peter Carnegie*

Turbulence in the lock is noticeable when the gates open so a delay in entering is advisable.

Bassin No.1 on the port hand after leaving the lock is commercial. Bassin No.2 is formed by the canalised part of Rivière de Gouet and is entered through a swing bridge which opens twice a day around lock opening. Proceed through it and towards the viaduct to find a berth alongside the wall preferably on the N side where the shops and cafés are situated. (See photograph).

Ashore in St Brieuc/Le Légué

St Brieuc is a provincial university town with an airport and is a focus for road and rail links. There is considerable light industry on the outskirts and the city is divided by two deep, wooded valleys which are crossed by several viaducts. There are some shops, bars and cafés down in Le Légué but the surroundings are not attractive and it is a long walk up (300 feet, 1 mile) to the city.

Facilities

Water: Occasional points on the quays, otherwise from the bars or cafés; fuel in cans from garage on N side of basin; boatyard, chandlery and repairs on the S side of basin; 30-ton travel-lift, 10-ton crane; a small *supermarché* and shops including a chemist and post office on the N side of the basin; cafés and bars on N side. The best eating area up in St Brieuc is in the old quarter up the hill behind the cathedral.

Travel

Good road and rail connections with the rest of France. Twice daily flights to Paris from local airport; also to Channel Islands. Taxi ☎ 002 96 94 70 70

History

The inundation of the Baie de St Brieuc by the sea has only occurred in the last 2000 years. In Roman times forests and cultivated land existed where there is now only drying sand out in the bay.

Le Tour de Cesson, on the hill above the entrance at its narrowest part, was built originally in 1395 but has been blown up, knocked down and rebuilt over the centuries.

St Brieuc is an old cathedral town named after the Celtic monk who arrived with his disciples in the 5th-century and converted the district to Christianity. Much of the cathedral is 13th- and 14th-century.

Le Légué was formerly the base for a fleet of goëlettes, the fine two-masted topsail schooners that fished off Greenland and Iceland until the last century.

Port Le Légué   *Peter Carnegie*

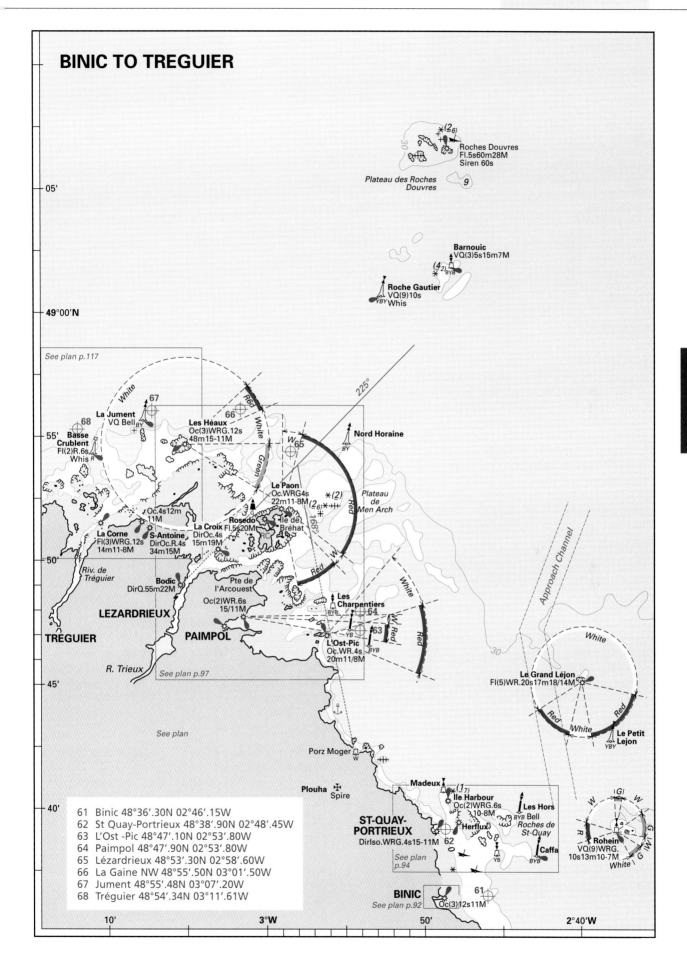

BINIC TO TREGUIER

Roches Douvres
Fl.5s60m28M
Siren 60s

Plateau des Roches
Douvres

9

Barnouic
VQ(3)5s15m7M

Roche Gautier
VQ(9)10s
Whis

49°00'N

See plan p.117

White

67

La Jument
VQ Bell

68

Basse
Crublent
Fl(2)R.6s
Whis

Les Héaux
Oc(3)WRG.12s
48m15-11M

66

White

Green

Nord Horaine

W 65

White

55'

Le Paon
Oc.WRG4s
22m11-8M

Plateau
de
Men Arch

225°

Red

168°

Approach Channel

30

Oc.4s12m
11M

La Corne
Fl(3)WRG.12s
14m11-8M

S-Antoine
DirOc.R.4s
34m15M

La Croix
DirOc.4s
15m19M

Rosedo
Fl.5s20M

Ile de
Bréhat

Riv. de
Tréguier

Bodic
DirQ.55m22M

50'

LEZARDRIEUX

TREGUIER

PAIMPOL

Pte de
l'Arcouest

Oc(2)WR.6s
15/11M

Les
Charpentiers

W. Red

64

63

White

Red

Le Grand Léjon
Fl(5)WR.20s17m18/14M

White

Red

Red

R. Trieux

See plan p.97

L'Ost-Pic
Oc.WR.4s
20m11/8M

45'

See plan

White

Le Petit
Lejon

Porz Moger

Plouha
Spire

Madeux

(1₇)

Ile Harbour
Oc(2)WRG.6s
10-8M

Les Hors
Bell

Rohein
VQ(9)WRG.
10s13m10-7M
White

40'

ST-QUAY-
PORTRIEUX
DirIso.WRG.4s15-11M

Herflux

62

Roches de
St-Quay

Caffa

See plan
p.94

BINIC
See plan p.92

61

Oc(3)12s11M

61 Binic 48°36'.30N 02°46'.15W
62 St Quay-Portrieux 48°38'.90N 02°48'.45W
63 L'Ost -Pic 48°47'.10N 02°53'.80W
64 Paimpol 48°47'.90N 02°53'.80W
65 Lézardrieux 48°53'.30N 02°58'.60W
66 La Gaine NW 48°55'.50N 03°01'.50W
67 Jument 48°55'.48N 03°07'.20W
68 Tréguier 48°54'.34N 03°11'.61W

10'   3°W   50'   2°40'W

III. ST MALO TO LEZARDRIEUX AND PONTRIEUX

149 Binic

An attractive little port with a locked basin in the middle of the town which is in rural surroundings. Gate sill dries 5.5m.

Location
6M NW of Le Légué, 3M S of St Quay

Shelter
Good inside the lock

Depth restrictions
Dries 5m in approach; sill dries 5.5m

Night entry
Just possible if lock open

Tidal information
HW St Malo -0008
LW St Malo -0025

Mean height of tide (m)

HWS	HWN	LWN	LWS
11.4	8.6	4.0	1.3

Tidal streams
HW St Helier -0430 SSE-going
HW St Helier 0000 NNW-going

Berthing
Alongside pontoon

Facilities
Most available

Charts
BA 3674 (50)
SHOM 7154 (48), 7128 (7.5)
Imray C33B

Weather
Cap Fréhel on Ch 79 at 0545, 0803, 1203, 1633 and 2003

Radio/Telephone
Ch 09 (Working hours)
☎ 02 96 73 61 86

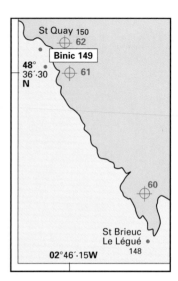

PILOTAGE

Approaches

See pages 93 and 94 if coming from the N.

There are no dangers in the immediate vicinity of Binic except Basse Gouin a rock about 1½M ENE of the harbour with 1.6m over it which should not present a problem unless anchoring in the vicinity.

The least depth on any approach in the E sector is drying 5m with a shallow and steady gradient from the 5m line.

From ⊕61 the breakwater light (White tower, green top, Oc(3)12s) and the church spire close N of the harbour may be identified.

Entrance

The outer harbour has many moorings in it on the N side but a fairway is kept clear for access to the lock, and access for fishing boats to berth on the S pier. See photo on next page.

The gate opens when the tide rises to 8.5m and stays open until HW. It will not operate outside these limits so take care not to be caught inside if approaching neaps.

Red and green lights control entry and exit.

A timetable of opening is displayed outside the Harbour Office. There is a sliding bridge by the gate which is operated by the Harbourmaster.

Berthing

There are 60 visitors' berths either on the first pontoon inside the gate (max 10m) or alongside the long pontoon running along the N wall (max 15m). Depths in the basin vary from 2.5m near the gate to 1.5m further in.

There are no provisions for visitors on the moorings in the outer harbour but a drying berth may be found along the N mole drying 4.5m, sand and mud where it is quieter than in the basin.

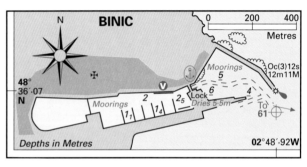

61   Binic 48°36′.30N 02°46′.15W

Anchorage

In westerly or settled weather an anchorage may be selected in a suitable depth of water anywhere off the port except in the vicinity of Basse Gouin.

Ashore in Binic

There is still some fishing activity here but mostly confined to the outer harbour. Binic tries hard to please yachtsmen and is a good deal more agreeable from their point of view than Le Légué although rather more tidally limited. St Quay just to the N is much more expensive but available at all states of the tide.

Facilities

Water and electricity on the pontoons; showers and heads behind the Harbourmaster's Office just N of the gate; fuel from garage 300m away in the town; launderette near the basin; 10-ton crane; slip at head of the basin; chandlery two close by; mechanics, electrician, sailmaker available, ask at the Harbourmaster's Office; many shops of all qualities close by in the town; a good selection of hotels and restaurants; there is an active yacht club in the unusual building just S of the gate.

Binic   *Peter Carnegie*

Travel

Bus service to St Brieuc whence there are frequent departures in all directions by road or rail. The nearby airport has twice daily flights to Paris. Taxi ☎ 02 96 70 59 46.

Leisure

The Zoological Gardens of Brittany are 6km W with many wild animals in natural surroundings; open 1000–1900 in the season. Good beaches to the N and S.

History

Binic used to be a considerable port and was the first to break the Basque monopoly of the Newfoundland cod fishery. Hundreds of *terres-neuviens* made the round trip of several months each year to the fishery and then to the south of France to sell their catches.

Binic. The basin from the lock

III. ST MALO TO LEZARDRIEUX AND PONTRIEUX

Rade de St Quay-Portrieux

Passage through and approaches to St Quay Marina (Port d'Amour)

Tidal streams
HW St Helier -0430 SSE-going starts
HW St Helier + 0115 NNW-going starts

PILOTAGE

Approaches

From N by day

This entrance goes close to a 1.6m patch and this depth should be allowed for.

From ⊕63 L'Ost-Pic make good a track of 155° towards ⊕62. When to the W of Madeaux W cardinal beacon pick up the line Moulières E cardinal beacon/Breakwater end light (White metallic structure) 172° (Line N) and turn down it. When Herflux S cardinal beacon tower comes into line with La Longue S cardinal beacon tower (both on Roches de Saint Quay) 119° (Line P) turn on to it. After 0.3M turn to starboard to 182° (Line Q) with Breakwater end in transit with Le Four white beacon tower. Follow this to round the breakwater end and enter the marina.

If continuing S, turn off Line Q to pass through ⊕62 to pick up the back transit Breakwater light/Semaphore tower 315° and proceed on 135° (Line R) to leave the unnamed E cardinal spindle buoy marking a wreck to starboard. This track then passes close to a 0.3m patch to leave La Rosilière W cardinal buoy to port, and away. To avoid this patch or go towards ⊕61 adjust the track to 150° by the E cardinal buoy.

From N by night

Approach as for By Day from ⊕63 until the white sector of Marina Elbow light Iso WRG.4s 172° is entered.

Note that in the red sector you will be too far to starboard, not port. (Line N). Shortly after Herflux light on the port bow (Fl(2)WRG.6s) turns from red to white, alter to 119° to bring it ahead and continue until the white sector of Ile Harbour light Oc(2)WRG.6s on the port quarter is entered when turn to 182° (Line Q) for the Breakwater end (Fl(3)G.12s to enter the Marina. A least depth of 0.3m should be allowed for on this approach.

If continuing S, turn off Line Q to pass through ⊕62 to pick up the white sector of the Breakwater Elbow light (Dir.Iso WRG.4s) 315° and proceed down it on 135° (Line R) to leave La Rosilière buoy VQ(9.10s) to port. This track passes close to a 0.3m patch. To avoid this or go to ⊕61 adjust the track to 150° by the E cardinal buoy.

From S by day

Approaching from ⊕61 or the SE identify La Longue S cardinal and La Ronde W cardinal beacon towers to pass close to La Rosilière W cardinal buoy

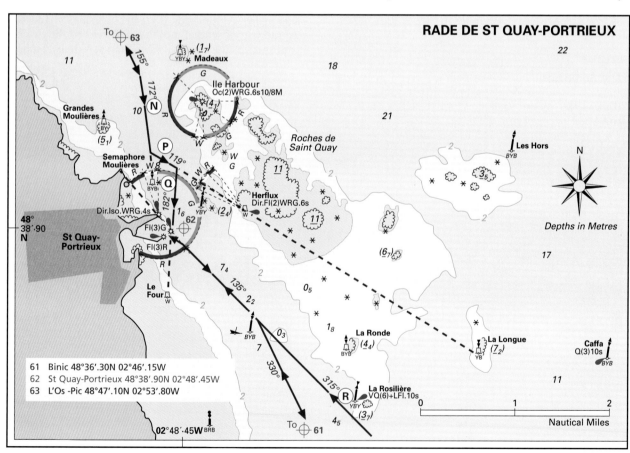

61   Binic 48°36'.30N 02°46'.15W
62   St Quay-Portrieux 48°38'.90N 02°48'.45W
63   L'Os -Pic 48°47'.10N 02°53'.80W

RADE DE ST QUAY-PORTRIEUX

Depths in Metres

to pick up the transit Breakwater End light (Green and white metal structure) Semaphore Tower 315° (Line R). Then leave an E cardinal spindle buoy to port and Le Four white beacon tower 800m to port to round the breakwater end.

To avoid a 0.3m patch close to this track, approach the E cardinal buoy on 330° from ⊕61.

From S by night

From ⊕61 proceed towards La Rosilière buoy VQ(9)10s and pick up the white sector of the Breakwater Elbow light Iso.WRG.4s 315° and alter up it (Line R). This passes close to a 0.3m patch; to avoid it, make good 330° from ⊕61 on the right hand edge of the red sector until the unlit E cardinal buoy is passed to port when the Marina entrance lights (Fl(3)R.12s and Fl(3)G.12s) can be made for.

If continuing N, pass through ⊕62 and turn in to the white sector of Ile Harbour light Oc(2).WRG.6s on 002° (Line Q) to leave Les Noirs unlit W cardinal buoy to starboard. When Herflux (Dir.Fl(2).WRG.6s) turns from green to white steer up this sector on 299° (Line P) until in the N white sector of the Breakwater elbow light Dir.Iso.WRG.4s when alter to 352° (Line N) to proceed N out of the Rade.

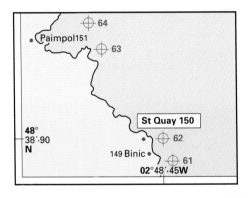

150 St Quay-Portrieux Marina (Port d'Amour)

One of the largest and best appointed marinas on the coast and probably the most expensive, backed up by a pleasant resort.

Location
3M N of Binic, 9M S of L'Ost-Pic

Shelter
Good

Depth restrictions
Marina dredged to 3m; old harbour dries between 3.5–7m

Night entry
Well lit

Tidal information
HW St Malo -0010
LW St Malo -0035

Mean height of tide (m)

HWS	HWN	LWN	LWS
11.3	8.6	4.0	1.4

Berthing
On pontoons with fingers

Facilities
All those of a modern marina and town

Charts
BA 3674 (25), 3674 (50)
SHOM 7128 (7.5)
Imray C34
An all-weather lifeboat is kept here

Weather
From Bodic on Ch 79 at 0533, 0745, 1145, 1615, 1945

Radio/Telephone
Ch 09 (24 hours)
☎ 02 96 70 81 30

62   St Quay-Portrieux 48°38'.90N 02°48'.45W

St Quay-Portrieux Marina

Entrance and Berthing

Turn to port on entry, leave all the yacht berths to port and secure to the arrivals pontoon which is the centre one at the W end. The one to the N of this is used by the vedettes and one to the S is the fuelling pontoon. Go to the Marina Office to be allocated a berth. There are 100 visitors' berths up to 18m and multihulls are catered for. Visitors are usually put on pontoon 7 and most of the area is dredged to 3m. There are substantial fingers on the pontoons.

In addition to vedette traffic which runs to Bréhat, one of the leading fishing complexes in Brittany occupies the N side of the harbour and is a principal scallop fishery.

Anchorage

An anchorage can be found to the E of the old southern harbour breakwater in any desired depth, clear of the entrance, sand and mud, good holding. Avoid the area of the 1.2m sounding S of the marina entrance on the chart and Plan which is rock, and another of 0.2m 200m to the SW of it. The tidal stream falls off appreciably the further W one goes.

Old Harbour

Yachts are not allowed to berth alongside the quays but those with bilge keels or legs can dry out on hard sand in the harbour, clear of the entrance and many moorings. There is not much spare space. The harbour dries from 3.5m to 7m.

Ashore in St Quay

Facilities

Water and electricity on the pontoons; fuel diesel and petrol from the fuel berth with a credit card or call Ch 9; showers and heads 20 of each situated at W end of the S mole; slip in the NW corner; full maintenance and repair facilities; ice from the Marina Office; chandler on the Marina; shops some in the Marina, the nearest supermarché is on the front by the old harbour where there are also a number of food shops; restaurants, cafés, bars and hotels of all styles and qualities, some in the Marina; a new YC is on the N side of the old harbour; bicycle hire through the Marina Office.

Travel

A bus runs to St Brieuc whence there are connections to the national road and bus network. Twice daily flights to Paris from St Brieuc airport.

Leisure

The usual *divertissements* of a bustling holiday resort but little of cultural interest.

History

Another Brittany port whose history is steeped in fishing. Like Binic, it was in the forefront of the Newfoundland fishery and there was once a large fleet of *terre-neuviens* many of whom spent the winters hauled well up the beach in the old harbour.

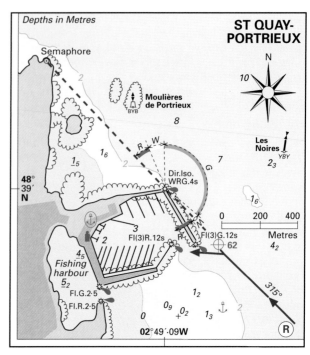

62   St Quay-Portrieux 48°38'.90N 02°48'.45W

St Quay entrance   *Peter Taylor*

St Quay reception and fuel berth   *Peter Taylor*

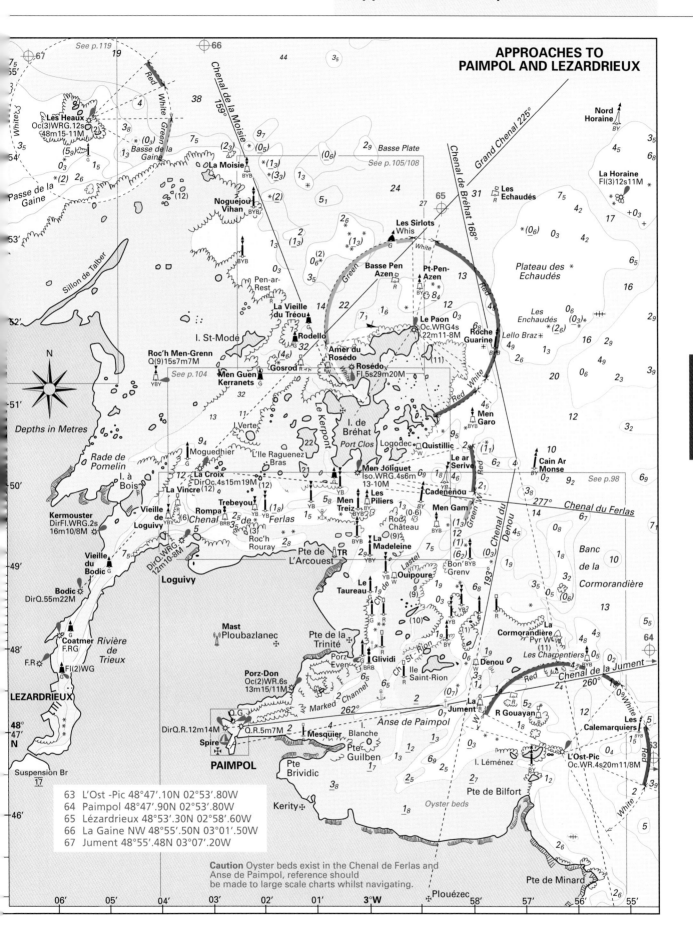

See p.119

Nord
Horaine
BY

Chenal de la Moisie 159°

Grand Chenal 225°

Chenal de Bréhat 168°

Les
Echaudés

La Horaine
Fl(3)12s11M

Les Heaux
Oc(3)WRG.12s
48m15-11M

Basse de la Gaine

Passe de la
Gaine

Basse Plate
See p.105/108

Plateau des
Echaudés

La Moisie
BYB

Noguejou
Vihan
BYB

Les Sirlots
Whis
White

Basse Pen
Azen
R

Pt-Pen-
Azen
BY

Les
Enchaudés

Lello Braz

Pen-ar-
Rest

La Vieille
du Tréou

Le Paon
Oc.WRG4s
22m11-8M

Roche
Guarine
BYB

Rodello

Amer du
Rosédo

Men
Garo
BYB

Sillon de Talber

I. St-Modé

Roc'h Men-Grenn
Q(9)15s7m7M
YBY

Gosrod

Men Guen
Kerranets
YBY

Rosédo
Fl.5s29m20M

See p.104

Cain Ar
Monse
BY

Depths in Metres

N

Rade de
Pomelin

I. à
Bois

Moguedhier

I. Verte

L'Île Raguenez
Bras

I. de
Bréhat
Port Clos

Logodec
W

Quistillic

Le ar
Serive

See p.98

Chenal du Ferlas 277°

Men Joliguet
Iso.WRG.4s6m
13-10M

Men
Treiz

Les
Piliers
BYB

Cadenenou
YB

Banc
de la
Cormorandière

La Croix
DirOc.4s15m19M

Kermouster
DirFl.WRG.2s
16m10/8M

Vieille
de
Loguivy

Trebeyou

Rompa

Chenal de Ferlas

Roc'h
Rouray

La
Vincre

Roc
Château

Men Gam
BY

Chenal du Denou 193°

Vieille
du
Bodic

DirQ.WRG
12m10-8M

Pte de
L'Arcouest
TR

La
Madeleine

Bon'
Grenv
BYB

La
Cormorandière
Pyr W

Les Chappentiers

Bodic
DirQ.55m22M

Loguivy

Le
Taureau

Ouipoure
YB

Denou

Coatmer
F.RG

Mast
Ploubazlanec

Pte de la
Trinité

Glividi
BRB

Ch St-Rion

Ile
Saint-Rion

Chenal de la Jument 260°

La Cormorandière

Les
Calemarquiers
BYB

F.R

Fl(2)WG

Rivière
de
Trieux

Porz
Even

Porz-Don
Oc(2)WR.6s
13m15/11M

La
Jument

R Gouayan

LEZARDRIEUX

48°
47'
N

Q.G.

Mesquier

I.
Blanche

Anse de Paimpol

L'Ost-Pic
Oc.WR.4s20m11/8M

DirQ.R.12m14M
Q.R.5m7M

Spire

Marked Channel 262°

Pte
Guilben

I. Léménez

PAIMPOL

Pte
Brividic

Suspension Br
17

Kerity

Pte de Bilfort

Oyster beds

Pte de Minard

63 L'Ost -Pic 48°47'.10N 02°53'.80W
64 Paimpol 48°47'.90N 02°53'.80W
65 Lézardrieux 48°53'.30N 02°58'.60W
66 La Gaine NW 48°55'.50N 03°01'.50W
67 Jument 48°55'.48N 03°07'.20W

Caution Oyster beds exist in the Chenal de Ferlas and
Anse de Paimpol, reference should
be made to large scale charts whilst navigating.

Plouézec

Approaches to Paimpol

There are two outer and five inner approach channels to Paimpol. Of the two outer, Chenal de Ferlas is described on page 104 and Chenal de Bréhat briefly below. This section describes the five inner approaches.

PILOTAGE

Only Chenal de la Jument is navigable at night provided the unlit buoys in the final approaches can be seen. (Some have reflective strips)

Chenal de Bréhat

This approach is from the N passing E of Ile de Bréhat and leads to Chenals de Lastel, St Rion, Dénou or La Jument. It may be followed on BA 3673(20) or SHOM 7127 and accessed from ⊕65 or the Lézardrieux approach line.

Warnings

Either BA 3673 or SHOM 7127 charts should be used when navigating these channels as all details cannot be shown on these scales of Plans.

Chenal de la Jument (Lines Z and K)

All the other channels lead in to La Jument which carries a least depth of drying 3m; however drying

4.9m will be found close outside the narrow channel and this should be allowed for in the final 2M.

From ⊕64 to the NE of L'Ost-Pic identify the first leading line of Paimpol church spire/Pointe Brividic (a woody hill in front of the town) bearing 260° and follow this. At night the F.R leading lights are intensified between 261° and 266° and lead right up to the breakwater end.

The Porz Don light's Oc.WR.6s white sector indicates clearance from La Jument until this is passed when the red sector indicates progress along the leading line.

These lines will leave:

Les Charpentiers E cardinal unlit beacon tower 300m to starboard.
Roc'h Gouayan port unlit beacon tower 800m to port.
Roc'h Gueule port unlit buoy 200m to port.
La Jument port unlit beacon tower 150m to port.
Roc'h ar Zel port unlit beacon tower 300m to port. At this point align with the final leading line if not on it (White hut, red top on breakwater end/white tower with red top behind, F.R *Front* and *Rear* intensified) bearing 264°.

The final 1½M to the entrance will leave:

An Uhel starboard unlit beacon to starboard.
Mesquier port unlit beacon 300m to port.

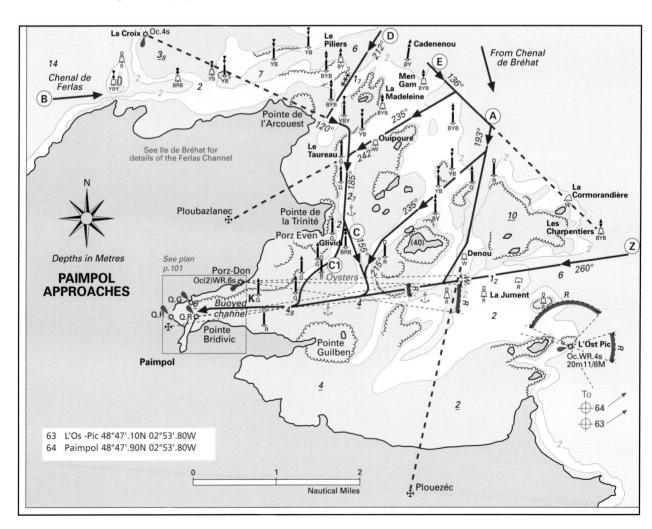

63	L'Os -Pic 48°47'.10N 02°53'.80W
64	Paimpol 48°47'.90N 02°53'.80W

El Bras starboard unlit beacon to starboard. Thereafter the channel is marked with unlit port and starboard buoys (with reflective strips) and beacons up to the breakwater end (See plan on page 101).

Chenal de la Trinité (Lines D & C)

The least depth in this channel is drying 2.2m at the N end. It shallows to drying 4.9m in the final stages of the approach to the lock at Paimpol.

Navigate to a position 400m to the E of Les Piliers N cardinal beacon tower. From here Quistillic white pyramid (12m) to the NE will be open to the right of Men Bras Logodec (a rock which never covers (4m) on a bearing of 032°. Make good the reciprocal 212° keeping Quistillic open to the right to avoid the three Lel-Ouene rocks drying 2.2m if the depth is not enough to clear. Then leave:

Men Treiz E cardinal beacon 300m to starboard.
Roc'h Chateau 250m to port.
Roc'h Lème E cardinal beacon 350m to starboard.
La Madeleine W cardinal beacon 200m to port.
At this point look to the NNW and when La Croix lighthouse comes into line with the coast on the NW side of Pointe de l'Arcouest bearing 300° alter to 120° to leave Les Fillettes S cardinal beacon to port. When Le Taureau starboard beacon bears 180° alter to 155° to leave it to starboard (Line C). From here leave:

**Rollic starboard beacon 100m to starboard.
Min Treuse port beacon 100m to port.
Roc'h ar Gerroc port beacon 150m to port.
When Pointe de la Trinité bears 335° make good 155° (Line C) with Roc'h ar Zel port beacon almost ahead. This leaves **Glividi** isolated danger beacon 200m to starboard and leads in to the main La Jument channel. Note Plan for Alt C1.

Chenal de Lastel (Lines E & C)

This leads in from the NE and has a least depth of 1.2m and is subject to cross sets.

From the NE of Cardenenou N cardinal buoy make good 136°on the transit La Cormorandière white pyramid/Les Charpentiers E cardinal beacon tower leaving Men Gam E cardinal beacon tower 600m to starboard.

When Ouipoure white beacon tower bears 235° alter to this to leave it 100m to port. From here keep a steady bearing on Le Taureau starboard beacon before turning 200m short of it to 185° (Line C). Then proceed as from ** above for Chenal de la Trinité.

Chenal St Rion (Lines A & C)

This channel has a least depth of drying 0.4m but is very narrow and has no leading marks for the most part.

Pick up the transit La Cormorandière/Les Charpentiers 136° and proceed down it until the leading marks for Chenal du Denou (Plouezec spire/Denou white pyramid 193°) (see photo page 100) come into line and turn down it. Shortly after, Roc'h Petite Moisie port beacon will align with La

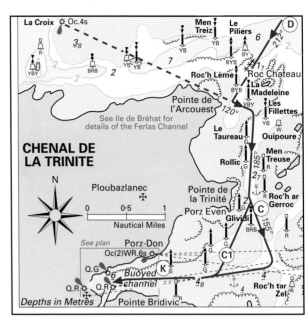

CHENAL DE LA TRINITE

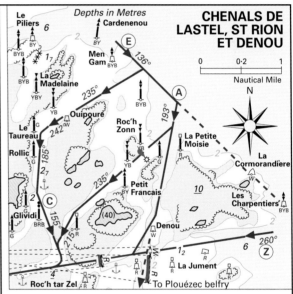

CHENALS DE LASTEL, ST RION ET DENOU

Cormorandière white pyramid when the track should be altered to 235° and held to leave:

Roc'h Zonn S cardinal beacon 150m to starboard.
An unnamed S cardinal beacon 100m to starboard.
Petit Francais N cardinal beacon 200m to port.
Pass between the Ile St Rion to the SE and the group of rocks to the NW in the narrowest part of the channel on 235° with an unnamed port beacon fine on the port bow. Pass close to this and join the main channel on a track of 215°.

Chenal du Denou (Line A)

The least depth in this channel is 0.5m.

Proceed as for Chenal St Rion and hold the leading line of Plouezec spire/Denou white pyramid on 193° to leave the pyramid 100m to port whence the track may be altered to 205° to rejoin the main La Jument channel.

III. ST MALO TO LEZARDRIEUX AND PONTRIEUX

Paimpol. Leading line for Chenal du Dénou. Dénou white beacon tower and Plouézec spire in transit bearing 193°

Tidal streams

A. Between La Jument and Dénou beacon towers:
HW St Helier -0340 SSE-going starts
HW St Helier +0405 NNW-going starts
The maximum rate in each direction is 3½ knots.

B. At the N end of Chenals Trinité, Lastel and Denou, the S-going stream starts about 15 minutes earlier and the N-going 15 minutes later than the times above.

C. At the W end of the bay:
HW St Helier -0515 W-going starts
HW St Helier +0215 E-going starts
The maximum rate is 1½ knots

Paimpol. L'Ost-Pic lighthouse bearing 240°

151 Paimpol

A substantial port at the head of an extensive estuary. The locks open up to ±2½ hours HW and there are good yacht facilities in a fishing and commercial port.

Location
11M NNW of St Quay, 4M S of Ile de Bréhat

Shelter
Good inside port

Depth restrictions
See under 'Pilotage' on page 98

Night entry
Only possible via the main channel

Tidal information
HW St Malo -0010
LW St Malo -0035

Mean height of tide (m)

HWS	HWN	LWN	LWS
10.8	8.3	3.8	1.3

Berthing
On pontoons in the port

Facilities
Those of a medium-sized town

Charts
BA 3673 (10), 3670 (50)
SHOM 7127 (49)
Imray C34 (Plan)

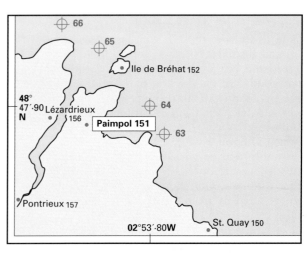

64   Paimpol 48°47′.90N 02°53′.80W

Weather
From Bodic on Ch 79 at 0533, 0745, 1145, 1615 and 1945

Radio/Telephone
Ch 09 HW±2 hours
Harbourmaster ☎ 02 96 20 80 77
Lock ☎ 02 96 20 90 02

Anse de Paimpol
looking E at LW

Entrance

The channel and sill dry 3m but drying 4.9m will be found close to the channel and this should be allowed for in the final 2M of approach.

Turn close round the breakwater end and secure on the W side of the lock if necessary to wait for it. The lock works for up to 2½ hours either side of HW, is 60m long and 12m wide. With the depth above 8.5m the gates are left open over HW for varying times depending on the height of the tide. In this situation before HW there is often a strong inward flow through the gates.

Berthing

Bassin No.1 is on the E side of the docks and is reached through another lock that is generally left open. It is for fishing and commercial vessel.

Bassin No.2 is for yachts and has 20 visitors' berths. The reception pontoon is 'A', the first one ahead from the locks and to the W of the Harbour Office on the central quay. Maximum length 20m.

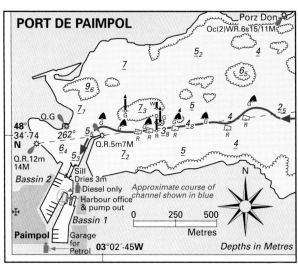

(See plan on page 96)

Paimpol   *Peter Carnegie*

Lock entrance at half-tide

Anchorage

In the outer approaches

Anse de Bréhec is 3M S of L'Ost-Pic with a long sandy beach sheltered from S through W to NE. It can be approached from Le Taureau beacon tower (Isolated danger mark) 1M to the E.

In Anse de Paimpol

It is possible to anchor almost anywhere in the Anse clear of the shellfish beds although there are few sheltered areas for yachts. The following are possibilities (See plan page 98):

- Near Line Z with La Jument bearing E and Ile St Rion bearing N in a suitable depth 0–8m. Take care to avoid the 0.7m rock near this position. Little shelter and a long way from anywhere.

- NNE of Pointe Guilben at the head of the deep approach channel with restricted swinging room. It is roughly on the following transits:
  La Vierge de Kerroch monument (to the W of Porz Don) open to the right of Le Vahel beacon. Kerity church and the W side of the hillock on the end of Point Guilben.
  An anchor light at night would be a wise precaution as this is on or near the leading line. There is a dinghy landing on the N side of Pointe Guilben above half tide.

- Off Porz Even in 2.7m with Glividi beacon bearing 190° 200m, to the E of the moorings. This is the most sheltered anchorage from the W. Dinghy landing at Porz Even, a small drying harbour for fishing boats.

Ashore in Paimpol

Facilities

Water and electricity on the pontoons; fuel and pump-out at the end of central quay; showers and heads by the harbourmaster; slip, wi-fi; cranes up to 45 tonnes; repairs and chandlery – there are several private yacht yards and chandlers round the basin. It would be a good place to lay up although security arrangements ashore may be suspect; many shops round the basins, *supermarché* at the S end of No.2 basin will deliver; there are many cafés, restaurants and bars to suit all tastes and pockets.

Leisure

A lively town with a tangle of narrow streets lined by grey granite houses. The harbour is still very much the centre of things; a college in the town ensures a young population.

Travel

Rail and bus to St Brieuc where there is also an airport with twice daily flights to Paris.

History

Paimpol used to be the great base for the Icelandic cod and whaling fleets that left every February for northern waters. Their departure was the occasion for a famous 'pardon', a religious ceremony lasting for a few days. Until September the town would be empty of young men whose return was greeted with great celebrations. The ships were either *goëlettes* (topsail schooners) or *dundees* (ketches). Hand lines were worked from the ships themselves, hove-to in deep water.

The fishery started in 1852 and grew to as many as 50 vessels with 25 crew from this port alone. The last of the *goëlettes*, La Glycine made her final voyage to Iceland in 1935.

152 Ile de Bréhat

An enchanting island,crowded during the day from the many vedettes that ply there. For those who can dry out there is plenty of space; neaps are best for deep draught boats to anchor.

Location
4M N of Paimpol, 6M from Lézardrieux

Shelter
Some in anchorages

Depth restrictions
Anchorages dry out

Night entry
Unlit except for Chenal de Ferlas

Tidal information
HW St Malo -0010
LW St Malo -0045

Mean height of tide (m)

HWS	HWN	LWN	LWS
10.3	7.9	3.8	1.3

Tidal streams
To NE of Ile de Bréhat
HW St Helier +0610 SE flood
HW St Helier +0005 NW ebb
In Chenal de Ferlas
HW St Helier +0610 E flood
HW St Helier +0005 W ebb
In Kerpont Channel
HW St Helier +0610 S flood
HW St Helier +0005 N ebb

Berthing
Anchoring or drying out

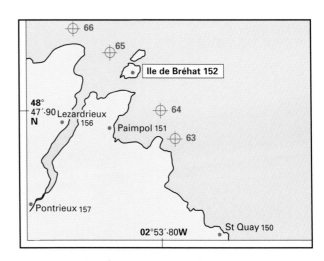

65 Lézardrieux   48°53'.30N 02°58'.60W

Facilities
Basic provisions

Charts
BA 3673 (10), SHOM 7127 (20)

Weather
From Bodic on Ch 79 at 0533, 0745, 1145, 1615 and 1945

Radio/Telephone
None

Ile de Bréhat looking N

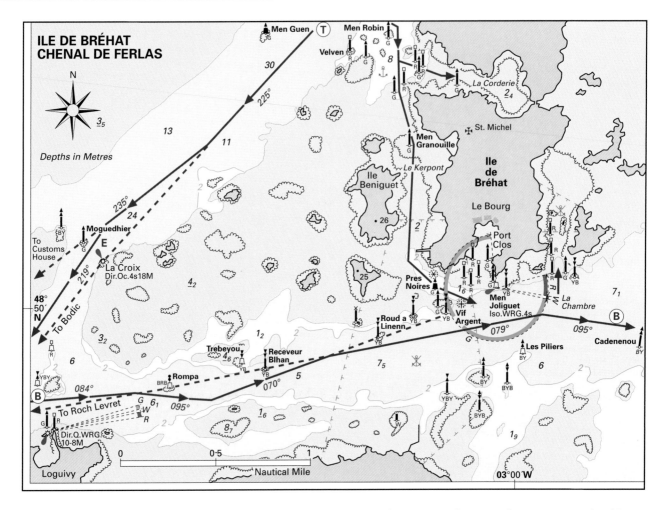

ILE DE BRÉHAT
CHENAL DE FERLAS

Depths in Metres

PILOTAGE

Chenal de Ferlas

Approaches

From W by day

From the Grand Chenal de Trieux identify Veille de Loguivi W cardinal beacon and approach it on a track of 084° to leave it 100m to port, aligning Rompa isolated danger mark with Les Piliers N cardinal beacon on the same bearing. Continue until 150m from Rompa and alter to 095° to leave Rompa at least 100m to port as there is an outlier drying 3m 50m to the S of it. After 400m align the S cardinal beacons of Roud ar Linenn and Vif Argent on 070° and hold this to leave:

Trebeyou S cardinal beacon tower 200m to port.
Receveur Bihan S cardinal beacon 100m to port.
Roud ar Linenn S cardinal beacon 100m to port.
Vif Argent S cardinal beacon 250m to port.
Men Joliguet W cardinal beacon tower (lit) 300m to port.
Les Piliers N cardinal beacon tower 300m to starboard.

Thence the track can be maintained on 070° out to the ENE or through Chenal de Bréhat leaving the unlit Lel ar Skrey S cardinal buoy to starboard (marking a shoal drying 0.2m just to the N), or altered to 095° to leave Cadenenou N cardinal buoy to starboard. The latter alternative leads to the Paimpol entrance channels of Lastel, St.Rion, Denou and La Jument.

To proceed to Paimpol through Chenal de la Trinité turn to starboard to the S round Les Piliers beacon tower and proceed as on page 98.

From W by night

Only with difficulty as the directional leading lights are aligned to be used from the E.

From E by day

Reverse the tracks and transits for the passage from the W.

From E by night

There are three directional leading lights which lead through the Chenal from E to W. Be warned that the sided sectors are inconsistent from one to another.

From a position 1½M N of ⊕64 pick up the white sector of Men Joliguet (Iso.WRG.4s) on a track of 280° (Green to the S, Red to the N) and proceed until between the unlit buoys of Cadenenou and Lel ar Skrey when the red sector of Roc'h Quinonec at the W end of the Chenal will become visible; continue into the very narrow white sector (0.7° 257°) and proceed down it exactly until Rompa (unlit) is abeam to starboard (Red to the S, Green to the N). The white sector of Kermouster

(Dir.Fl.WRG.2s) will then be entered on 272° to lead in to Grande Passe de Trieux (Red to the S, Green to the N) leaving Vielle de Loguivy unlit beacon well to starboard.

Approaches

To La Corderie
(See photo on page 106).
From ⊕65 proceed up the Grande Passe de Trieux leading line 225° until Vieille de Tréou starboard beacon tower bears N when alter to 177° to leave Gosrod port beacon tower well to starboard and pass between Men Robin starboard beacon and Amer du Rosedo white pyramid. When the drying rocks to port are cleared, alter to leave Moncello Richard port beacon 100m to port and pass between the next port and starboard beacons in to La Corderie.

153 La Corderie

This offers a restricted anchorage to deep draught vessels at springs but there is more scope at neaps. The inner harbour dries about 2.4m which gives about 1.2m at MLWN. Deeper draughts can anchor in the pool outside the entrance beacons, sounding as close in to the sides as possible to avoid the strong streams that run through the Kerpont Channel. At neaps it may be possible to find enough water inside the entrance beacons and clear of the channel to anchor. Bilge keelers or yachts with legs can proceed further E to dry out on the bottom which, except in a few rocky places, is hard sand. There is a power line across the harbour marked by beacons which should be avoided.

The landing slip is on the N side of the harbour but the beaches and rocks on the S side are nearer to the shops. An anchor light is recommended at night especially outside the harbour as fishing boats use the Kerpont Channel.

Kerpont Channel

This is an interesting short cut by day and near HW. The stream runs hard through the channel but always true to the fairway. From the N, proceed as for La Corderie but continue on a southerly track to pass through the port and starboard beacons at the N end of the passage and leave the following marks on the sides indicated:

Men Granouille starboard beacon 10m to starboard. This is the narrowest and shallowest part of the channel.

The isolated above water rock on the E side of Ile Beniquet 60m to starboard.

The isolated above water rock off Ile Beniquet's SE corner 100m to starboard.

Follow the deep water round to the N of Les Pierres Noires starboard beacon tower, taking care to avoid the end of the slip to the N and the rocks extending to the SE from Les Pierres Noires. And so into Rade de Bréhat.

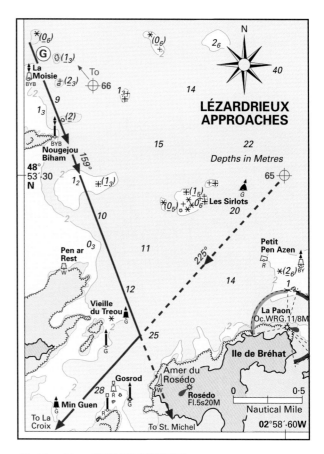

65 Lézardrieux 48°53′.30N 02°58′.60W
66 La Gaine NW 48°55′.50N 03°01′.50W

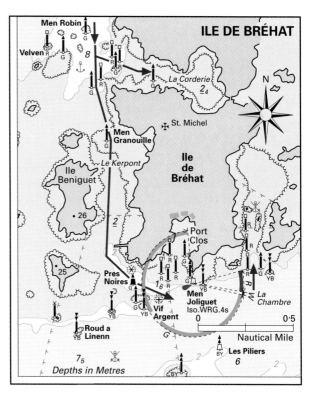

III. ST MALO TO LEZARDRIEUX AND PONTRIEUX

Ile de Bréhat. Port de la Corderie looking E at LW

Kerpont Channel from the S

An indication of the depth in the channel is that the passage is clear for a 1.8m draught when the slip on the SW corner of Ile de Bréhat is covered.

154 La Chambre

(See photo on page 107).
A small drying harbour on the SE corner of the island. It is now very crowded with moorings and difficult to find an anchorage out of the stream even at neaps. There are sometimes moorings placed outside and to seaward of Men Allan bay just to the W but these and the anchorage are subject to any swell from the E. Craft with legs or bilge keelers can dry out further in but note the prohibited anchorage further N. There is a landing slip on the W side and another further N which is nearer to the village Le Bourg.

Men Allan bay to the W is an alternative anchorage; sound in as far N as depth allows but outside the buoyed swimming area.

155 Port Clos

(See photo on page 107).
A small drying harbour on the S side much used by the *vedettes*. Do not obstruct the slips and jetties. 2M or more can be found at MLWN to the NW of Men Joliguet beacon tower. Craft able to take the ground can use the inner harbour where there is perfect shelter. Note the prohibited anchorage which covers the W side of the outer harbour. The vedette traffic ceases in the evening. Land at any of the slips.

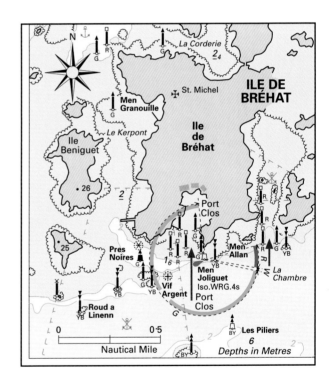

Ile de Bréhat. La Chambre looking N, Men Allan Bay- bottom left

Ashore in Ile de Bréhat

The island is worth walking over. It is virtually divided into two with a short, narrow isthmus to the N of Le Bourg. There is no traffic apart from the occasional small tractor. Bicycles can be hired in the village. There are fine views from St Michel chapel over the surroundings with varied seascapes. Le Bourg village is in the centre and has a post office and a surprising number of restaurants, créperies and some shops. There are also restaurants at Port Clos as well as a hotel. There is a small and thriving sailing club at La Chambre.

The chaplain of HMS *Charybdis*, sunk in 1943 off Les Sept Iles is buried in St Michel churchyard.

Ile de Bréhat. Port Clos at LWS looking SSW

Vif Argent

Les Pierres Noires

III. ST MALO TO LEZARDRIEUX AND PONTRIEUX

156 Lézardrieux

The main approach from the NE and Chenal de Ferlas from the E can be taken in most weathers by day or night. The river to Pontrieux, Ile de Bréhat and the Anse de Paimpol offer many miles of sheltered water for a holiday. Good facilities at Lézardrieux and Pontrieux.

Location
The town is 5M upstream from Ile Bréhat

Shelter
Good at Lézardrieux

Warning
Heavy seas in approaches in wind over tide conditions

Depth restrictions
Deep water all the way to marina

Night entry
Well lit with good leading lights

Tidal information
HW St Malo -0020
LW St Malo -0050

Mean height of tide (m)

HWS	HWN	LWN	LWS
10.5	8.0	3.7	1.3

Tidal streams in river

HW St Helier +0610 in-going flood starts
HW St Helier +0005 out-going ebb starts
Average spring rate 2½ knots

Berthing
On pontoons in marina

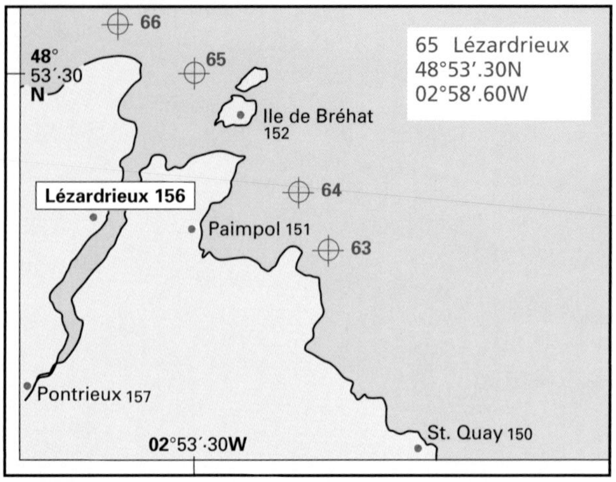

PILOTAGE
Outer Approaches (Line T)

Tidal streams

HW St Helier +0610 SE-going flood starts
HW St Helier +0005 NW-going ebb starts

From NE by day or night

The spring rates attain 3¾ knots, the bottom outside the entrance is rocky and uneven and the seas on the approaches can be unpleasant.

From ⊕65 identify the first leading line which is La Croix double white towers with red tops (Dir.Oc.W.4s) and Bodic green and white light structure on the skyline (Dir.Q.W) 225° (See photo page 109). Follow this track allowing for any cross set to leave:

Les Sirlots unlit starboard buoy to starboard.
Petit Pen Azen N cardinal beacon tower ½M to port.
Pen Azen unlit port buoy ¼M to port.
Vieille du Tréou starboard beacon tower ¼M to starboard.
Rodello starboard beacon on base of old tower ¼M to starboard.
Amer du Rosédo white pyramid ½M to port.
Gosrod port beacon tower 200m to port.
Men Guen starboard beacon tower 300m to starboard.
When about 1M from La Croix, leave Line T and head for the red roofed old Customs House building (not CG as on BA 3673) or Moguedhir starboard beacon to pick up the marks for Line E which are

The map at the top right shows:

```
          ⊕ 66
48°
53'.30        ⊕ 65
N
                    Ile de Bréhat
                    152
Lézardrieux 156           ⊕ 64
          • Paimpol 151
                          ⊕ 63

                              St. Quay 150 •
• Pontrieux 157
        02°53'.30W
```

65 Lézardrieux
48°53'.30N
02°58'.60W

Facilities
Those of a small town and marina

Weather
From Bodic on Ch 79 at 0533, 0745, 1145, 1615 and 1945

Charts
BA 3673 (10), SHOM 7127 (20)
Imray C34

Radio/Telephone
Ch 09 (Working hours)
Harbourmaster ☎ 02 96 20 14 22

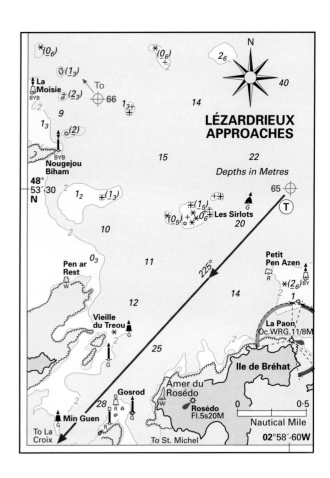

LÉZARDRIEUX APPROACHES
Depths in Metres

Lézardrieux. Leading marks for Grand Chenal. La Croix lighthouse with Bodic on skyline to right

Coatmer Aval white gable light structure (F.RG) and Coatmer Amont a similar white gable end (F.R) bearing 219°. This line (partly obscured by trees) leaves the following marks:

Moguedhier unlit starboard beacon 120m to starboard.

La Croix lighthouse 200m to port.

Vincre unlit port beacon tower 300m to port.

Vieille de Loguivy unlit W cardinal beacon tower 150m to port.

Custom House Island 500m to starboard.

Olénoyère unlit port beacon tower 100m to port.

The leading line can be left when Olénoyère is abeam and a convenient course taken up channel to leave Lostmer unlit starboard beacon tower and Perdrix starboard beacon tower Fl(2)WG.6s 100m to starboard. The white sector of the latter leads upriver in deep water. From here the prominent Roches Donan can be seen and rounded 30m to port to head for the marina pontoons.

From E by day or night

Details of Chenal de Ferlas which runs S of Ile de Bréhat in to Grande Passe de Trieux close S of Vielle de Loguivi beacon tower can be found on page 104.

Proceeding to Lézardrieux from Chenal de Ferlas, turn to port after passing Vielle de Loguivi unlit W cardinal beacon tower to pick up the Coatmer leading line 219° (*Front*, F.R.G, *Rear*, F.R) to continue upriver.

The passage through the Chenal de Ferlas by day is not difficult nor by night from the E. From the W by night the problem is that the three very narrow sectored lights will be astern.

Chenal de la Moisie

From N by day

This carries a least depth of 1.3m and is useful as a short cut from Tréguier to Lézardrieux, Ile de Bréhat or Paimpol. Its only disadvantage is seeing the line in poor light. It would be prudent to allow a least depth of drying 2.3m if there was any doubt about losing

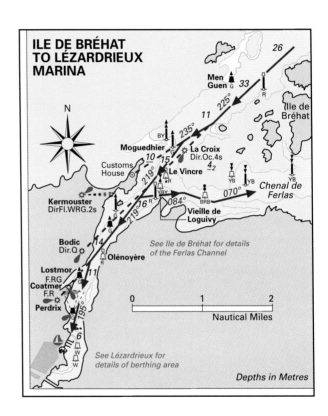

Lézardrieux. Leading marks for Chenal de la Moisie just open right. St-Michel chapel and Rosédo white beacon tower. La Vieille du Trou starboard beacon tower on right

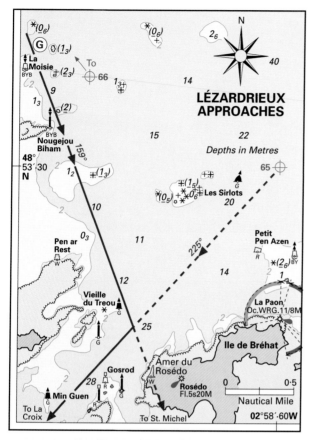

LÉZARDRIEUX APPROACHES

Depths in Metres

65   Lézardrieux 48°53'.30N 02°58'.60W
66   La Gaine NW   48°55'.50N 03°01'.50W

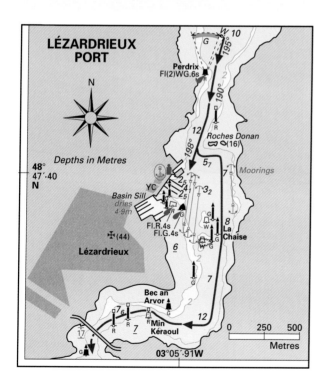

LÉZARDRIEUX PORT

Depths in Metres

sight of the line on the way out, or not being able to pick it up the leading marks at the start of the inward passage.

From the vicinity of ⊕66 align Amer du Rosédo white pyramid with St Michel's chapel on 159° checking that this passes about 150m E of La Moisie E cardinal beacon tower. Follow this line closely to leave:

La Moisie E cardinal beacon tower 150m to starboard.

Nougejou Bihan E cardinal beacon tower 50m to starboard and a shoal drying 2m close to the NE.

Pen ar Rest white beacon tower 0.4M to starboard Then leave **Vieille de Tréou** starboard beacon tower close to starboard and turn to join the La Croix/Bodic transit 225° up-river.

Entrance and Berthing at marina

The marina pontoons will be seen from abeam of Perdrix to the right of the conspicuous Roches Donan and are well lit at night. There are 70 visitor spaces, maximum 15m. There appears to be at least 2.5m at these pontoons but it is shallower at the fuel berth at the innermost end of the north arm. There are fingers on the pontoons and berthing near slack water is recommended as the stream runs through them.

The wet basin to the SW has a sill that dries 4.9m and a berth may be allocated here but entry and departure will be restricted to the top part of the tide.

Moorings

There are some visitors' moorings between Perdrix and Roches Donan but check with the harbour office before picking one up.

The main visitors' moorings for those not using the pontoons are between the marina and La Chaise; there is one at least for those over 20m. Some have pontoons on them to berth on and some are of the dumbell type. They attract a charge. Most of the area has at least 3m and the stream runs strongly through it.

Anchorage

- At the side of the main channel between Bodic and Roches Donan clear of the shellfish beds, mostly sand and mud.

- On the E side of the channel clear of moorings between Roches Donan and the first bend at Bec an Arvor.

Ashore in Lézardrieux

Facilities

Water and electricity on the pontoons; fuel at the root of the N pontoon; dinghy landing on the pontoons and at the slip; 50-ton crane; yacht club is welcoming and has a bar and café; showers and heads in block by harbour office; shops are all in the small country town ½ up the hill; there is a

Lézardrieux yacht harbours looking WNW

Pontrieux basin looking NNW

supermarché 50m beyond the far side of the square; there are a number of restaurants, bars and cafés on the road up to and in the town with a well known restaurant over the bridge. The town hall can be hired for larger functions.

Travel

The town is on the main E/W coast road between St Brieuc and Morlaix both of which have airports. The nearest railway stations are at Paimpol and Pontrieux.

History

Lézardrieux has been popular with yachtsmen, especially the English since the turn of the 19th-century and has prospered in spite of the fishing moving downriver to Loguivi. It is a popular venue for yacht rallies and the lesser offshore races. There used to be a Ponts et Chaussées depot on the E bank by Roches Donan and there is still a large mooring there which is sometimes used by small naval or service craft.

157 Pontrieux and upper reaches de Rivière de Trieux

A pleasant 3M river trip on a rising tide to an accommodating market town with a welcome and good facilities for visiting yachts inside the lock.

Location
3M upriver from Lézardrieux

Depth restrictions
Sill dries 3.5m
Height restrictions
Bridge 17m

Night entry
No lights

Tidal information
HW and LW at the lock same as St Malo

Mean height of tide (m)

HWS	HWN	LWN	LWS
10.5	8.0	3.7	1.3

Tidal streams
The spring ebb under the bridge at Lézardrieux is 3¾ knots but eases off up-river

Berthing
Alongside wall

Facilities
Those of small town

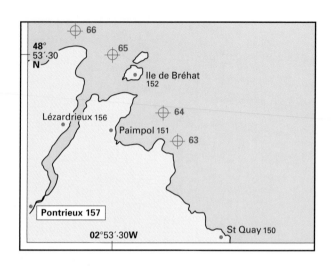

Charts
No official charts

Weather
From Bodic on Ch 79 at 0533, 0745, 1145, 1615 and 1945

Radio/Telephone
Lock Ch 12 (HW -2 to +1)
Harbourmaster ☎ 02 96 95 34 87
Lock ☎ 02 96 95 60 70

PILOTAGE

Upriver to the lock and Entrance

The suspension bridge at Lézardrieux has a clearance of 17m and above this are two beacon towers marking the sides of the channel before the valley opens out. Provided this section is taken on the first half of the flood, the channel will be visible for the first mile after which the banks close in and the channel follows the outside of the bends. A high-tension cable crosses the river just above a wreck on the E bank whose clearance is believed to be 20m+. 1½M above the bridge the river takes a sharp bend to port below Chateau Roche Jagu where there is sometimes a mooring and an anchorage to await the lock opening. Beware if staying over a tide as the banks are steep and it is possible to swing on to a drying bank as the tide falls, even at the mooring. See *Facilities* below for more details of the chateau.

An anchor light should be exhibited if staying in the river overnight as there is occasional coaster, dredger or *vedette* traffic.

Above the chateau take the right fork for the lock (the other arm is spanned by the railway). There are port and starboard buoys 200m below the lock which should be left close on the appropriate sides. Just outside the lock the river takes a sharp turn to port round a port beacon. There is a waiting buoy here. The bed of the river is rocky and uneven and if it is necessary to dry out the best place is alongside the wall by the entrance to the gates.

The sill dries 3.5m, the lock is 65m long and 11m wide; the gates will stay open if the tide level exceeds 10m. The high-tension cable over the lock has a clearance of 25m. The basin has between 2m and 4m throughout the length.

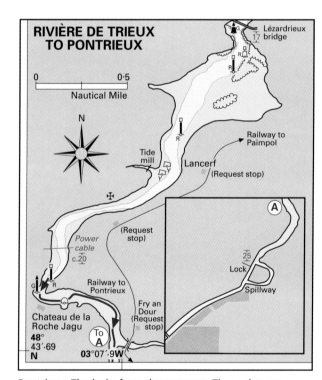

Pontrieux. The locks from downstream. The yachts are waiting to enter

Pontrieux. Château Roche Jagu showing moorings and slip

Pontrieux. The lock into Pontrieux basin looking WNW. The river dries at LW from the spillway downwards

Berthing

There are 160 berths with 40 for visitors, maximum length 25m, round the first bend beyond the aggregate works. There are also moorings in the basin. It is customary to double up at berths and moorings.

Tell the harbourmaster if there are elderly or children on board and he will try to get you alongside.

Ashore in Pontrieux

A suitable place to leave the boat or to change crews.

Facilities

Water and electricity points on the quay; showers and heads by Harbourmaster's Office; slip; 5-ton crane; chandlery; fuel from garage in town but delivery possible; shops none near the quay but plenty in town ½M up the hill; market day is Monday; restaurants: two near the quay and a selection in town; laying up either ashore or afloat, mast can be removed and guardianage arranged, security is said to be adequate.

Travel

A Michelin (diesel railcar) runs from Paimpol through Pontrieux to Guingamp and back – allowing access to the TGV to Paris etc.

Leisure

There are excursions to Château Roche Jagu which has a programme of theatrical and musical events 1 June to 31 August. It is worth a visit to see the house and gardens even without an event. There is a restaurant outside the gates.

There is a fête in town on third Sunday in July.

Pontrieux looking NE

III. ST MALO TO LEZARDRIEUX AND PONTRIEUX

IV. TRÉGUIER TO OUESSANT

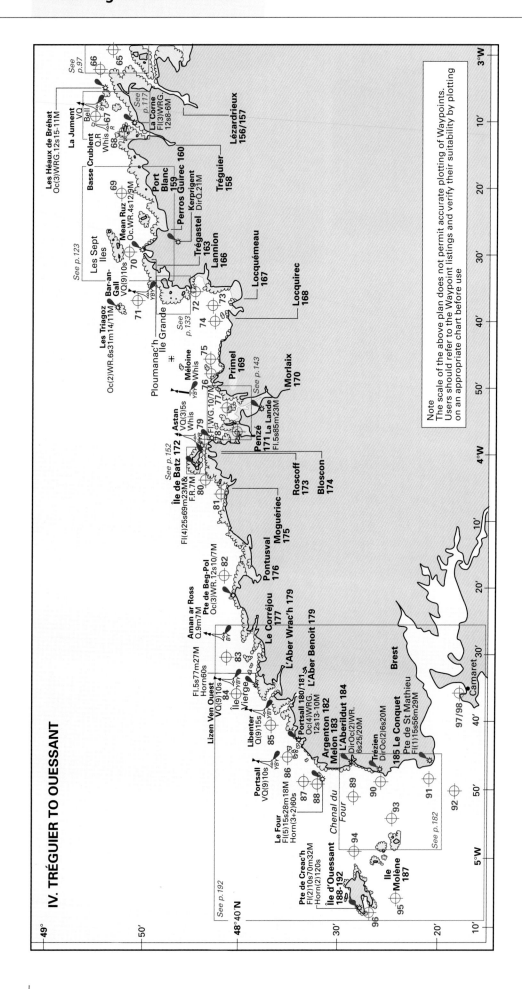

Les Héaux de Bréhat
Oc(3)WRG.12s15-11M

La Jument
VQ

Bell
Q.R
BY

66
65

See p.97

67

68

La Corne
Fl(3)WRG.
12s8-6M

See p.117

Lézardrieux
156/157

Basse Crublent
Q.R
R

69

Mean Ruz
Oc.WR.4s12/9M

Port
Blanc
159

Perros Guirec 160

Kerprigent
DirQ.21M

Tréguier
158

Les Sept
Iles

Baran-
Gall
VQ(9)10s

70

Trégastel
163

Lannion
166

Locquémeau
167

See p.123

Les Triagoz
Oc(2)WR.6s31m14/11M

71

Île Grande

72

73

74

Locquirec
168

Ploumanac'h

See p.133

Méloine
Whis

75

76

Primel
169

Morlaix
170

See p.143

Astan
VQ(3)5s
Whis

77

78

79

Fl.WG.10/7M

La Lande
Fl.5s85m23M

Penzé
171

See p.152

Île de Batz 172
Fl(4)25s69m23M&
F.R.7M

80

81

Roscoff
173

Bloscon
174

Moguériec
175

Pontusval
176

Aman ar Ross
Q.9m7M

Pte de Beg-Pol
Oc(3)WR.12s10/7M

82

Le Corréjou
177

L'Aber Wrac'h 179

L'Aber Benoît 179

Fl.5s77m27M
Horn60s

83

Lizen Ven Ouest
VQ(9)15s

84

Libenter
Q(9)15s

85

Île
Vierge

Portsall 180/181
Oc(4)WRG.
12s13-10M

Argenton 182
Melon 183

L'Aberildut 184
DirOc(2)WR.
6s25/20M

Trézien
DirOc(2)6s20M

185 Le Conquet

Pte de St Mathieu
Fl(1)15s56m29M

Brest

97/98

Carnaret

Portsall
VQ(9)10s

86

Le Four
Fl(5)15s28m18M
Horn(3+2)60s

87

88

Chenal du
Four

89

90

91

92

See p.182

94

Pte de Creac'h
Fl(2)10s70m32M
Horn(2)120s

Île d'Ouessant
188–192

See p.192

95

96

Île
Molène
187

93

See p.192

48° 40 N

49°

50'

30'

20'

10'

See p.97
See p.117
See p.123
See p.133
See p.143
See p.152
See p.182
See p.192

Note
The scale of the above plan does not permit accurate plotting of Waypoints.
Users should refer to the Waypoint listings and verify their suitability by plotting
on an appropriate chart before use

3°W
10'
20'
30'
40'
50'
4°W
10'
20'
30'
40'
5°W

IV. Tréguier to Ile d'Ouessant

⊕65	Lézardrieux	48°53'.30N 02°58'.60W
⊕66	La Gaine NW	48°55'.50N 03°01'.50W
⊕67	Jument	48°55'.48N 03°07'.20W
⊕68	Tréguier	48°54'.34N 03°11'.61W
⊕69	Port Blanc P. Guirec	48°52'.20N 03°20'.01W
⊕70	Ploumanac'h Sept I.	48°51'.05N 03°29'.20W
⊕71	Triagoz	48°49'.90N 03°38'.75W
⊕72	Trébeurden	48°46'.06N 03°37'.31W
⊕73	Lannion	48°44'.35N 03°37'.60W
⊕74	Locquirec	48°42'.75N 03°37'.80W
⊕75	Les Chaises	48°44'.57N 03°46'.72W
⊕76	Primel	48°43'.50N 03°49'.92W
⊕77	Morlaix	48°43'.35N 03°53'.50W
⊕78	Duons	48°43'.25N 03°55'.40W
⊕79	Roscoff. Bloscon	48°43'.80N 03°57'.20W
⊕80	Ile de Batz W	48°44'.45N 04°03'.00W
⊕81	Moguériec	48°43'.50N 04°05'.45W
⊕82	Pontusval	48°41'.60N 04°19'.20W
⊕83	Le Corréjou	48°41'.40N 04°29'.21W
⊕84	Vierge	48°40'.05N 04°34'.10W
⊕85	Libenter (for L'Aberwrac'h and L'Aber Benoit)	48°37'.50N 04°38'.85W
⊕86	Portsall NE	48°36'.90N 04°39'.40W
⊕87	Portsall W	48°34'.30N 04°47'.25W
⊕88	Le Four (Argenton)	48°30'.90N 04°49'.10W
⊕89	L'Aberildut	48°27'.90N 04°49'.05W
⊕90	Chenal du Four N	48°25'.69N 04°49'.62W
⊕91	Le Conquet	48°21'.30N 04°47'.75W
⊕92	Chenal du Four S	48°19'.25N 04°47'.75W
⊕93	Molène	48°25'.80N 04°56'.50W
⊕94	Fromveur NE	48°27'.50N 05°00'.00W
⊕95	Fromveur S	48°24'.08N 05°07'.48W
⊕96	Ouessant (Lampaul)	48°26'.01N 05°09'.20W
⊕97	Camaret	48°17'.44N 04°36'.08W

La Côte de Granit Rose from Port Blanc to Trébeurden deserves its name not only for the colour of the rocks but the strange shapes that wind and weather have fashioned them into. From Lannion westwards the more sombre grey granite is evident and the coast becomes rockier and more rugged until the westernmost outlier is reached at Ile d'Ouessant. In between there is no major port apart from the ferry terminal at Roscoff/Bloscon but a number of deep harbours in estuaries such as Morlaix, Penzé and the Abers. A number of coastal paths have been opened in the area which are well marked and used. The tidal streams ease off but are still significant especially round Ouessant where the Atlantic swell can combine to create unpleasant seas. Industry has not made its mark on this part of Brittany; agriculture, fishing and accommodating the holiday trade are the chief pursuits in an unspoilt rural region.

Ile Vierge looking SW across the approach to L'Aber Wrac'h
(page 163)

DISTANCE TABLE

	Guernsey	Tréguier	Port Blanc	Perros Guirec	Ploumanac'h	Les Sept Isles	Trégastel St-A	Trébeurden	Lannion	Primel	Morlaix	Penzé River	Roscoff	Ile de Batz	Moguériec	Pontusval	Le Correjou	L'Aber Wrac'h	L'Aber Benôit	Portsall	Argenton	L'Aber-Ildut	Le Conquet	Ile de Molène	I d'Ouessant
Guernsey		51	49	53	54	53	58	62	66	71	82	78	75	77	81	90	100	105	108	109	113	116	124	124	129
Tréguier	51		15	19	21	21	24	28	32	37	48	44	41	44	49	61	72	79	80	81	85	88	96	96	101
Port Blanc	49	15		7	8	8	11	15	19	24	35	31	28	31	36	48	59	64	67	68	72	75	83	83	88
Perros Guirec	53	19	7		6	6	9	13	17	22	33	29	26	29	34	46	57	62	65	66	70	73	81	81	86
Ploumanac'h	54	21	8	6		3	4	8	12	17	28	24	21	24	29	41	52	57	60	61	65	68	76	76	81
Les Sept Isles	53	21	8	6	3		5	9	13	18	29	25	22	25	30	42	53	58	61	62	66	69	77	77	81
Trégastel St-A	58	24	11	9	4	5		4	12	19	24	21	18	20	25	37	48	53	56	57	61	64	72	72	77
Trébeurden	62	28	15	13	8	9	4		4	14	23	20	17	19	24	36	47	52	55	56	60	63	71	71	76
Lannion	66	32	19	17	12	13	12	4		12	23	20	17	19	24	36	47	52	55	56	60	63	71	71	76
Primel	71	37	24	22	17	18	19	14	12		11	8	6	8	13	25	36	41	44	45	49	52	60	60	65
Morlaix	82	48	35	33	28	29	24	23	23	11		11	11	13	18	30	41	46	49	50	54	57	65	65	70
Penzé River	78	44	31	29	24	25	21	20	20	8	11		6	8	13	25	36	41	44	45	49	52	60	60	65
Roscoff	75	41	28	26	21	22	18	17	17	6	11	6		2	7	19	30	35	38	39	43	46	54	54	59
Ile de Batz	77	44	31	29	24	25	20	19	19	8	13	8	2		5	17	28	33	36	37	41	44	52	52	57
Moguériec	81	49	36	34	29	30	25	24	24	13	18	13	7	5		12	23	28	31	32	36	39	47	47	52
Pontusval	90	61	48	46	41	42	37	36	36	25	30	25	19	17	12		11	16	19	20	24	27	35	35	40
Le Correjou	100	72	59	57	52	53	48	47	47	36	41	37	30	28	23	11		5	8	9	13	16	24	24	29
L'Aber Wrac'h	105	77	64	62	57	58	53	52	52	41	46	42	35	32	28	16	5		3	4	8	11	19	19	24
L'Aber Benôit	108	80	67	65	60	61	56	55	55	44	49	45	38	35	31	19	8	3		1	5	8	16	16	21
Portsall	109	81	68	66	61	62	57	56	56	45	50	46	39	36	32	20	9	4	1		4	7	15	15	20
Argenton	113	85	72	70	65	66	61	60	60	49	54	50	43	40	36	24	13	8	5	4		3	11	11	16
L'Aber-Ildut	116	88	75	73	68	69	64	63	63	52	57	53	46	43	39	27	16	11	8	7	3		8	8	13
Le Conquet	124	96	83	81	76	77	72	71	71	60	65	61	54	51	47	35	24	19	16	15	11	8		7	17
Ile de Molène	124	96	83	81	76	77	72	71	71	60	65	61	54	51	47	35	24	19	16	15	11	8	7		10
I d'Ouessant	129	101	88	86	81	82	77	76	76	65	70	66	59	56	52	40	29	24	21	20	16	13	17	10	

Distances are given over the shortest navigable route and are measured to and from inner harbour or anchorage

158 Tréguier and Rivière de Tréguier

There is 9M of attractive river and estuary from the outer approaches to Tréguier town with a small marina and the usual facilities; entry is possible in most weathers by day or night.

Location
18M W of Lézardrieux (by sea)
15M E of Port Blanc (by sea)

Shelter
Good inside

Depth restrictions
Least depth 2m

Night entry
Only one lit ldg line; lit buoys

Tidal information
HW St Malo -0020
LW St Malo -0050

Mean height of tide (m)

HWS	HWN	LWN	LWS
9.9	7.7	3.6	1.3

Tidal streams
The streams in the river turn at about HW and LW with the ebb at up to 2½ knots.

Berthing
At fingers, waiting pontoon 1.8m- see plan on page 121; only a few berths for over 10m.

Facilities
Adequate; good shops

Charts
BA 3672 (25/15), 3670 (50)
SHOM 7126 (20)
Imray C34 (Plan)

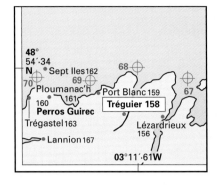

Weather
From Bodic on Ch 79 at 0533, 0745, 1145, 1615 and 1945

Radio
Ch 09 (working hours)
Harbourmaster ☎ 02 96 92 42 37
YC ☎ 02 96 92 42 08 *Mobile* 00 33 6 72 70

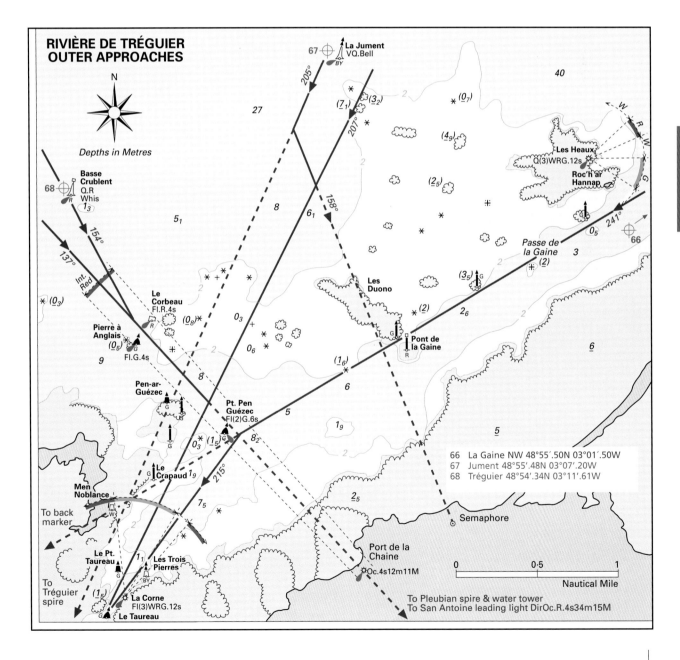

PILOTAGE

Approaches

There are three approaches to the estuary:

Grande Passe in all conditions by day or night in visibility of 2M or more. Least depth to La Corne 1.1m.

Passe de la Gaine which is narrow and dependent on seeing the marks 5M or more; by day only. Least depth to La Corne drying 2m.

Passe du Nord Est is not so narrow as Passe de la Gaine but 10M visibility is needed to see the rear leading marks; by day only. Least depth 0.5m.

Grande Passe (Line A)

The leading marks for this channel are the light structures of Port de la Chaine (*Front*, Oc.4.11M) and St Antoine (*Rear*, Dir.Oc.R.4s.15M) bearing 137°. Port de la Chaine is a white house with a red lantern near the shore, and St Antoine is a white house with a small red lantern elevation 34m. Both are difficult to identify by day and another line may be used in the early stages. This is Pleubian water tower (not on BA 3672) and Pleubian spire on 154° which passes close to Basse Crublent buoy and ⊕68 (see photograph below). This transit leads between Le Corbeau unlit port buoy and Pierre à Anglais unlit starboard buoy from where the Port de la Chaine/St Antoine transit of 137° should be identifiable.

At night the strong leading lights of Port de la Chaine/St Antoine, the latter of which is intensified from 134° to 140°, will lead in from well to seaward of Basse Crublent buoy on Line A.

Continue on 137° and do not stray to the E to keep clear of Le Corbeau shoal. This leaves Pen ar Guézec beacon tower and beacon 400m to starboard and at night will be in the green sector of La Corne. ** Round the unlit Petit Pen ar Guézec starboard buoy when La Corne bears 215° and changes to the white sector. Continue down this white sector; by day keep the E edge of La Corne white lighthouse with red base in line with Skeiviec white beacon tower (see photograph below) leaving the following marks:

Two starboard beacons 600m to starboard.

Men Noblance black and white beacon tower ½M to starboard. (This is the front mark for Passe de la Gaine).

Les Trois Pierres N cardinal beacon tower 100m to port.

Note that there is a 1.1m patch just to the NW.

Le Petit Taureau starboard beacon tower 200m to starboard.

La Corne lighthouse 100m to port; round the lighthouse in its green sector and enter the narrow SW white sector keeping to its SE side on about 235° to pass the Banc de Taureau unlit starboard buoy close to starboard.

From here the SE edge of the white sector on 235° will lead to Guarivinon port buoy (Fl.R) which will be visible by day, and so up the buoyed and lit channel. See page 120 for La Corne inwards.

Tidal streams

Outside the estuary to the N of Basse Crublent and La Jument buoys the streams start as follows:
HW Brest -0350 E–going
HW Brest +0220 W–going
Maximum spring rate is 3¼ knots
In Passe de la Gaine S of Les Heaux the streams start as follows:
HW Brest -0450 ENE–going
HW Brest +0130 WSW–going
Maximum spring rate 2½ knots

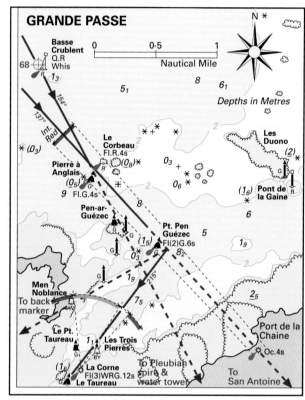

Tréguier. Outer approach to Grande Passe. From Le Crublent buoy, left foreground keep Pleubian spire (front) in transit with water tower (rear) on 154°

Tréguier. La Corne light tower with Skeiviec white beacon open left. Banc de Taureau buoy to left of yacht on far right

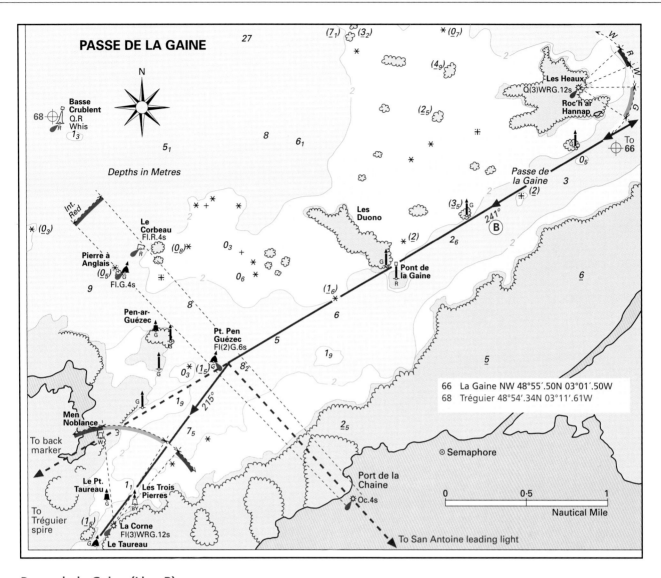

Passe de la Gaine (Line B)

(See photo on page 120).

Use only in daylight and good visibility; the rear mark is 6M from the E entrance and the line is difficult to see especially in the afternoon sun. The least depth is 0.3m but a 30m diversion from the line will find drying 2m in places and this should be allowed for.

Approach Les Heaux from ⊕66 and identify Roc'h ar Harrap, a rock steep-sided on the SE side which lies ¼M SSE of the lighthouse and never covers. With this bearing N and the first starboard beacon bearing 290° the leading marks should be in line. They are Men Noblance, a white beacon tower with a black stripe across its middle in line with a white wall beacon with a vertical black stripe just below the skyline bearing 241°. The latter is some 500m to the W of the prominent Plougrescant church spire. (See photograph on page 120).

Follow this line leaving the first starboard hand beacon 200m to starboard (*Note* the 0.5m patch just to the SE), the second beacon 150m to starboard and pass in the middle between the two beacons at Pont de la Gaine; leave the line slightly to the N at this point to hit the middle but return to the line when through the Pont to avoid a drying 1.5m rock on the NW side shortly after. Continue on the line up to Petit Pen ar Guézec starboard hand buoy and then proceed down the next leading line of 215° as from ** in Grande Passe above.

The passage from W to E presents fewer problems as the leading marks can be identified before becoming committed and alternative exits via Grande Passe or Passe du Nord Est are immediately available options.

The tidal streams run at up to 2½ knots and a cross-set must be watched for. The extensive rocks and shoals of Les Heaux and Les Duono are an efficient barrier at most states of the tide to any swell in the passage.

Plougrescant spire

Rear mark just open left of Men Noblance

Tréguier. Leading marks for Passe de la Gaine (just open left) on a clear day. Plougrescant spire far left

Passe du Nord Est (Line C)

By day only, and if coming from the E or NE, afternoon sun may prevent the Passe de la Gaine leading marks being identified. Visibility needs to be 10M to see the rear mark of Tréguier church spire. Least depth 0.5m.

From ⊕67 or La Jument des Heaux N cardinal buoy, position Tréguier church spire (the right hand of the two spires visible between the river banks) between the beacon tower and beacon on Penn ar Guézec bearing 205°. The S beacon is a spindly affair and if not visible keep the church spire just open left of the NW beacon tower. Follow this line for about 0.75M.

When the summit of the middle rock in Le Duono group is in line with the old semaphore building bearing 158°, alter to follow this line for about 0.3M until Skeiviec white beacon tower comes in to line with the church spire bearing 207° (Line C). This line can then be followed until La Corne is reached but it passes very close to a drying 1.5m rock. If necessary to avoid this, turn to port on to the Grande Passe leading line and then to 215° round the starboard Petit Pen ar Guézec buoy to follow the tracks as from ** in Grande Passe above.

From La Corne inwards

See plan opposite. A track of 240° from Banc de Taureau starboard unlit buoy and the SE edge of the white sector of La Corne light (Fl(3)WRG.12s) will carry to Guarivinou port hand buoy (Fl.R). From here course may be altered to 195° up the channel. As Roche Jaune is approached the channel is further defined by the number of moorings on either side of it. See over for the final approach to the town.

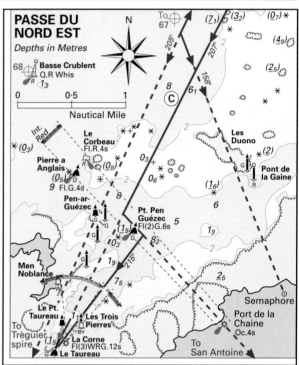

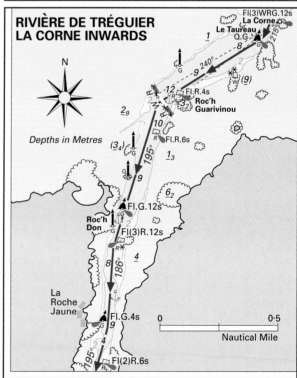

Anchorages

It is possible to anchor in good holding almost anywhere in the channel but room must be left for the occasional coaster, fishing boats and the fish farm craft. A riding light is advisable. Consider:

- Near the Guarivinou buoy in 5m sandy mud. Avoid the rock close to the S of the buoy.
- Towards the W of the channel between the starboard Fl.G buoy and Roc'h Don beacon in 5m, mud.
- Clear of the moorings and fish farms off Roche Jaune village.
- Below the chateau opposite Banc de Ven below the town in 5m, mud but the banks are steep to and the channel narrow.

Anchorage is prohibited between the chateau and the bridge above the marina.

Moorings

There is one mooring suitable for the larger yacht off the town quay below the marina and more are planned.

Berthing

There are 5 pontoons with 45 berths kept for visitors. Maximum length 12m but the fingers are only 7m long. The outer berths are dredged to 2m but this shallows towards the wall. There is one berth only for a longer boat at the end of the first pontoon but doubling up here especially at springs is not encouraged.

The stream runs strongly through the pontoons and it is advisable to arrive at or near slack water to berth and the inner berths should not be attempted outside these times. If an arrival occurs outside slack water times, always berth head to stream and adjust if necessary before departure.

It might be possible to take the ground alongside the commercial quay downstream of the pontoons.

Dinghy landing

The only dinghy landings at all stages of the tide are at the root of the pontoons or at the slip just downstream of them.

Ashore in Tréguier

Facilities

Water on the pontoons, electricity in places; diesel from the fuel berth, petrol in cans from garage opposite; showers and heads in the YC; pump-out, wi-fi in 2008, chandlers at each end of the quay; YC by pontoons is welcoming; there is a wide variety of shops and *supermarchés* up in the town, a 15 minute walk; there are few hotels and restaurants near the quay and more in the town.

Travel

Buses to Paimpol via Lézardrieux, and to Pontrieux and Lannion railways stations. Small airfield at Lannion.

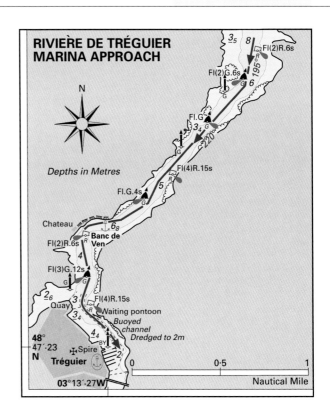

History and Leisure

This pleasant, quiet old town traces its history back to the monastery of Trécon, founded by St Tugdal of the 6th-century. There are many 17th-century buildings in the town. The fine church, formerly a cathedral, was founded in the 9th-century but mostly rebuilt in the 14th; there is an 11th-century tower on its N side. The strange granite spire, a sort of honeycomb of irregular openings, was finished in 1787. St Ives, the friend of the poor, lived in Tréguier in the 13th-century.

A procession from Tréguier church to his birthplace at the nearby village of Minihy takes place each year on 19 May known as 'the Pardon of the poor'.

Tréguier yacht berths

159 Port Blanc

A small natural harbour with shelter at anchor except from the N; a few facilities in a small seaside village.

Location
7M W of Tréguier entrance, 7M E of Perros Guirec

Shelter
Little from the N

Depth restrictions
7m to drying for anchoring

Night entry
Directional leading light

Tidal information
HW St Malo -0030
LW St Malo -0050

Mean height of tide (m)

HWS	HWN	LWN	LWS
9.6	7.5	3.6	1.3

Tidal streams
The streams to seaward start at the following times:
HW Brest -0450 E-going
HW Brest +0120 W-going
Maximum spring rate 2½ knots

Berthing
At anchor or mooring

Facilities
Minimal

Charts
BA 3670 (50), 3672 (20)
SHOM 7126 (20)
Imray C34 (Plan)

Weather
From Bodic on Ch 79 at 0533, 0745, 1145, 1615 and 1945

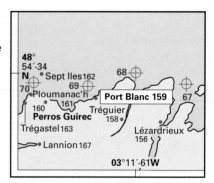

Radio/Telephone
The harbourmaster might be raised on Ch 09
☎ 02 96 92 64 96

PILOTAGE

Approaches

From ⊕69 the leading line of 150° is not easy to pick out by day and will depend on how recently the trees have been cut back and the tower painted. Le Voleur (White tower, square window, Fl.WRG.4s 14/11M) has a strong light and will be easily visible by night.

By day the following features will help identify Le Voleur:

Ile Chateau Neuf with a white pyramid to the W of the line
Note In 2006 this was no longer 'conspicuous' but was grey, dirty and partially obscured by trees.

A white house with a grey roof just to the E of Le Voleur.

A white pyramid on the W side of Ile St Gildas.

The 30m line clears all dangers outside comfortably until the leading line can be identified.

Entrance

Le Voleur on 150° or the centre of the white sector at night leads into the anchorage passing:
Basse Gauzier unlit port buoy 0.7M to starboard.
Le Four white painted rock 0.5M to starboard.
Ile Chateau Neuf and white pyramid 300m to starboard.
Ile St Gildas and its white beacon 300m to port.
Roc'h Ruz port beacon 100m to port.
Ron Glas starboard beacon 150m to starboard.

Anchorages

The W part of the inner anchorage is occupied by a number of white mooring buoys to the E of Ron Glas starboard beacon, one of which may be vacant. If not, there is room to anchor clear of them in 1 to 3m sand, but do not anchor in the channel as you will be asked to move.

Ashore in Port Blanc

There is a slip and jetty drying 1.3m alongside just to the E of Le Voleur. This could be used to dry out

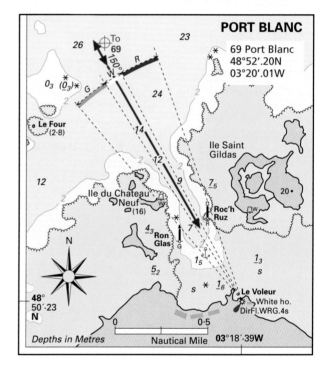

alongside. The slip can be used to land or the beach anywhere between Le Voleur and the Sailing School. There is another slip to the W of the Sailing School which is a long building 300m W of Le Voleur where the Harbourmaster may also be found.

Facilities

Water from taps at both slips; bar and *boulangerie* a short distance from W slip; fuel from garage at Penvénan 3km S from E slip where the only shops are; taxi from the café; public WCs and showers at the Sailing School; Grand Hotel has a restaurant with post box in its side wall.

History

The 16th-century chapel of Notre Dame de Port Blanc stands above the village, and is the scene of a Pardon held on 8 September attended mainly by seafarers and fishermen.

Port Blanc *Peter Carnegie*

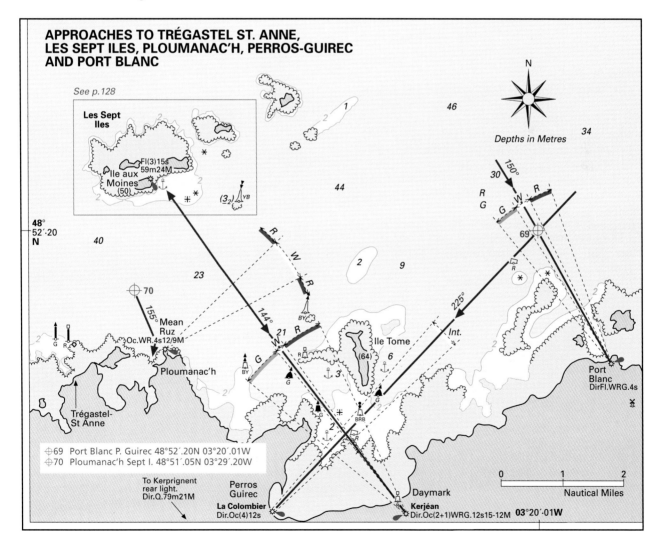

APPROACHES TO TRÉGASTEL ST. ANNE, LES SEPT ILES, PLOUMANAC'H, PERROS-GUIREC AND PORT BLANC

See p.128

Les Sept Iles

Fl(3)15s 59m24M

Ile aux Moines (50)

N

Depths in Metres

150°

30

R G

G W R

69

R

46

34

44

2 9

(3₂) YB

⊕70

155°

144°

Mean Ruz
Oc.WR.4s12/9M

Ploumanac'h

48°
52'·20
N

40

23

21 R

W

R

W R

BY

G

BY

R

Ile Tome
(64)

6

225°

Int.

Port Blanc
DirFl.WRG.4s

Trégastel-
St Anne

3

G

G

BRB

G

R

2

⊕69 Port Blanc P. Guirec 48°52'.20N 03°20'.01W
⊕70 Ploumanac'h Sept I. 48°51'.05N 03°29'.20W

To Kerprignent
rear light.
Dir.Q.79m21M

Perros
Guirec
La Colombier
Dir.Oc(4)12s

Daymark
Kerjéan
Dir.Oc(2+1)WRG.12s15-12M **03°20'·01W**

0   1   2

Nautical Miles

IV. TREGUIER TO ILE D'OUESSANT

160 Perros Guirec

A substantial marina at the head of a drying bay with all weather access, backed by a holiday town of some size with most facilities; sill dries 3.5m.

Location
4M W of Port Blanc, 3½M E of Ploumanac'h

Shelter
Total inside; some at anchor outside

Warning

Marina gate only 6m wide.

Depth restrictions
Much of the bay dries

Night entry
Lit ldg or directional lines; entry lit

Tidal information
HW St Malo -0040
LW St Malo -0110

Mean height of tide (m)

HWS	HWN	LWN	LWS
9.3	7.3	3.8	1.2

Tidal streams
The streams in Chenal des Sept Iles start at the following times:
HW Brest -0435 SE going
HW Brest +0130 NW going

Berthing
On fingers on pontoons

Facilities
Usual for small town and marina

Charts
BA 3670 (50), 3672 (20)
SHOM 7126 (20)

Weather
From Bodic on Ch 79 at 0533, 0745, 1145, 1615 and 1945

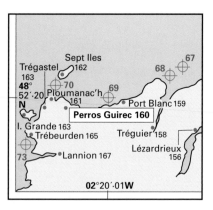

Radio/Telephone
Ch 09, 16 (working hours)
Harbourmaster ☎ 02 96 23 37 82
Marina ☎ 02 96 49 80 50

PILOTAGE

Approaches

The buoys and beacons in the outer reaches of both approaches are sufficient to navigate if the leading marks cannot be identified. The least depth in the final 1M to the gate is drying 3m.

Passe de l'Est (Line D)

From ⊕69 identify the leading line Le Colombier (white house with name on it (Dir.Oc(4)12s28m15M, *Front*) and Kerpigent (white tower on skyline (Dir.Q.79m**21M** Intense 221°-228°), *Rear*) on 225°. Make good this track to leave:
Basse Guazer port buoy 200m to port.
Roc'h Morville (dries 1.5m) the seaward end of an unmarked shoal 300m to port. (See plan on previous page).
Pierre à Rouzic starboard buoy 50m to starboard.
La Durante port beacon 400m to port.
Pierre du Chenal isolated danger beacon tower 150m to starboard.
Cribineyer port buoy 100m to port.
The line now passes over a 0.4m patch and if avoidance is needed, alter to 270° before reaching Cribineyer and regain the 225° line when Roc'h Hu du Perros port beacon tower bears 180°, or well in to the green sector of Kerjean light Dir.Oc(2+1)WRG.12s.
Continue along the line if the tide serves to leave:
Roc'h Hu du Perros port beacon tower 250m to port.
Lost ar C'hraou starboard beacon 50m to starboard. The depths now shallow to drying 3m and the head of Jetée du Linkin (Fl(2)G.5s) should be rounded close to starboard. The deeper water from here to the lock gate is close to the W side of the Jetée.

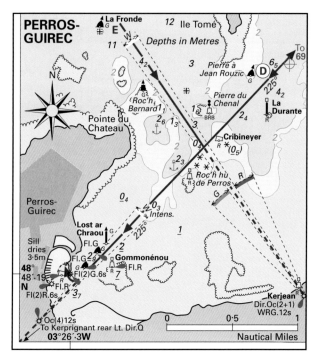

69 Port Blanc 48°52'.20N 03°20'.01W

Passe de l'Ouest (Line E)

Navigate to a position about ½M SW of Toull Carr W cardinal buoy and identify the leading line (White tower on house near shore *Front*; Kerjean, white tower with grey roof on skyline (Dir.Oc(2+1)WRG.12s78m12M), *Rear*) bearing 144°. White sector is 1.6° wide, red to NE, green to SW. Least depth on this line is 1m. Leave the following on the sides indicated:
Bilzic port beacon tower 200m to port.
La Fronde starboard buoy 250m to starboard.
Roc'h Bernard starboard beacon tower 250m to starboard.

Perros Gate   *Peter Taylor*

Pierre du Chenal isolated danger beacon tower 400m to port. As soon as Pierre du Chenal is abeam alter to 190° or more to pick up the Passe del'Est leading line 225° and avoid the 0.4m patch. Continue as for Passe de l'Est.

Entrance and Berthing

The marina is enclosed by a wall that dries 7m and is marked by a few red and white poles. The narrow (6m) entrance is at the NE end of the wall and dries 3.5m. The gate is open when the level reaches 7m which is approximately HW ±1½ hours at springs but this reduces to ±30 minutes towards neaps. At slack neaps it will not open and may be closed for a few days; beware not to get caught inside. 2.5m is maintained through most of the basin.

There are 70 berths for visitors with most on the N pontoon.

The W side of Jetée Linkin outside the gate dries and is used by fishing boats and coasters.

Moorings

There are 10 white visitors' buoys in a minimum of 3m just to the E of Pointe du Château but they can be uncomfortable around HW. There are three waiting buoys outside the harbour entrance, drying about 3m.

Anchorages

There is generally good holding throughout the Anse de Perros with shelter from the SE through S to NW.

- With Roc'h Hu de Perros tower bearing 130°, 250m. Least depth 2.4m, sand.
- With Roc'h Hu de Perros tower bearing 120° and with Bilzic port beacon tower just open W of Roc'h Bernard tower in a least depth of 0.6m.
- At neaps anywhere to the SW of these anchorages as depth allows.
- In westerly weather on the SE side of Ile Tomé about 200m offshore in 3.5m, sand and shells. The island is precipitous and uninhabited.
- In easterly weather on the W side of Ile Tomé well S of Bilzic and its offlyers in about 3m.

Ashore in Perros Guirec

Facilities

Water and electricity on the pontoons; fuel from the fuel berth on the N shore; showers and heads included in the berthing price, entry code needed from office; launderette within 50m of office; 40 tonne mobile crane; slip; chandlers nearby; shops, restaurants and cafés: basic needs down by the marina but a full range including a *supermarché* up the hill in the attractive town (15 minute walk).

Travel

Buses to Lannion or Pontrieux railway stations which join with the national network at St Brieuc and Morlaix. Small airfield at Lannion.

Leisure

The Tourist Office produce an excellent brochure in English.

There is an interesting 12th-century church and nice coastal and cliff walks.

In a park, close uphill from the town centre towards Pointe du Château is a small memorial to the 500 lost in H.M. Ships *Charybdis* and *Limbourne* to the N of Les Sept Iles in 1943. Many of the bodies are buried where they came ashore between here and the Cotentin peninsula.

161 Ploumanac'h

The epitome of La Côte de Granit Rose in a beautiful but shallow landlocked bay. Small but crowded marina, sill depth drying 2.55m. Few berths for deep draught yachts.

Location
3½M W of Perros Guirec, 2½M S of Les Sept Iles

Shelter
Good inside

Depth restrictions
Harbour dries outside entrance channel and anchoring prohibited

Night entry
Unlit

Tidal information
HW St Malo -0035
LW St Malo -0110

Mean height of tide (m)

HWS	HWN	LWN	LWS
9.3	7.3	2.5	1.3

Tidal streams
Tidal streams in Chenal des Sept Iles start at the following times:
HW Brest -0435 SE-going
HW Brest +0130 NW-going
Up to 4 knots spring rate in centre

Berthing
Dumbell moorings in marina

Facilities
Those of small village

Charts
BA 3670 (50)
SHOM 7125 (20)

Weather
From Bodic on Ch 79 at 0533, 0745, 1145, 1615 and 1945

Radio
None
Harbourmaster ☎ 02 96 91 44 31

Lifeboat
A lifeboat is stationed just to the W of Mean Ruz

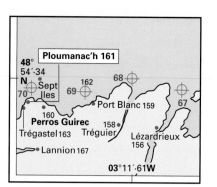

PILOTAGE

Approaches and Entrance

From ⊕70 make good a track to place Mean Ruz lighthouse bearing 110°, ½M and continue on this track until the first port beacon No.2 bears 215°. Turn onto this bearing into the entrance with the conspicuous Château Costaérès on the starboard bow. SHOM chart 7125 is the only one of sufficiently large scale for use and because there is no leading line a least depth of drying 2.1m should be allowed for safety although the channel carries 2.5m to beyond No.2 beacon. From here the channel shallows to drying 1.9m outside the sill.

There are 11 numbered beacons marking the channel, Nos8 and 12 having tide gauges showing depths over the sill. The gauge on No.12 covers near HW (there is no No.11) when there will be at least 2m over the sill. There are two white waiting buoys between Nos.8 and 8b beacons drying about 1.7m but they are frequently occupied. The sill is between Nos7 and 12 beacons and dries 2.55m.

If intending to enter the basin, an entry should be timed so there is enough water over the sill to pass straight in. Waiting anchorages outside may be found at Trégastel-St Anne (Page 130), Les Sept Iles (Page 129) or off Perros Guirec (Page 125).

Berthing

There are several rows of dumbbell moorings inside the basin. There is up to 2m on the middle outer ones but fishing boats tend to occupy them. The water shallows progressively towards the SE corner. There are ostensibly 20 places for visitors up to 12m. In 2006 there was a minimum depth of 1.8m but the bottom is subject to change.

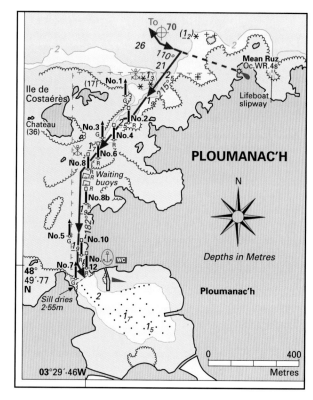

⊕70 Ploumanac'h Sept Iles 48°51'.05N 03°29'.20W

Anchorages

Anchoring is prohibited as shown on the plan and SHOM 7125. For those able to dry out anchorages may be found on generally firm sand either inside the basin or to the W of the prohibited area.

Ploumanac'h entrance bearing 215° with boat ahead in channel. Château Costaérès far right

Ploumanac'h   *Peter Carnegie*

Ashore in Ploumanac'h

The colour and beautiful shapes of the rocks in the landlocked bay has made it popular and led to the anchoring and other prohibitions. Nevertheless well worth a visit.

Facilities

Water and electricity at head of both slips; fuel nearest garage a good kilometre to the SW; there are a few hotels, bars and restaurants around the harbour and a few shops scattered through the village; the main slip by the office has been extended to LW.

Travel

Buses to Perros Guirec, and to Lannion railway station. There is a small airfield at Lannion.

Leisure

Pleasant cliff and coastal walks especially around LW. See Perros-Guirec English brochure for details.

The Satellite Telecom Centre 3M away with a planetarium and hourly shows is worth a visit on a rainy day. ☎ 02 96 91 83 78

Ploumanac'h Harbour sill No12 depth mark   *Robin Rundle*

162 Les Sept Iles

A group of uninhabited islands except for the lighthouse keepers. Landing allowed only on Ile aux Moines, all the rest is nature reserve. Fine weather anchorages on S side of group.

Location
2½ M N of Ploumanac'h

Shelter
From W through N to NE

Warning
Tidal streams run at up to 4 knots in Chenal des Sept Iles and can be high and steep with wind over tide

Depth restrictions
Adequate to anchor

Night entry
Possible to anchorage

Tidal information
HW St Malo -0040
LW St Malo -0110

Mean height of tide (m)

HWS	HWN	LWN	LWS
9.3	7.3	2.5	1.3

Tidal streams
Streams start in the Chenal des Sept Iles at the following times:
HW Brest -0322 ENE-going
HW Brest +0250 WSW-going

Charts
BA 3670 (50)
SHOM 7125 (20)

Weather
From Bodic on Ch 79 at 0533, 0745, 1145, 1615 and 1945.

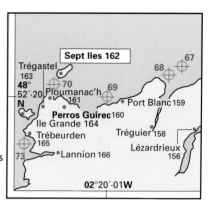

Radio/Telephone
None

PILOTAGE

Approaches

From E

Pass close S of Les Dervinis unlit S cardinal buoy and hold a track of 285° on Ile aux Moines lighthouse Fl(3)15s passing between two shoal patches as on the Plan. When the W end of Ile Bono bears 345° make good this into the anchorage.

From S

Pick up Line D 225° (See plans pages 123 and 124) provided the Kerjean marks can be seen or the white sector of the directional light Oc(2+1)WRG.12s can be identified. The white sector is 1.6° wide and leads in to the anchorage (red to NE, green to SW) but passes close W of the drying 0.1m rock.

From W

Keeping outside the 30m line, pass 500m S of the western outliers and Ile aux Moines until the W end of Ile Bono bears 345° when hold this track in to the anchorage.

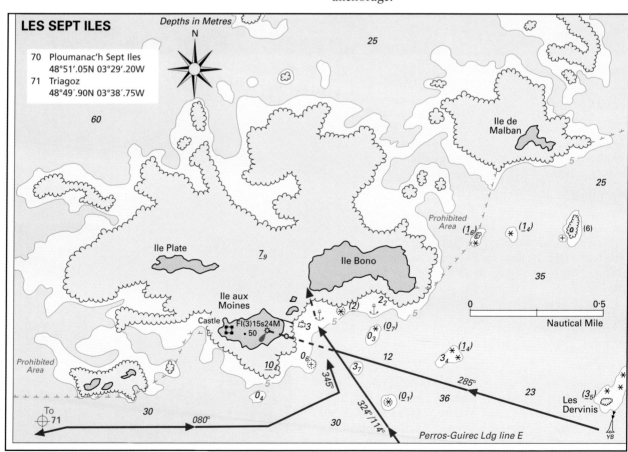

Les Sept Iles looking N at half tide

Les Sept Iles looking NNE

Anchorage

The main anchorage lies SE of the gap between Ile aux Moines and Ile Bono with the lighthouse bearing about 270° and the W end of Ile Bono 000°. There is a mooring buoy in the anchorage which is used by the vedettes.

Anchor between the buoy and the pier which has a beacon on the end of it. Do not proceed far N of the buoy towards the strand between the islands as there are two rocks which cover towards HW. The anchorage is protected from the NNE and NE by Ile Bono and from the W by Ile aux Moines. The strand

of sand and stones which dries out between the islands, breaks the sea from that direction but otherwise is quite open to southerly winds and should only be used in settled weather. The anchorage is often crowded in daytime especially at weekends.

Another less frequented anchorage lies to the S of the centre of Ile Bono which is less sheltered from the W (See photograph above). SHOM 7125 is really needed to avoid the drying rocks (drying 0.7m and 0.1m) to the S and a rocky drying area drying 2.2m off the centre of the beach. Landing is not allowed on Ile Bono.

Ashore in Les Sept Iles

At one time the islands were the resort of corsairs but the fort at the W end was built to dissuade them; it was occupied until 1875 and is worth a walk to for the view. In the season a *buvette* is opened by day on the terrace above the anchorage.

Les Sept Iles

163 Trégastel-St Anne

A more sheltered anchorage than the chart indicates but not from the N; a small but select resort in attractive surroundings suitable for children.

Location
2 M W of Ploumanac'h, 2 M NE of Ile Grande

Shelter
Little from the N or NW

Depth restrictions
Anchorage in 7m to drying

Night entry
No lights

Tidal information
HW Brest +0105
LW Brest +0110

Mean height of tide (m)

HWS	HWN	LWN	LWS
9.2	7.3	3.5	1.4

Tidal streams
Streams start off the entrance at the following times:
HW Brest -0335 ENE-going
HW Brest +0230 WSW-going
Maximum rate 3¼ knots

Berthing
At anchor or mooring

Facilities
Those of small resort

Charts
BA 3670 (50)
SHOM 7124 (25)

Weather
From Bodic on Ch 79 at 0533, 0745, 1145, 1615 and 1945

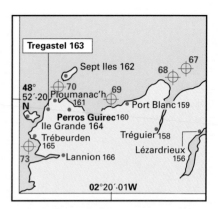

Radio/Telephone
July & August ☎ 02 96 23 49 51

PILOTAGE

Approaches

From ⊕70 or 71 navigate to a position ½M to the NW of the prominent Pierre Pendue and identify Ile Dhu (6m) with its port beacon, and Le Taureau (drying 4.6m) whose starboard beacon is sometime missing with its base remaining. Between the two align No.6 port beacon (the third one in) with a prominent house on 164° and proceed down this track allowing for any cross set. Leave:

Le Taureau N cardinal beacon 300m to starboard.
Ile Dhu port beacon 100m to port.
No.4 port beacon 100m to port.
No.3 starboard beacon 50m to starboard.
No.6 port beacon to the W of Ile Ronde 50m to port.

Anchorages and Moorings

The western bay is full of white mooring buoys for locals but outside these there is a row of red buoys for visitors. To the S of beacons Nos.3 and 6 depths shallow from 6m to drying and an anchorage may be found in a suitable depth clear of the moorings.

The area is sheltered from the E through S to SW. There are no lights to facilitate a departure in the dark if the wind comes away from the N sector or a swell develops, and the anchorage would be dangerous in these conditions.

The bay to the E of Ile Ronde dries 1.1m and also has many small boat moorings in it (See photograph on next page).

Ashore in Trégastel-St Anne

Facilities

Water in cans from the café; fuel from garage in St Anne ½M inland; slip on the sands; reataurants and hotels on the front; several shops including *supermarchés* in St Anne.

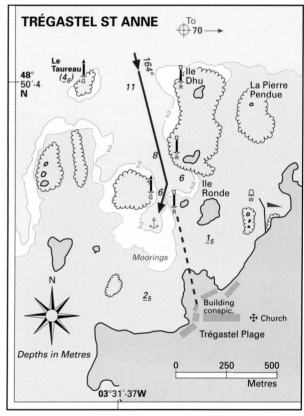

70   Ploumanac'h Sept Iles 48°51'.05N 03°29'.20W
71   Triagoz 48°49'.90N 03°38'.75W

Leisure

The bay is almost completely landlocked at LW and a good place for children where all the strangely shaped rocks have names. There is an interesting little aquarium in caves under a pile of rocks aptly called The Turtles which is topped by a saintly figure in white.

Trégastel St-Anne looking WSW

Tregastel Coz-Pors looking NW   *Robin Rundle*

IV. TREGUIER TO ILE D'OUESSANT

164 Ile Grande

A delightful area for a holiday in a shoal draught craft with some scope for those of deeper draught at neaps. Trébeurden is the nearest place with any facilities.

Location
2M S of Trégastel, 2M N of Trébeurden

Shelter
Nearest at Trébeurden

Depth restrictions
Much of area dries

Night entry
Unlit

Tidal information
HW Brest +0105
LW Brest +0110

Mean height of tide (m)

HWS	HWN	LWN	LWS
9.2	7.3	3.5	1.4

Tidal streams
Streams off Le Crapaud shoal to the W turn as follows:
HW Brest -0405 SE/E-going
HW Brest +0220 SW/W-going

Berthing
Anchoring only

Facilities
Minimal except at Trébeurden

Charts
BA 3669 (50)
SHOM 7124 (25)

Weather
From Bodic on Ch 79 at 0533, 0745, 1145, 1615 and 1945

Radio/Telephone
None

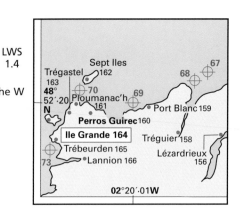

PILOTAGE

Approaches and Anchorages

From S

From ⊕72 identify Kerellec grey tower light structure and approach it on a track of 067° with Ile Milliau on the starboard bow. Leave Ar Guradec S cardinal buoy 100m to port and when 200m short of An Ervennou W cardinal buoy align Les Trois Frères E cardinal beacon (NE of Ile Molène) with the E edge of Ile Losket on 358°. Follow this track for about ¼M until Karreg ar Jantil S cardinal beacon and Karreg ar Merk E cardinal beacon tower are in transit bearing 043°. This line leads close to or over two rocks drying 2.2m and 2.4m and this depth should be allowed for. Once N of Karreg ar Merk beacon tower, select an anchorage clear of the moorings S of the slip and jetty on the SW corner of the island.

From N Chenal de Toull ar Peulven

It is recommended that SHOM chart 7124 is used for this passage, or that one leaves rather than enters on the first visit. In either event it is essential that all marks are identified before becoming committed.

Proceed to a position 1M W of Ile Losket – which is flat and steep-sided. Identify Penven water tower which from this position will appear just S of the conspicuous radome. With the water tower bearing 101° it will be in transit with the right hand edge of Ile Fougère and over the grey roof of a long white building with two rows of windows behind the island. Proceed down this transit with any allowance for set across, leaving the rocks drying 2.1m 100m to port and Morguen N cardinal beacon (drying 3.4m) 50m to starboard.

Ile Grande slip and anchorage   *Peter Taylor*

Now steer 120° to pass midway between Ile Fougère and Ar Jalvotenn E cardinal beacon to pick up the transit 043° of Karreg ar Gentil/Karreg ar Merk into the anchorage off Ile Grande allowing for a least depth of drying 2.4m as above on the transit.

From Chenal de Toull ar Peulven to Trébeurden

Follow the entrance as above until Morguen N cardinal beacon has been left to starboard and pick up the transit on the port quarter of Ar Volenneg just clear of the E edge of Ile Losket bearing 344°; make 164° on this line to follow the transits for the entrance from the S on their reciprocals. Leaving An Evennou W cardinal beacon to port before turning on to the Trébeurden approach line of 067° on Kerrelec light.

Ashore in Ile Grande

Facilities

Water from a tap at the head of the slip; two small *supermarchés*, a butcher and baker at Kervolant village which is 15 minutes' walk from the slip; restaurant and café at Kervolant.

Any other requirements or diversions must be found in Trébeurden (See next page).

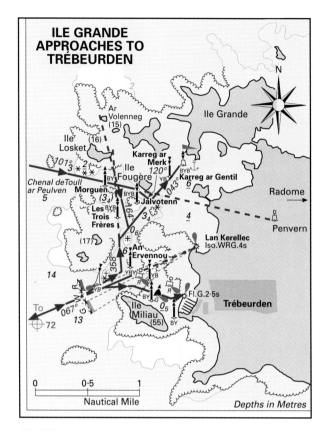

72   Trébeurden 48°46'.06N 03°37'.31W

Ile Grande. Looking S over Ile Grande slipway towards Trébeurden

165 Trébeurden

An upmarket seaside resort with a large marina and ample berthing for visitors. Sill dries 2.1m

Location
2 M S of Ile Grande, 3 M N of Lannion

Shelter
Good inside

Depth restrictions
Dries 1.1m on approach

Night entry
One directional light on outer approach; no ldg lts

Tidal information
HW Brest +0105
LW Brest +0110

Mean height of tide (m)

HWS	HWN	LWN	LWS
9.2	7.3	3.5	1.4

Tidal streams
Streams off Le Crapaud shoal to the W turn as follows:
HW Brest -0405 SE/E-going
HW Brest +0220 SW/W-going

Berthing
On fingers on pontoons

Facilities
Those of good marina and small town

Charts
BA 3669 (50)
SHOM 7124 (20)

Weather
From Bodic on Ch 79 at 0533, 0745, 1145, 1615, 1945

Radio
Ch 09 (0600(2200)
C/s Bureau du Port
Telephone
Marina ☎ 02 96 47 40 15
YC ☎ 02 96 15 45 97
Email port-trebeurden@wanadoo.fr

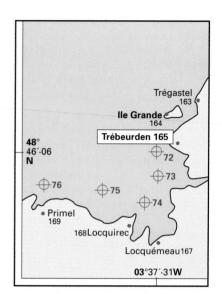

PILOTAGE

Approaches

From W

See page 133 for plan of outer approaches.

From ⊕72 make good a track of 067° on Lan Kerellec light having avoided the extensive Le Crapaud shoal to the WNW. Lan Kerellec is an inconspicuous grey tower (Iso.WRG.4s15m8/5M; red to the N, green to the S, white sector 5° centred on 067°). By day the prominent Ile Milliau will be on the starboard bow, and is well visible at night in front of the town lights. Leave Ar Gouredec buoy (S cardinal VQ(6)+Fl.10s) 200m to port and short of the port hand buoy in the white sector Fl(2)R.6s turn to about 110° to leave:

Men Radence S cardinal beacon 200m to port.
Starboard buoy Q.(3)G.10s close to starboard.
Roche Derrien port buoy Q.(3)R.10s to port.
Roche du Hont S cardinal beacon 300m to port.
Head then for the end of the breakwater Fl.G.2.5s. *Note* that there is a rocky patch drying 1.6m 100m WNW of the breakwater end but there will be water to carry over it if the sill can be crossed.

From N

See directions for Chenal du Toull ar Peulven on page 133. The use of this rock-strewn and winding route if coming from the N will barely save 1M in distance rather than passing outside and to the E of Le Crapaud shoal.

Entrance

Call *bureau du port* on Ch 09 on the approach for a berth. G pontoon for visitors.

The deeper water is close to the breakwater and round its end which involves a 360° turn to line up

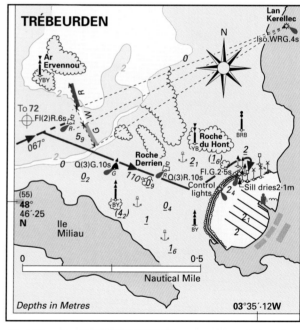

72   Trébeurden 48°46'.06N 03°37'.31W

with the gate. This should be taken slowly in case boats without masts are leaving. The control lights 100m along the breakwater are:

3R	Entry and departure prohibited.
2G + 1Wh	Entry and departure allowed (1.5m+ over the sill).

The maintained depths in the marina are from 2.5m near the entrance, to 2m towards the S corner. The water is retained by a wall which dries 3.8m and the height of the sill in the entrance dries 2.1m. The wall on either side of the entrance is marked by port and

Trébeurden looking S at LW

starboard beacons and there is a depth gauge on either side. The pontoon for visitors is the first one (G) and there appears to be 2.5m along its length.

There is considerable turbulence near the outer end of the two pontoons for up to 10 minutes after the gate has opened. Yachts here should be well secured and movements through the gate should not be attempted during this time.

Moorings

There are a number of moorings to the N of Ile Milliau 10 of which are for visitors. The yellow ones marked 1 to 10 are specifically for those waiting to go on to the marina.

Anchorages

Anchor on sand where there is water to the N of Ile Milliau between the moorings and the approach channel. At springs this will be exposed to the W and the whole area is open to any NW swell particularly near HW. There is a slip to land on at Ile Milliau on the N side but beware of a rock drying 4.2m just to the N of it marked by a N cardinal beacon (See photograph above).

Ashore in Trébeurden

Facilities

Water and electricity on the pontoons; fuel at the fuel berth in the E corner of the marina; showers and heads by the marina office; launderette nearby in the rue de Trouzol; slip and crane up to 20 tonnes, pump-out 2008; shops are mainly up the hill in the town; the large *supermarché* is some distance but there is a free marina shuttle bus to town; restaurants and *créperies* some by the marina and many more in town.

Travel

Nearest free railway station is at Lannion which connects with the national network. There is a small airfield at Lannion and bus services to there and the rest of France.

Leisure

This is a good place for a family with a bilge keeler. SHOM 7124 would allow full use to be made of the area. 3 miles away is the conspicuous radome of the Satellite Telecom Centre where there are guided tours (in French); there is also a modern planetarium on the site with exciting effects and hourly shows (☎ 02 96 91 83 78).

Trébeurden Marina entrance   *Peter Taylor*

166 Lannion

The town lies 4M up the narrow and winding Rivière Léguer and dries 5.5m so can only be reached towards springs where one can dry out, but not comfortably. Some anchoring places in the river.

Location
3M S of Trébeurden, 3½ M ENE of Locquémeau

Shelter
Only well inside the river

Warning
Not an entrance in strong NW or westerlies

Depth restrictions
0.1m in outer channel; then dries progressively inwards

Night entry
No lights

Tidal information
HW Brest +0100
LW Brest +0110
Add 2 hours for Lannion Town

Tidal information
HW Brest +0100
LW Brest +0110

Mean height of tide (m)

HWS	HWN	LWN	LWS
9.1	8.2	3.5	1.4

Berthing
See above

Facilities
Lannion is a big town but with little for yachts

Charts
BA 3669 (50)
SHOM 7124 (20)

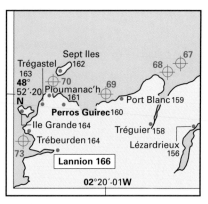

Weather
From Bodic on Ch 79 at 0533, 0745, 1145, 1615 and 1945

Radio/Telephone
None

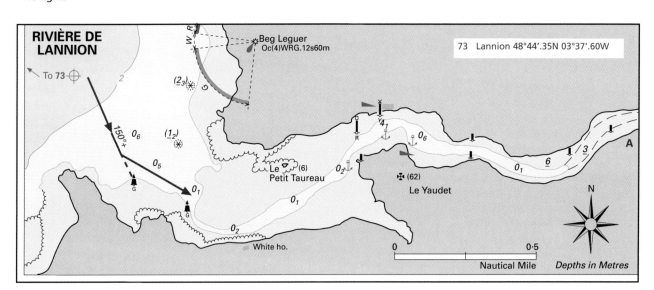

PILOTAGE

An entry by night would only be possible with a full moon but an anchorage outside can be found by approaching Beg-Léguer light (Oc(4) WRG.12s) on a track of between 070° and 090° in the green or white sectors, and anchoring in 2m+ as the depth dictates.

Approaches and Entrance

From ⊕73 make good a track of 095° on Ben-Léguer light structure (white house amongst trees on a ridge) to leave Kinierbel starboard buoy 400m to starboard. To avoid a rocky patch drying 0.1m, continue until the two green beacon towers are well open and the W one bears 150° or more; turn to leave the W one 100m to starboard and then the E one 50m to starboard. Keep about 100m off the S bank until the white house among the trees is abaft the beam and slowly turn to head for the slipway and house on the N bank. Leave Le Petit Taureau islet 200m to port and the beacon on the W point close to starboard. The moorings will then show where the channel lies.

Anchorage

Not easy in this congested area.

- Between Le Petit Taureau and the W point and SW of the slip before the moorings start.
- Above the slip, where there is an active sailing school, outside the moorings. Take care at turn of the tide not to swing in to the neighbouring moorings.
- In the pool E of Le Yaudet slip in 1.2m+ but again care will be needed at the turn of the tide.
- Sound until a pool is found. It does not appear than any exist about ½M above Le Yaudet. In some parts of the river the bed is rocky.

Berthing

There are three quays projecting from the rough, sloping stone walls that line both sides of the last mile of the river. Only one is of any practical use with safety.

- The old sand dredger jetty at Loguivy but not to dry out on as the bottom is very uneven; it is two miles from anywhere.

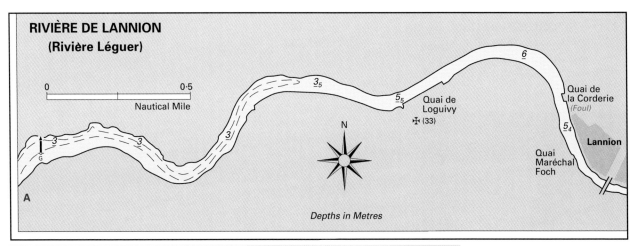

RIVIÈRE DE LANNION
(Rivière Léguer)

0   0·5
Nautical Mile

N

3₅

5₅ Quai de
      Loguivy
      ⌖ (33)

6

Quai de
la Corderie
(Foul)

5₄

Lannion

3   3   3

G

A

Quai
Maréchal
Foch

Depths in Metres

Lannion. Lannion river
entrance looking E

- Quai de Corderie on the N bank just before the town. There is the remains of a wreck alongside it which is submerged above half tide and the quay should not be used.
- A longer jetty on the S side and 200m below the first bridge (Quai Maréchal Foch) has a reasonable surface, a ladder and a couple of bollards. It might be possible to dry out alongside on steep, soft mud but a recce first would be advisable whatever the keel configuration.
  A yacht drawing 2m should have enough water for a 3 hour run ashore over HW before returning down river to avoid drying out.

Ashore

Facilities at Le Yaudet

A mobile shop visits the village up the hill from the slip; restaurant (in the Logis de France hotel) and *créperie*; the picturesque little church has a curious statue of the Virgin Mary with the infant Jesus.

Facilities at Lannion

Water hydrant on the quay; fuel from garage in town; many shops and restaurants in this large town.

Leisure

The Place de Centre is flanked by 15th- and 16th-century houses and the 12th-century church at Brévélenez is worth the climb up.

Travel

Lannion is on a branch railway line. Buses connect to St Brieuc and Morlaix and beyond. There is a small airfield 10km to the E of the town.

Lannion. The last reach below bridge. Looking downstream from quay on S side

IV. TREGUIER TO ILE D'OUESSANT

167 Locquémeau

A small haven with a few alongside drying berths; minimal facilities; two handy restaurants and a fish market.

Location
3½M WSW of Lannion entrance; 3½M ESE of Locquirec

Shelter
Little

Depth restrictions
Dries from outer beacon inwards

Night entry
Lit ldg line but not recommended

Tidal information
HW Brest +0105
LW Brest +0110

Mean height of tide (m)

HWS	HWN	LWN	LWS
9.1	8.2	3.5	1.4

Berthing
Drying alongside jetty

Facilities
1 M to village with small shops

Charts
Only SHOM 7124 (20) serves

Weather
From Bodic on Ch 09 at 0533, 0745, 1145, 1615 and 1945

Radio/Telephone
None

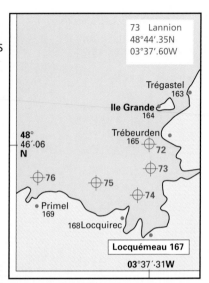

Locquémeau at LW

PILOTAGE

Approaches, Entrance and Berthing

From ⊕73 locate Locquémeau starboard buoy bearing 105° and leave it to starboard to pick up the leading line 121° (White lattice pylon, red top, *Front*; white gabled house, red gallery, *Rear*). There is 0m at the outer starboard beacon, shallowing gradually from therein. This beacon marks the outer end of the slip/breakwater with the next beacon on the elbow; the leading line must be borrowed to port to leave these two to starboard. When the second is abeam, take a jink to starboard to regain the line and pass between the next two beacons. Continue then until the line of of the inner jetty opens up and go alongside on the S side. It has a smooth surface, there are bollards and it dries 5.5m. The bottom is hard, smooth sand and shingle.

Facilities

Restaurant by the jetty; sub post office in the net store; some small shops in the village 1M along the shore.

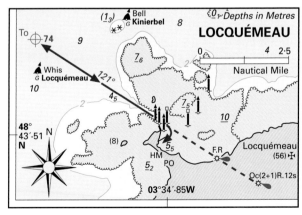

74 Locquirec 48°42'.75N 03°37'.80W

168 Locquirec Toull an Héry

Two small drying harbours in a shallow bay. Locquirec is an attractive, good-sized village with a deep water anchorage off it sheltered from the W.

Location
3½M WSW of Locquémeau; 9M E of Primel

Shelter
Only from the W

Depth restrictions
Both harbours and much of bay dry

Night entry
Not lit

Tidal information
HW Brest +0105
LW Brest +0110

Mean height of tide (m)

HWS	HWN	LWN	LWS
9.1	8.2	3.5	1.4

Berthing
Drying alongside quay; at anchor

Facilities
Shops and restaurants in village

Charts
BA 3669 (50)
SHOM 7124 (20)

Weather
From Bodic on Ch 09 at 0533, 0745, 1145, 1615 and 1945

Radio/Telephone
None

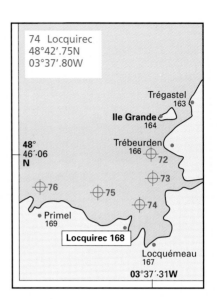

PILOTAGE

Approaches, Moorings and Anchorages

From ⊕74 identify the prominent Pointe du Château and the N cardinal buoy marking its northern outlyers (not on plan). Shape a course to pass about 400m to the E of Ile Verte and La Roche Tombée. Beware of a 1m patch 700m E of Ile Verte if of deep draft.

Locquirec

There are 30 moorings E of Pointe du Château, 5 for visitors and some in deep water. Either pick one up or anchor to the E or S of them.

If proceeding further in to the bay or to the harbour approach on a course of at least 230° and leave La Roche Tombée (8) at least 50m to starboard. The harbour has a short jetty with a smooth inner wall which dries about 5.5m. On the W side is another wall with wooden piles and ladders also suitable to dry out against (See photograph on next page).

Toull an Héry

This is nothing more than a jetty at the mouth of Rivière de Douron with a long and winding approach through the sands marked by two beacon towers and a beacon. The plan and SHOM 7124 show the run of the channel. The jetty is substantial and the E side smooth but the bottom is uneven, dries 5m and it would be unwise to dry out without a prior recce (see photograph on next page). The sand between the jetty and the bridge above is smooth and suitable to dry out on.

Ashore

Many shops and restaurants.

In both places it would be possible to berth alongside before HW, have a meal ashore and be away before grounding on the ebb, otherwise suitable for multihulls and yachts which can take the ground.

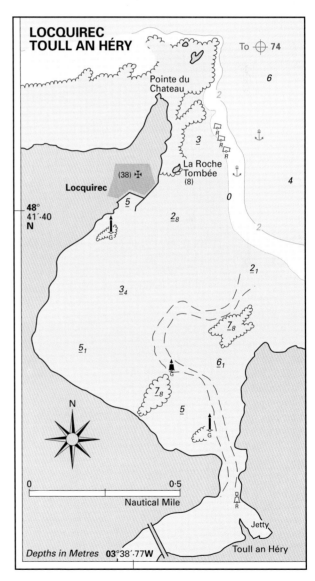

74   Locquirec 48°42′.75N 03°37′.80W

IV. TREGUIER TO ILE D'OUESSANT

The harbour at Locquirec near LW looking SW

At Locquirec

Water tap on the jetty; fuel garage in the village; a baker and chemist but light on provision shops; tourist office by the harbour; a restaurant and café.

At Toull an Héry

A restaurant and créperie near the jetty; no shops.

Toull an Héry. The jetty looking N to final beacon on approach

Baie de Lannion
Primel to Ile Grande

(See location plan on page 141).
This large bay extends some 11 miles between Primel and Ile Grande. With its neighbour to the W, Baie de Morlaix there are several dangers offshore which must be avoided if on passage from Chenal des Sept Iles to Roscoff/Morlaix/Penzé or to Primel, Locquirec, Locquémeau, Lannion, Trébeurden and Ile Grande in the bay. There are no lights in the bay away from the harbour entrances except for a buoy on the W side of Le Crapaud on the E side of the bay.

BA chart 3669 or SHOM 7124 should be consulted and used if entering the area.
The dangers from E to W are:
Les Roches and An. Taro Braz 1M to the SW of Trébeurden with a least depth of drying 6.7m. There is a further isolated rock Le Four drying 3.5m ½M to the W of these shoals.

Le Crapaud shoal 3M to the W of Trébeurden has a least depth of drying 3.7m but the shallows are 1½M wide. It is marked at its W extremity by a W cardinal buoy Q(9)15s. There is a clear passage N/S inside Le Crapaud between it and the shoals off Ile Molène.

A shoal drying 0.1m ¾M NNE of Locquémeau on the W approach to Lannion and just in the green sector of Bèg-Léguer light.

Various unmarked rocks in Baie de Plestin on the approaches to Locquirec shown on the charts.

Various drying rocks and shoals within 1M from the shore between Pointe du Château at Locquirec and Pointe de Primel.

Les Chaises de Primel (14) which extend 2M ENE from Pointe de Primel.

Plateau de la Meloine, an area of scattered shoals and above-water rocks up to 19m extending for 2M in a NE/SW direction 3–5M N of Pointe de Primel. The SW end is marked by a W cardinal buoy.

There are clear passages avoiding these dangers between the following waypoints:

71 Triagoz to 72 Trébeurden passing to the E of Le Crapaud.
72 Trébeurden to 73 Lannion to 74 Locquirec to 75 Les Chaises to 76 Primel.
71 Triagoz to 75 Les Chaises to 76 Primel.
76 Primel to 77 Morlaix to 78 Duons to 79 Roscoff/Bloscon.

Tidal streams

Start at the following times in the centre of the bay:
HW Brest -0345 S – E – S The spring rates in either direction are 1½ knots which increases to 2 knots near the coast.
HW Brest +0145 S – W – S

169 Primel-Trégastel

A natural, well-marked and lit fishing harbour with few facilities for yachts and not much shelter from the N. Marina development under active construction.

Location
9M W of Locquirec; 6M E of Roscoff

Shelter
Limited from the N

Depth restrictions
Inner harbour dries

Night entry
Well lit and lit ldg line

Tidal information
HW Brest +0105
LW Brest +0115

Mean height of tide (m)

HWS	HWN	LWN	LWS
9.0	7.1	3.4	1.3

Tidal streams
The stream turn as follows to the N of Primel:
HW Brest -0430 E-going
HW Brest +0145 W-going

Berthing
Some visitors' moorings; otherwise at anchor

Facilities
Some shops at Trégastel

Charts
BA 3669 (50)
SHOM 7124 (20)
Imray C34 (Plan)

Weather
Ile de Batz on Ch 79 at 0515, 0733, 1133, 1603 and 1933

Radio/Telephone
Ch 09 (Working hours)
Harbourmaster ☎ 06 22 43 77 58

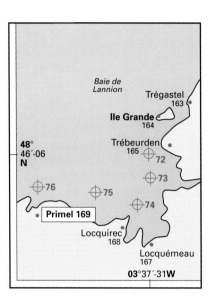

PILOTAGE

Approaches and Entrance

See previous page for details of dangers in the approaches to Primel in Baie de Lannion.

From ⊕76 identify Pointe de Primel (46) and the leading line 152° (White pylon with vertical red stripe, *Front*; white board with vertical red stripe, *Middle*; white pylon with vertical red strip, *Rear*; F.R on *Front* and *Rear* marks). Follow this line closely noting that submerged dangers lie to port, and leave:
Ar Zammeguez a prominent rock with green and white patch and a starboard beacon 30m to starboard.
Roc'h Cramm a port beacon 30m to port.
Raoul starboard beacon 20m to starboard.
The breakwater end (Fl.G.4s) 50m to starboard looking out for vessels leaving.

Moorings

There are 9 visitors' moorings E of Roc'h au Trez Bras in depths that do not dry and these should be used in preference to anchoring.

Anchorages

• Near the leading line outside the breakwater in 9m. Anchor light essential as there can be much fishing boat traffic.

• To the SE of the breakwater as far from it as depths and moorings allow. 2 anchors may be needed to restrict swing.

• In the vicinity of Roc'h au Trez Bras where depths and mooring allow.

• If drying out further up the harbour the line of Roc'h au Trez Bras beacon and left hand edge of Pointe de Primel give the line.

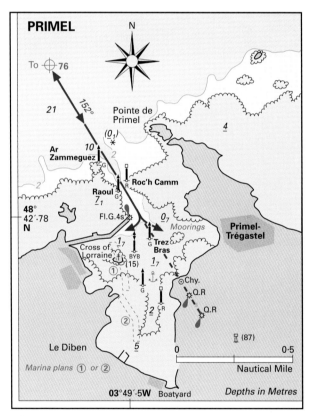

⊕76 Primel 48°43'.50N 03°49'.92W

Berthing

The outer stretch of the breakwater as far as the slip is used by fishing boats but a berth may be found here. Ask at the Harbourmaster at the root of the breakwater. This jetty is high and a ladder will be needed unless a berth by one of the ladders is available.

IV. TREGUIER TO ILE D'OUESSANT

Primel

Ashore in Primel-Trégastel

There is not much of Le Diben on the W side of the harbour except for fish processing units. Trégastel is a minor resort of little cachet.

Facilities

Water tap at root of breakwater; fuel from garage over a mile away; shops a good walk away in Trégastel; dinghy landings at the slip on the breakwater, at a small slip on Trégastel beach and at a slip at Le Diben; fish and shellfish can be bought from the freezer building; boatyard and chandler at the head of the harbour.

Leisure

Imagination required.

Travel

Buses run to Morlaix whence Roscoff with its ferries to Plymouth is a further 10M. Morlaix is also on the railway and has a small airport, as does Lannion 20M to the E.

Primel. Leading line 152°, just off to the right

170 Morlaix

The town lies 8M up a large, complex estuary and river which has a locked basin with a sill drying 2.2m. All the facilities of a large town.

Location
9M from Primel; 10M from Roscoff

Shelter
Not much until well up the river

Depth restrictions
Dries 2.7m in upper reaches

Night entry
Unlit for upper 3M; no lit ldg lines.

Tidal information
HW Brest +0100 Add 20 mins for LW Brest +0110 times at lock

Mean height of tide (m)

HWS	HWN	LWN	LWS
8.9	7.1	3.4	1.3

Subtract 0.2m for heights at lock

Tidal streams
In the vicinity of Chateau du Taureau the streams start as follows:
Flood HW Brest -0450
Ebb HW Brest +0105
Maximum rate on ebb 2½ knots which reduces to 1 knot in Rade de Morlaix with no discernible flood in upper reaches

Berthing
On pontoons in marina

Facilities
First class including pump out

Weather
From Ile de Batz on Ch 79 at 0515, 0733, 1133, 1603 and 1933

Charts
BA 2745 (20)
SHOM 7095 (20)

Radio/Telephone
Ch 09,16 HW ±2
Harbourmaster ☎ 02 98 62 13 14
Lock ☎ 02 98 85 54 92

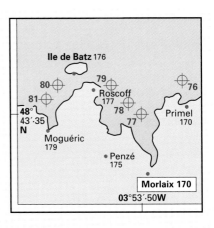

76 Primel 48°43′.50N 03°49′.92W
77 Morlaix 48°43′.35N 03°53′.50W
78 Duons 48°43′.25N 03°55′.40W
79 Roscoff-Bloscon 48°43′.80N 03°57′.20W

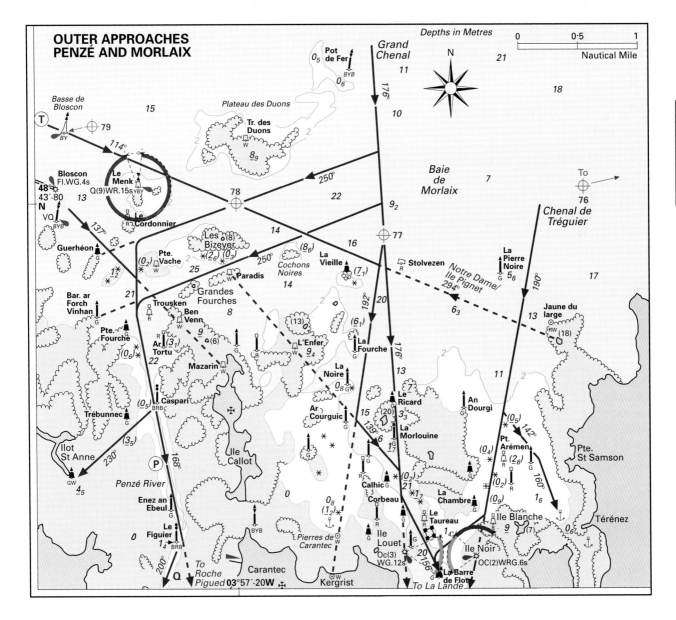

PILOTAGE

Grand Chenal to Penn ar Lann (Line J)

(Note photos on pages 146 & 147).

Leaving Pot de Fer E cardinal buoy 300m to starboard proceed through ⊕77 on the transit 176° of Line J Ile Louet (Oc(3)WG.12s) and La Lande (White square tower, black top near skyline (Fl.5s) leaving the following marks as indicated:

Stolvezen unlit port buoy 200m to port.

La Vieille starboard beacon tower 600m to starboard.

La Fourche starboard beacon 600m to starboard.

Le Ricard starboard beacon tower 50m to starboard.

La Morlouine starboard beacon 50m to starboard.

Calhic starboard beacon tower 100m to starboard.

When Calhic bears about 290° leave the leading line and make 156° to leave:

Le Corbeau starboard beacon tower 100m to starboard.

** **Le Taureau** port beacon tower 100m to port.

Then pass midway between Ile Louet and the conspicuous Chateau de Taureau continuing to leave Barre de Flot unlit starboard buoy close to starboard to proceed up the river. (See next page). If bound for the Penn ar Lann anchorage leave Barre de Flot buoy well to port.

Chenal Ouest de Ricard (Line K)

By day

From ⊕77 identify in the bay to the W of Penn ar Lann two small white painted rocks of the Pierre Carentec in transit with a white wall mark on the shore at Kergrist 188° (Line K) and proceed down it leaving:

La Vieille starboard beacon tower 400m to starboard.

La Fourche starboard beacon tower 140m to starboard.

La Noire starboard beacon 140m to starboard.

Ar Courguic starboard beacon 140m to starboard.

When Ar Courguic is abeam alter to make good 139° on a stern transit of L'Enfer white beacon tower in line with Le Paradis white beacon tower (not on Plan) bearing 319°. This line leaves:

A starboard beacon 250m to starboard

Calhic starboard beacon 250m to starboard.

As soon as Ile Louet aligns with La Lande again alter to make good 176° and proceed, as at ** above, up river or to Penn ar Lann anchorage.

Chenal de Tréguier to Penn ar Lann (Line M)

Least depth in this channel is drying 1m.

From ⊕76 or 77 navigate to a position 300m E of Pierre Noire unlit starboard beacon and align Ile Noire lighthouse (White square tower, red lantern, Oc(2)WRG.6s, *Front*) with La Lande (White square tower, black top near skyline, Fl.5s, *Rear*) on 190° (Line M) and follow this to leave:

Jaune du Large red and white mark on rock 400m to port.

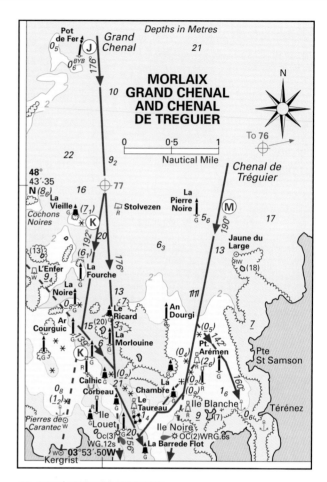

76 Primel 48°43'.50N 03°49'.92W
77 Morlaix 48°43'.35N 03°53'.50W

An Dourgi starboard beacon 400m to starboard.

At this point turn off the leading line to 142° if going to Térénez (See Anchoring below for directions).

Petit Arémen port beacon tower 200m to port.

Grand Arémen starboard beacon tower 300m to starboard.

La Chambre starboard beacon tower 100m to starboard.

Skirt La Chambre at this distance to align it and Petit Arémen port beacon tower beacon astern on 031° and make good the reciprocal of 211°. Continue on this to the vicinity of Barre de Flot and proceed up river or to the Penn ar Lann anchorage.

Anchorages

• A popular spot is between Barre de Flot buoy and Penn ar Lann in depths of 9m downwards. This is well sheltered from the W but not from other quarters and it is difficult to creep in far enough to get out of the stream. There are sometimes mooring buoys here which are ostensibly for visitors, There is a dinghy landing at all states of the tide at the NE corner of Penn ar Lann. From here a footpath climbs the hill and it is then a mile further to the town of Carantec which has shops and facilities.

- In settled weather and neap tides an anchorage may be found near Pierres de Carantec (see plan on previous page).

- In easterly weather and neaps there is an anchorage close S or SW of **Pointe de Térénez** where there is about 2.1m at neaps. (See approach and details on plan on previous page). There is a busy sailing school and a port office here with some drying moorings for visitors. An anchorage between here and Pointe St Samson is another alternative. There are two cafés and a restaurant ashore, and a water tap but no shops.

- In the Rade de Morlaix between Barre de Flot and Dourduff it is possible to anchor in good holding on either side of the fairway but there is no reasonable landing for dinghies near LW. An anchor light should be exhibited at night. Alternatively leave the main channel to the S of Barre de Flot buoy and anchor in the Mouillage des Herbiers.

Anchoring is prohibited in the channel above Dourduff.

Rade de Morlaix and the upper river

The alignment of the E side of Chateau de Taureau and the W side of Ile Ricard on 336°/156° leads down the channel of the Rade de Morlaix. This is wide and deep shallowing from 24m to 2m by No.4 buoy. Inward from here it shallows quickly to drying at CD by No.5 buoy. From here it progressively gets shallower to drying 2m off Locquénolé and shoals gradually to drying 2.7m in the upper reaches.

The track of 156° should be continued from No.5 buoy until the next buoyed channel of 220° is opened up leading to Loquénolé. From here it is well marked by beacons until the final stretches when conspicuous transit posts indicate the channel and should be closely kept to. The buoys are all on the edge of the deepwater channel but some of the beacons are set back.

Navigation above Dourduff at night is not allowed unless fitted with a searchlight with an effective beam of at least 200m.

Entrance

The lock is 63m long, 16m wide, the lower sill dries 2.2m and the upper 3.1m. The gate opens 3 times each HW at HW −1½ hours, HW and HW +1 hour. The tide gauge shows the depth over the lower sill. The bridge below the lock has a clearance of 26m and the power line shown on older charts has been removed. Whilst waiting for the gates to open go alongside the quay on the W side about 150m from the lower gate. Yachts may safely dry out here but not nearer to the lock where there are drying rocks. The aggregate jetty below this quay is a better place to go alongside provided it is not occupied by coasters. The best place to dry out is below the weir alongside the E side of the old entrance where the wall is smooth, has two ladders and a soft mud bottom.

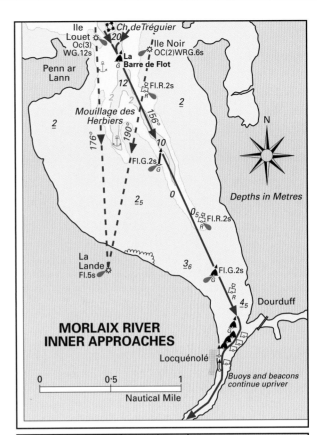

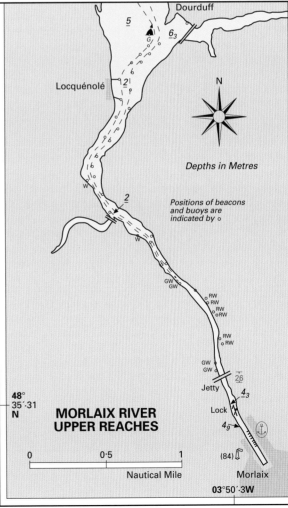

When locking through do not be in a hurry to let go warps and proceed. There is considerable turbulence as the gates open which takes a minute or two to subside.

Berthing

Depths in the basin which is over ½M long vary from 2.4m to 5.4m alongside the quays. At the southern end are the pontoons of the marina. The basin narrows appreciably towards the southern end and large yachts may find some difficulty in turning round if they progress too far in. There is a mobile walkway across the basin halfway down which is pulled aside around lock opening times. There are some 180 pontoon berths and 40 on the quays; maximum length on the pontoons 12m with 30 for visitors, larger yachts go alongside the quays. The arrival berth where one should first go to unless directed otherwise, is alongside the E bank before the Harbour Office.

Ashore in Morlaix

Facilities

Water points at base of pontoons, use own hose; fuel berth by harbour office; pump-out facilities, diesel on west side, showers and heads by the harbour office; ice machine near the same place; launderette close by; the main shopping centre is beyond the end of the basin under the viaduct. Morlaix is a major town able to satisfy most needs; many hotels and restaurants in town; boatyard, chandlers and repairs, all is possible. Ask initially at the YC or the Harbour Office. This is a good place to lay up ashore or afloat and close to the ferry to Plymouth; yacht club E side of the basin welcomes visitors.

Travel

Morlaix is one of the main communication centres of Brittany and there is a good train service to Roscoff, Brest and Paris with connections to St Malo and Dinard. There are similar bus services. The nearest airport is at Ploujean just outside the town with other airports at Brest and Dinard. Roscoff with its twice daily ferries to Plymouth is 10 miles away.

Leisure

Much of the lower town dates back to the 15th-century and is worth a look round. There are connections with Mary Queen of Scots, Duchesse Anne and a Musée des Jacobins. The locally brewed beer coreff is based on dark Welsh brews and is a feature of the bars and cafés. The tobacco factory near the basin is open to visitors on Wednesdays.

History

In Roman times there was a fortress and the town was called Mons Relaxus; in the Middle Ages it was an important port and shipbuilding centre with interest in piracy and the tobacco trade. There were many warlike as well as trading exchanges with the English. The Fontaine des Anglais on the E bank of

Morlaix. Térénez looking SE (see Plan on page 144)

Morlaix. Château du Taureau and Ile Louet looking E

the river marks the place where in 1522, 600 English who had disembarked to attack the town were surprised while asleep and killed. They had arrived to find all the inhabitants away at a fair and had helped themselves to all they wanted, especially the wine. This is commemorated in the Morlaix coat of

Morlaix lock looking N   *Robin Rundle*

Morlaix outer estuary looking S

Morlaix lock looking N   *Peter Carnegie*

arms; the lion facing the English leopard and the legend *S'ils te mordent, mords-les* – 'If they bite you, bite them'.

Two years later the town was captured and occupied by the English but in 1542 the merchants of the town built Chateau de Taureau to discourage any further raids.

171 Rivière de Penzé. Carantec, Pen Poull and Penzé

An unspoilt estuary given over to the cultivation of oysters running 8 miles inland through a rural area. Bridge clearance of 10m limits navigation of the last 3M to Penzé town. Only small town facilities.

Location
19M from Morlaix (by water); 3M from Roscoff

Shelter
Adequate inside river

Depth restrictions
At least 0.9m to Pont de la Corde, shallowing to drying 5m at Penzé

Night entry
No lights, not possible

Tidal information
HW Brest +0100
LW Brest +0110

Mean height of tide (m)

HWS	HWN	LWN	LWS
8.9	7.1	3.4	1.3

Tidal streams
Spring ebb up to 2½ knots in river

Berthing
Anchoring, or drying alongside

Facilities
Shops at Carantec, Pen Poull and Penzé

Charts
BA 2745 (20)
SHOM 7095 (20)

Weather
From Ile de Batz on Ch 79 at 0515, 0733, 1133, 1603 and 1933

Radio/Telephone
None

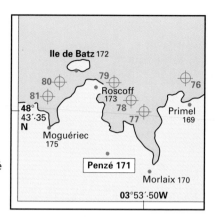

77 Morlaix 48°43'.35N 03°53'.50W

PILOTAGE

Approaches

From N

From ⊕79 and Basse de Bloscon N cardinal buoy make good 180° to leave the end of Bloscon breakwater 100m to starboard. From here align Benn Venn white beacon tower with Mazarin white beacon tower on the N end of Ile Callot bearing 137°. Follow this line closely to leave Guerhéon starboard beacon tower 100m to starboard and when La Petite Vache port beacon tower is abeam at 400m turn to 168° to pass between Trousken port beacon tower and La Petite Fourche starboard beacon tower.

** From here pick up Line P which aligns Roch Piguet bottle-shaped white pyramid with Amer de Stum black and white day mark bearing 168° (See details in plan on next page to continue). If these marks cannot be distinguished, the line passes close to Caspari BRB beacon and then to Le Figuer BRB beacon.

From E

(Line R) Navigate to ⊕78 and hold a line of 250° on **Guerhéon** starboard beacon tower to leave:
Les Bizeyer (8) group of rocks 400m to port.
La Petite Vache port beacon tower 400m to port.
Le Cordonnier port beacon tower 300m to starboard and when it is abeam turn to port to head between **Trousken** port beacon tower and **La Petite Fourche** starboard beacon tower and proceed on Line P as at ** above.

From E or from Morlaix

(Line S) From ⊕77 proceed towards ⊕78 leaving **La Vieille** starboard beacon tower 400m to port until **Bar ar Forc'h Vihan** starboard beacon bears 250° when turn down this track and hold it closely.

Leave **Les Cochons Noires** (drying 8.6m) to port, **Paradis** white beacon tower 50m to port, **Les Bizeyer** group of rocks to starboard, **La Petite Vache** port

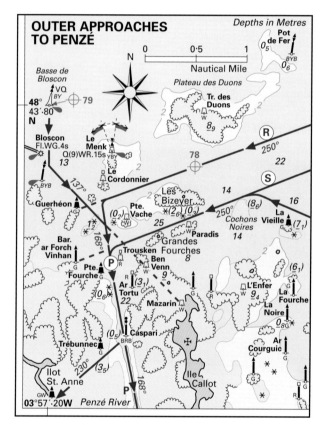

78 Duons 48°43'.25N 03°55'.40W
79 Roscoff-Bloscon 48°43'.80N 03°57'.20W

beacon tower 400m to starboard and **Trousken** port beacon tower to port before turning to Line P 168° and proceed as at ** above.

Le Figuer to Ponte de la Corde (Lines P & Q)

Leave Line P 168° (Roc'h Piguet, bottle shaped white pyramid; Amer de Stum, black and white daymark) at **Le Figuer** and continue down the channel marked by withies on 200° to pick up Line Q 210°. This is Pointe de Lingos (small white pyramid) and a white square on a wall at St Ives.

Leave **Les Cheminées** starboard beacon to starboard and enter the buoyed channel on about 232°. The buoys are small red and green plastic, many with missing topmarks. There is a least depth of about 0.9m from Pointe de Lingos as far as the old ferry slip.

Anchorages

- To the S of Le Figuer in 1–4m at the edge of the channel; convenient for Carantec.
- Between Les Cheminées and Pointe de Lingos clear of the moorings.
- S of the old ferry slip in about 1m, mud; this is the most sheltered and convenient for the restaurant at St Yves.

Pont de la Corde to Penzé town

The clearance below the bridge is 10m. The river winds through attractive rural surroundings for 4M to the town of Penzé. There are occasional buoys and beacons to assist. The railway bridge 2M above Pont de la Corde appears to have at least 30m under it and the main channel runs close to the E of the central pier; port and starboard marks are painted on the piers. 1 mile above this bridge, the main channel is the E branch which leads to Penzé.

There are some drying moorings just below the town bridge. Do not dry out at the quay on the E side where there is a rough and uneven bottom. The quay on the W side has a flat and unobstructed bottom, a smooth surface, two ladders and dries 5m. There is a slip here accessed through the car park (See photograph next page).

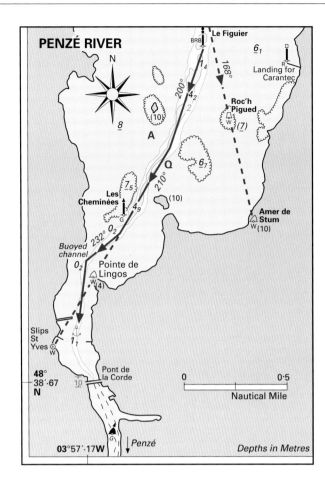

Carantec

Access to Carantec is via a stone jetty and slip below the town by two yacht yards. The slip dries about 4.6m and bilge keelers can dry alongside.

Rivière de Penzé. Carantec looking ESE

Rivière de Penzé. Pen Poul looking SSW

(image labels) Jetty and sailing school on Ilot St Andrew — Causeway to Pen Poull and St Pol de Leon — 230

Pen Poull

Pen Poull is a drying bay below St Pol de Leon with a slip and a hard. The approach is from Caspari beacon on a transit of a green and white beacon at the end of Ilot St Anne slip, and another green beacon and a gatehouse on the shore bearing 230° (See plan on previous page and photograph above). There is a busy sailing school on Ilot St Anne. It is possible to dry out alongside the slip/jetty on the Ilot on its W side where it dries about 4m. The approach dries 3.5m and the rest of the bay is all flat sand drying up to 5.5m.

Ashore

In Pen Poull

The village, which is a good walk from Ilot St Anne has few facilities and it is a further walk up the hill to the country town of St Pol de Leon with its impressive cathedral.

In Carantec

A good selection of shops and restaurants up in the town. Ile Callot is accessible below half tide and worth a visit (See History below).

In Penzé

Usual selection of shops and restaurants of a large village; At St Yves there is a restaurant on the main road above Pont de la Corde but no shops.

History

On Ile Callot stands the pilgrimage chapel of Notre Dame des Victoires, founded in the 6th century to commemorate a victory over Norse pirates. On 15th August seamen from the surrounding districts come to pay their devotions.

St Pol de Leon is an ancient cathedral town which lies about 1M W of the landing at Pen Poull. It has

Rivière de Penzé. The slip at Carantec

Rivière de Penzé. The jetty on W side at Penzé town looking downstream from town bridge

played a leading part in the history of Brittany. Its name is a corruption of St Paul Aurelian, the first missionary who came from Wales in AD530. The cathedral is entirely medieval and its twin spires are one of the most distinctive landmarks of the district. Close to the S of the cathedral is the thin spire of Kreisker, 79m high which was built to be the tallest in France, but was subsequently out-built.

Rivière de Penzé. The railway bridge between Penzé town and Pont de la Corde looking downstream. The channel passes through the right-hand arch

Rivière de Penzé. Looking W from Carantec anchorage. Sunset over Kreisker, and Pol de Leon twin spires

172 Chenal de l'Ile de Batz

A narrow channel with few leading marks and no leading lights which provides access to Roscoff and a short cut to Bloscon and Morlaix.

Location
Between Ile de Batz and Roscoff

Warning
Narrow channels, strong streams

Depth restrictions
Allow for least depth drying 0.8m
Night passage
No ldg lts. Not recommended

Tidal information
HW Brest +0100
LW Brest +0110

Mean height of tide (m)

HWS	HWN	LWN	LWS
8.9	7.1	3.4	1.3

Tidal streams
The streams start at the following times:
HW Brest -0435 E-going
HW Brest +0110 W-going
Both attain 3½ knots at springs

Berthing
Some moorings at E end; exposed anchorages

Charts
BA 2745 (20)
SHOM 7095 (20)

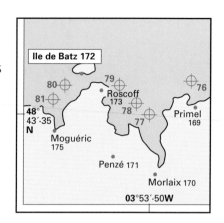

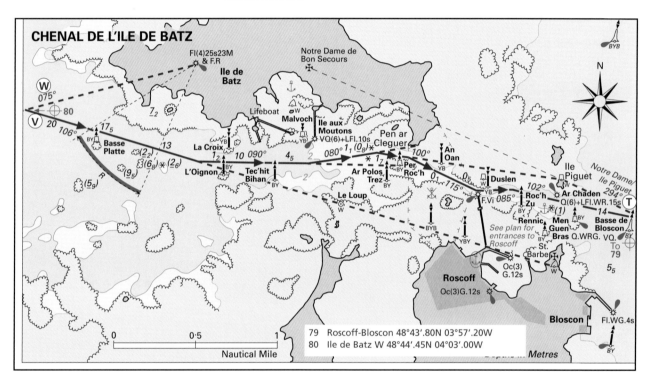

79	Roscoff-Bloscon 48°43'.80N 03°57'.20W
80	Ile de Batz W 48°44'.45N 04°03'.00W

PILOTAGE

From W

¾M visibility is needed in order to be able to see the next marks for safe transit. Approach from ⊕80 on a track of 075° on Ile de Batz light (Line W) until Basse Platte N cardinal beacon tower bears 110° and it can be left 100m to starboard on Line V. This is 106° with **Le Loup** (Small steep rock with white patch on N face) in transit with **St Barbe white pyramid** just to the S of the conspicuous St Barbe chapel. If the line cannot be identified steer to pass between **La Croix** S cardinal beacon and **L'Oignon** N cardinal beacon leaving a group of rocks the highest of which dries 9.5m and the nearest of which dries 2.2m, 150m to starboard. When between L'Oignon and La Croix alter to port to 090° on **Per Roc'h** N cardinal beacon tower leaving:

Tec'hit Bihan N cardinal beacon 200m to starboard.

Malvoch S cardinal beacon tower and **Ile aux Moutons** S cardinal beacon about 300m to port.

When the latter bears 000°, alter to port to 080° on **Pen ar Cleguer** the southernmost tip of Ile de Batz. This will pass between two rocks, one drying 0.8m which should not present a hazard above half tide.

When **An Oan** S cardinal beacon comes into line with **Ile Piguet** white pyramid on 100° alter to follow this line leaving **Per Roc'h** N cardinal beacon tower 100m to starboard.

When **Pen ar Cleguer** is abeam alter further to 115° to leave **An Oan** 80m to port and head for the purple beacon on the end of the long and spindly Roscoff/Batz ferry pier, leaving it 50m to starboard. Any cross component of the tidal stream should be watched on this leg.

From the ferry pier end make good 085° to leave **Duslen** S cardinal beacon about 50m and **Duslen**

Chenal de l'île de Batz   *Peter Carnegie*

IV. TREGUIER TO ILE D'OUESSANT

white tower 120m to port. When these are abeam, continue to make 085° towards **Ar Chaden** S cardinal lighthouse leaving **Roc'h Zu** N cardinal beacon 100m to starboard and altering to about 102° to leave Ar Chaden lighthouse 50m to port.

To continue E or to Morlaix, align **Ile Piguet** astern with **Notre Dame de Bon Secours** bearing 294° (Line T) and proceed via ⊕79 and 78 S of Duons leaving **Basse de Bloscon** N cardinal buoy and **Le Menck** W cardinal beacon tower to starboard (See plan on page 148).

To continue to Penzé River, from **Basse de Bloscon** N cardinal buoy proceed as on page 148 (Approaches from the N to Penzé).

From E

¾ M visibility is needed to be able to see the next marks for a safe transit.

Approach from ⊕79 and Basse de Bloscon N cardinal buoy either from the N, along Line T **Ile Piguet** in transit with **Notre Dame de Bon Secours** 294° (See plan on page 152) or from Penzé as on page 148. Make good a track to leave **Ar Chaden** S cardinal lighthouse 50m to starboard, leaving **Men Guen Bras** N cardinal lighthouse 250m to port (see photograph on the next page). From here adjust to pass 50m S of **Duslen** S cardinal beacon and 120m S of the white beacon tower of the same name leaving **Roc'h Zu** N cardinal beacon 100m to port.

When Duslen is abeam make for the purple and white beacon on the end of the long spindly ferry pier. Pass close to this, altering to a track of 295° and leave **An Oan** S cardinal beacon 80m to starboard. When this is on the starboard quarter align it with **Ile Piguet** white beacon tower bearing 100° and hold the reciprocal of 290°. Do not overshoot this transit and leave **Per Roc'h** N cardinal beacon tower 100m or less to port.

To avoid the rock drying 0.8m which may be a danger at half tide or below, when **Ar Porloz Trez** N cardinal beacon bears 160° make good 260° on **L'Oignon** N cardinal beacon to leave:

Ile aux Moutons slipway and **Malvoch** S cardinal beacon 300m to starboard.

Tec'hit Bihan N cardinal beacon 300m to port.

La Croix S cardinal beacon 200m to starboard.

At L'Oignon which is left to port, pick up the stern transit of **Le Loup** a small steep rock with a white patch on the N side and St Barbe white pyramid just S of the conspicuous chapel of St Barbe bearing 106° (Line V). Follow this transit out on 286° to leave **Basse Plate** N cardinal beacon tower and the rocks before it to the S of the track all to port.

If bound N follow this line for a further mile to clear the dangers on the W side of Ile de Batz.

If bound W put Ile de Batz lighthouse on a back bearing of 074° towards ⊕80.

Entering Chenal de l'Ile de Batz from the W

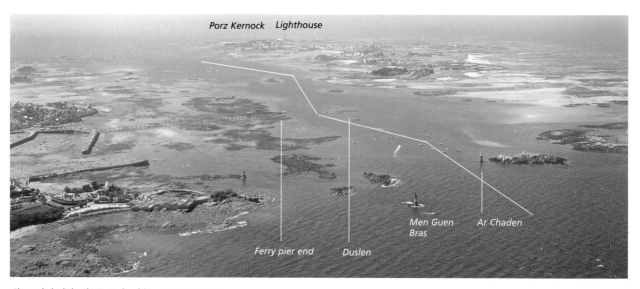

Chenal de l'Ile de Batz looking WNW at LW

Ile de Batz

A good, sheltered drying out area for shallow draught yachts but deep water anchoring only around neaps. There are many visitors during the day but they return to Roscoff in the evenings.

Anchorages

Anchoring is prohibited because of cables between Roscoff and the E end of Ile de Batz as indicated on the Plan and charts.

- Between Ar Chaden lighthouse and Duslen beacons as far N as depth will allow. This area has a growing number of moorings and it may be possible to use one. Otherwise at neaps it is possible to sound in to the N of them out of the stream.
- SW of Malvoch beacon tower (avoiding the 0.1m rock) or S of Ile aux Moutons and E of the causeway at neaps. The moorings in the area are much used by fishermen and it is uncomfortable in westerlies.
- In Porz Kernock if able to take the ground. A lot of rocks have been cleared from the harbour which is well sheltered. Enter leaving the Ile aux Moutons S cardinal beacon 15m to starboard and

head NNW to leave the white pyramid on Ile Kernock 50m to starboard and select a anchorage clear of moorings and floating fish boxes. Bow and stern anchors may be needed.

Facilities

The pier and slip in the NW corner are used by the ferries but can be used as a dinghy landing. Water tap and telephone on the front; showers in the hotel; a few bars and restaurants on the front; two small *supermarchés* and a baker.

Leisure

There are pleasant walks over the island which is given over to market gardening.

History

St Pol arrived on the island from Wales in the 6th-century, founded a monastery on the island. In Breton legend, he disposed of a dragon by tying his stole round its neck, leading it to the shore and throwing it into the sea. A fragment of material dating from the 8th-century that is kept in the 18th-century church Notre Dame de Bon Secours is believed to be part of that stole. The Monster's Hole on the NW shore beyond the lighthouse marks where the dragon was given his come-uppance.

173 Roscoff and Bloscon (174)

Only drying berths alongside for yachts except for three exposed and indifferent anchorages. A pity as it is a nice town and ferry port convenient to change crews. There are summer mooring buoys and a marina planned for 2010.

Location
3M from Penzé entrance, 6M from Moguéric

Shelter
Only in harbour

Depth restrictions
Dries 2m on approach, 5m at quay

Night entry
Well lit plus lit ldg line

Tidal information
HW Brest +0100
LW Brest +0110

Mean height of tide (m)

HWS	HWN	LWN	LWS
8.8	7.0	3.4	1.3

Berthing
Drying at quays, or at anchor

Facilities
Those of a medium sized town

Charts
BA 2745 (20)
SHOM 7095 (20)

Weather
From Ile de Batz on Ch 79 at 0515, 0733, 1133, 1603 and 1933

Radio
Harbourmaster Ch 09. Bloscon Ch 12
Telephone
Harbourmaster ☎ 02 98 69 76 37/ 02 98 63 73 07

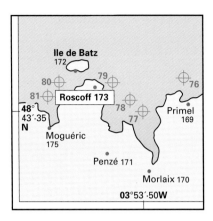

79   Roscoff-Bloscon 48°43'.80N 03°57'.20W

Roscoff entrance from N. Leading line open left

PILOTAGE

Approaches

See pages 152 to 153 for approaches through Chenal de l'Ile de Batz from W or E.

Passe à l'Est de Benven (Line Y)

Navigate to a position 150m SW of Ar Chaden, noting the rock drying 1m 200m S of Ar Chaden.

From here align the leading marks (White column on end of W mole (Oc(2+1)G.12s, *Front*; square white tower (Oc(2+1)W.12s), *Rear*) and stay close to this line until the end of the E mole is abeam when steer to enter the port. Least depth before the breakwater is drying 2m but the line goes very close to drying 4m rocks.

IV. TREGUIER TO ILE D'OUESSANT

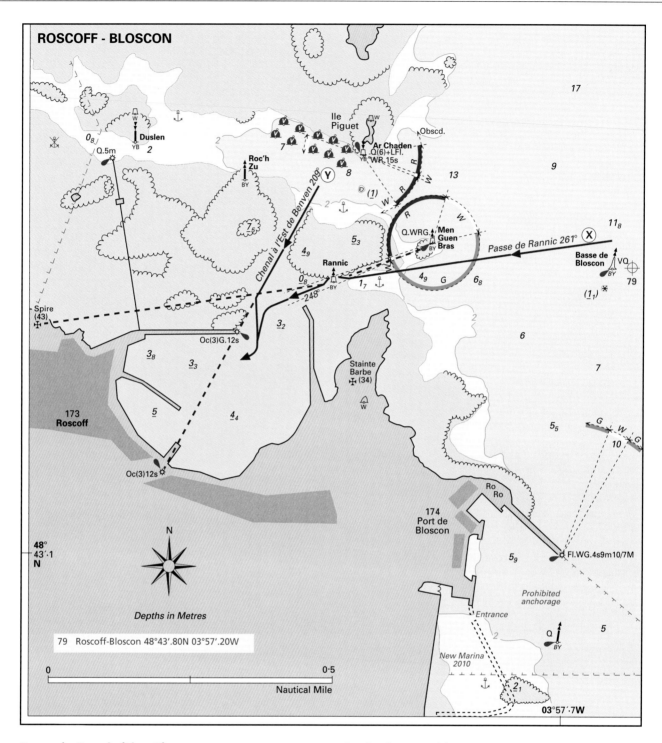

ROSCOFF - BLOSCON

Passe du Rannic (Line X)

From ⊕79 or Basse de Bloscon N cardinal buoy align Rannic N cardinal beacon tower with Roscoff church on 261° and proceed down it. Jink to the N round Rannic 30m off and then align Rannic with Men Guen Bras astern in its white sector at night (Q.WRG). When the head of E mole is abeam, alter to enter harbour. Least depth before the breakwater is drying 3.5m in the vicinity of Rannic.

Moorings

There are a number of moorings along the N edge of Chenal de l'Ile de Batz to the W of Ar Chaden which may be available to visitors.

Anchoring outside

No anchorage outside the port is clear of tidal streams except at Bloscon. All are open to the E. Selection will depend on wind direction and whether on springs or neaps.

- Between Ar Chaden and Duslen. Open to the N and only comfortable for deep draughts at neaps. See page 155.

- In about 1m just E of the Roscoff leading line with Roc'h Zu N cardinal beacon bearing 285° but note the rock drying 1m close E of this and the 1.9m patch.

Roscoff inner harbour looking W. Visitors lie alongside inner breakwater in centre of picture

- E of Rannic beacon tower in 1.7m to 5m, using the approach directions above. Some shelter from the W.
- Off Bloscon S of the prohibited area. Sheltered from the W but a long dinghy ride and walk to town.
- W of Ar Chaden 18 white visitors buoys laid May–September.

Berthing

The outer harbour has good drying berths along its N and W sides drying from 2.4m to 3m on hard sand but is reserved primarily for fishing boats and vedettes which use the steps. With the Harbourmaster's permission it may be possible to lie alongside the second or third ladder where a yacht with 1.8m draft will take the ground just after half tide. If the built-in ladders are occupied, a berth elsewhere alongside will require considerable agility at low water to get ashore without a ladder of one's own. These are good berths to shop from but longer stay visitors are expected to use the inner harbour.

The inner harbour dries from 3.6m to 5.1m. The old jetty is rather rough but there are good berths alongside with 6 ladders and two steps which may be unoccupied even if the outer harbour is full. The wall is high and the use of warps to hold the yacht in is preferable to masthead lines. Again, a long ladder is an asset.

The eastern part of the harbour is not recommended to dry out in as it is subject to surge with any swell.

Ashore in Roscoff

Facilities

Water from hydrants on the quay; fuel from garage in town; showers and heads tickets from tourist office by roundabout; turn right at end of quay for main street and shops; chandlery near lighthouse on S side of harbour; launderette up road from E end of front; restaurants and hotels many of all styles and prices.

Leisure

The aquarium has many forms of sea life. It is on the N front and is worth a visit as are the church and the chapel of St Barbe.

Travel

Rail and bus connections with Morlaix and the rest of France. Nearest airfield Morlaix (Ploujean). Ferries to Plymouth from Bloscon run up to three times daily in the summer, crossing time 6 hours.

History

Mary Queen of Scots landed at Roscoff in 1548, when she was 5 years old, to be married to the Dauphin in Paris. Here also came Prince Charles Edward Stuart in a French privateer following the battle of Culloden after a number of escapes including from English ships in the Channel.

The church has a remarkable Renaissance tower tower and spire (1550) decorated with carvings of ships and pieces of ordnance.

The Pardon of St Barbe takes place on the third Monday in July and the whole town is en fête.

The efficiency of Brittany ferries in opening up the English markets to the Breton farmer has, alas led to the disappearance of the beret-hatted onion men on their bicycles with strings of onions, many of whom came from the area.

174 Bloscon

An unattractive artificial harbour half a mile S of Basse de Bloscon buoy and a 1mile walk to town. It is completely open to the E but clear of the stream. It has the ferry terminal with acres of tarmac and a fishing complex; yachts are discouraged from an extensive controlled area. It is only useful as an emergency anchorage in strong westerlies and to change crews from the ferry. However 50 visitors' berths should be included in the new marina opening in 2010.

Approaches

Straight foward using BA 2745 or SHOM 7095 and the sectored Bloscon light at night.

Moorings and Anchorages

Some moorings for yachts have occasionally been put down in the S part of the controlled area. If not, anchor to the S of Ar Pourven buoy (VQ) but it shoals fairly quickly to drying 2.1m on Ar Pourven shoal.

Ashore in Bloscon

Facilities

Water tap by the ferry terminal; slipway at N end of fishing complex available at most stages of the tide and the best place to load/unload; no worthwhile shops in the terminal although there are the usual reataurants and cafés. Do not be fooled by the sign 'Supermarché 500m' – it is a good 2km.

175 Moguériec and Ile de Sieck

A useful anchorage in easterlies with two small drying harbours. Little shelter from the W. A small fishing fleet but few facilties.

Location
6M from Roscoff, 11M to Pontusval

Shelter
Only from the E

Depth restrictions
Both harbours dry about 5m

Night entry
Lit ldg lts and pier end at Moguéric

Tidal information
HW Brest +0050
LW Brest +0045

Mean height of tide (m)

HWS	HWN	LWN	LWS
8.9	7.1	3.4	1.3

Berthing
At anchor or dried out alongside

Facilities
Minimal

Charts
BA 2745 (20)
SHOM 7095 (20)

Weather
From Ile de Batz on Ch 79 at 0515, 0733, 1133, 1603 and 1933

Radio/Telephone
None

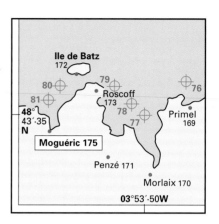

PILOTAGE

Approaches

From ⊕81 pick up the leading line 162°. The front mark is a white tower with green top on the jetty end (Iso.WG.4s in the white sector), and the rear another white beacon with a green top (F.G). Sibiril church spire on the skyline is also on the line. Follow this line to leave Golhédec (12) (just to the W of and joined at LW to Ile de Sieck) 400m to port, and various drying rocks 600m to starboard. If proceeding to the Sieck anchorage turn E after passing Golhédec and sound in with the jetty head bearing 080°. S of the jetty is a pile of rocks, Kerrec Levran which is some 300m E/W.

If proceeding to Moguériec, keep on the transit or in the white sector until about ½M short of the entrance and Ar Skeul W cardinal beacon bears 080°when turn to 160°. When the breakwater end bears 180° alter between the red and green beacons off the entrance. It dries some 5m off the entrance. Visibility at night of ½M will be needed to enter.

Anchorages

As above off Ile de Sieck. The space between Kerrec Levran and the jetty is limited and dries 2m.

To the N or S of Ar Skeul in a suitable depth on sand. The water is clear and any rock patches can be seen.

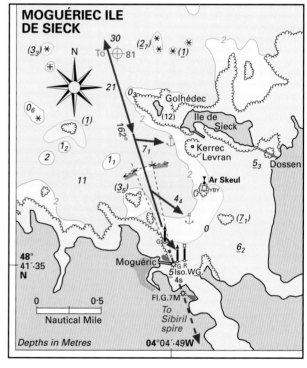

81 Moguéric 48°43'.50N 04°05'.45W

Moguériec looking S

Moguériec. The harbour at LW looking ENE. The yacht behind the second lamppost from right is dried on the bank to the S of the breakwater end

Berthing

Ile de Sieck The small harbour is protected by a low breakwater inside of which is a rough jetty. The outer part of this is a slipway running down to the end of the jetty but it is possible to berth at the inner end towards HW. The bottom inside consists of loose boulders and is not a place to dry out.

Moguériec The harbour lies on the W side of the mouth of the river Guillec. At LW the outflow turns W into the harbour and out along the wall. This often creates (but not every year) a mound of soft sand to the S of the breakwater end on which visitors' moorings are placed and provides a comfortable drying out area. There is a good length of quays to dry out on if they are not occupied by fishing boats.

Facilities

In Moguériec

Water tap, heads and telephone at the head of jetty; hotel/bar, restaurant by the quay; shop sometimes open in the camping site at W end of village.

Ile de Sieck

No resources but the sand spit (drying 5.5m) joins it to the village of Dossen where there are two café/restaurants, one telephone and no shops.

History

In 1944, two British airmen parachuted into the sea nearby and, as a reprisal for the help given to them by the inhabitants, all the buildings on Ile de Sieck were blown up by the Germans. Another version explaining the reason for the ruins on the island is that arms and explosives were being landed for the Resistance and cached on the island, causing a predictable reaction on discovery. 17 of the inhabitants, five from one family, were killed by the Germans and are commemorated on a memorial by the slip at Dossen.

Ile de Sieck harbour near HW. The yacht alongside is berthed above the slip

Looking S over Ile de Sieck and Kerrec Levran   *Peter Carnegie*

IV. TREGUIER TO ILE D'OUESSANT

176 Pontusval and Brignogan

An anchorage in pretty surroundings in an almost landlocked bay open to the N. Most of the bay dries and it is a long dinghy trip ashore if you cannot dry out.

Location
11M from Moguériec; 9M from Le Corréjou

Shelter
Little from the N around HW

Depth restrictions
Much of the bay dries

Night entry
No lights; departure at night difficult

Tidal information
HW Brest +0042
LW Brest +0048

Mean height of tide (m)

HWS	HWN	LWN	LWS
8.4	6.6	3.2	1.2

Tidal streams
Tidal streams off the entrance start at the following times:
HW Brest -0440 E-going
HW Brest +0125 W.going

Berthing
At anchor or dried out

Facilities
Minimal in the two villages

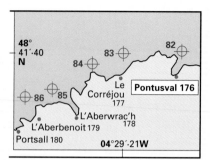

Charts
BA 2664 (50)
SHOM 7150 (48)

Radio/Telephone
None

PILOTAGE

Approaches

From ⊕82 or Basse Toulicot E cardinal buoy 1M N of the harbour pick up the leading line. This is Coatanguy white beacon tower (*Front*) and Plounéour-Trez church spire (*Rear*) 178°. The latter is the easternmost of two churches with its spire at the W end of the roof. Follow this line closely to leave Ar Peich starboard buoy close to starboard and An Neudenn port beacon tower close to port. To starboard there are then three rocks which are painted white from time to time. S of La Blanche, the second one, the channel shoals quickly and a deep draught yacht can only proceed further with sufficient rise of tide.

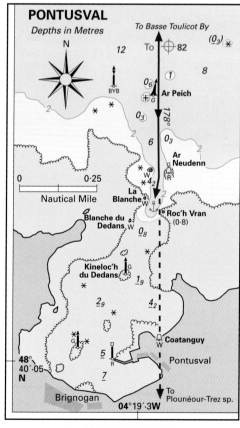

Anchorages and Moorings

The deepwater anchorage to the SSW of Ar Neudenn is defined by Ar Neudenn, La Blanche, Blanche de Dedans and Roc'h Vran (see Plan and photograph) and is rather restricted with rocks on either side drying 0.3m and six visitors' moorings. An anchor light would be advisable if staying over whether at anchor or mooring.

At neaps an anchorage further in can be found by sounding SE of Blanche du Dedans.

For those who can dry the rest of the bay is hard sand with rock patches. An isolated rock Kinloc'h du Dedans (dries 4.3m) is marked by a starboard beacon. Most of the bay dries about 3m and La Chambre on the E side where there are many small boat moorings, dries 4.2m. At Port de Pontusval in the SE corner there is a quay and a slip with rocks on the N side and sand on the S where it dries 5m.

Ashore in Pontusval and Brignogan

Facilities

Landing slip at Pontusval; or land anywhere over the beaches; shops, hotels and post office at the head of the bay at Brignogan. The nearest town of any size is Lesneven 5M south. Shower at Sailing School on the W side of the bay

Leisure

There is a pleasant walk over the dunes to Pointe de Pontusval past some standing stones. A good place for a beach holiday but not on a rainy day.

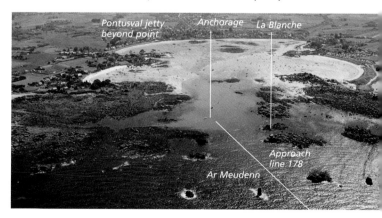

82 Pontusval 48°41'.60N 04°19'.20W

177 Le Corréjou

An open bay with shelter from the S and W for deep-keeled yachts and more scope for those able to dry out. Daylight and good visibility needed for entry; little shelter in easterlies; few facilities.

Location
9M from Pontusval; 8M from L'Aberwrac'h

Shelter
Only from the W and S

Depth restrictions
Dries in inner bay

Night entry
No lights, not on

Tidal information
HW Brest +0035
LW Brest +0040
An inshore lifeboat is kept here

Mean height of tide (m)

	HWS	HWN	LWN	LWS
	8.0	6.4	3.0	1.1

Tidal streams
Streams start off the entrance at about the following times:
HW Brest –0400 E-going
HW Brest +0200 W-going

Berthing
Only at anchor

Facilities
Few and 1½M away

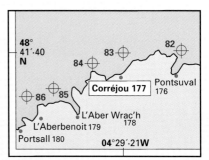

Charts
BA 2664 (50)
SHOM 7150 (48)

Radio/Telephone
None

PILOTAGE

Approaches

From N – Chenal Oriental

From ⊕83 identify Plouguerneau belfry which is just to the W of a prominent water tower. With this bearing 189° identify Men Yann, a small rock drying 7.1m with a green beacon and align this with the belfry on the bearing. Leave Basses Septentrionales port buoy to port and Penven rock (5) to starboard. Then deviate to port from the transit and leave Men Yann beacon 100m to starboard. Continue on a southerly track of less than 190° until 400m S of Men Yann where a starboard buoy must be left to starboard. Identify Barr ar Skoaz port can buoy and alter to starboard to leave it close to port. Then turn to port to leave the port beacon 250m E of the N end of Penhers Island close to port on a track of 170°. The channel is very narrow between this port beacon and Penhers but carries a least depth of 3.8m. This entrance is used most frequently by the fishing and kelp boats and it would be prudent to wait if one was leaving rather than meeting it in the narrows by the beacon.

There is a channel used by fishing boats near HW to the W of Penhers Island but it is unmarked and the depths unknown.

From W – Chenal Occidental

This channel is wider than Chenal Oriental and may be preferred. From ⊕84 proceed towards Ile Vierge lighhouse until Lazerez port buoy is identified and leave it to port on a track of 104° towards the two pinnacles of Karreg Cromm and Petit Cromm ahead. This track leaves Men Garo (2m) a conspicuous cottage-loaf-shaped rock ¼M to starboard. Chapel St Michel Noblet is hard to pick out in the trees but by then Bar ar Skoaz port hand buoy can be identified and steered for. Leave it close to port on a track of 170° and proceed as for Chenal Oriental.

Anchorages

SE of Penhers Island in from 0.6m and 4m sand.

An anchorage further in to the W may be found but there are several rocky patches to be avoided

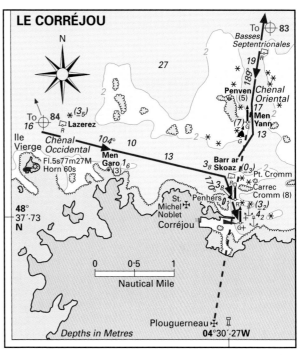

83 Le Corréjou 48°41′.40N 04°29′.21W
84 Vierge 48°40′.05N 04°34′.10W

which are usually visible in the clear water. There are a number of small moorings S and E of the slip.

The jetty to the W of the slip has fishery buildings on it and a sailing school. It would be possible to dry out on the end of the E side but ask first as fishermen and the kelp boats use it.

Ashore in Le Corréjou

The main industry here is kelp gathering which is carried out by specialist boats with articulated grabs. The kelp is landed at and transported from the jetty.

Facilities

Water tap on the jetty; showers at the sailing school; cafés and bars nearby on the main road; the nearest shops are at Plougerneau 1½M south but the distance can be shortened by taking a dinghy near HW to the S end of the bay.

IV. TREGUIER TO ILE D'OUESSANT

Le Corréjou looking SW

The coast from Ile Vierge to Anse de Kernic

The shores of these 15 miles of low-lying coastline are not very appealing to those with deep-draught vessels. Extensive shoals and dangers extend up to 2 miles offshore but apart from the semi-exposed achorages of Le Corréjou and Pontusval which are covered in detail above, there are other drying harbours and bays which bilge-keelers and multihulls may find interesting to explore in fine weather.

At the W end there is an inlet close (300m) to the SW of **Ile Vierge** running NW/SE with 3m in the outer part, up to 6.7m inside shoaling to drying and with some shelter from the NE and SW. Not a quiet place to be in foggy weather as the lighthouse has a 60s siren. BA chart 1432 and SHOM 7094 are just about adequate in scale.

Port de Trésény is a long drying inlet 3M to the E of Le Corréjou at the E end of the same bay. The approaches are much encumbered by rocks and BA chart 3668 and SHOM 7150 only give a rough indication of the problem. A rising tide, calm weather and a sun astern to see the rocky patches would be seamanlike aids with an approach from the vicinity of Basses Septentrionales buoy to the estuary. The inlet runs 2M inland in an easterly direction and dries 5.5m. The small village of Guessény lies on the southern bank.

Grève de Goulven is a large bay with extensive drying sands open to the NE 1M to the E of Pontusval. Parts of it are given over to a bird sanctuary and nature reserve and it dries up to 6m at its head.

Anse de Kernic is better known as it is part of a chart title. This is an enclosed bay to the E of Grève de Goulven drying 5m with a narrow entrance which is not marked or buoyed but is used by small local

Le Corréjou. Quay at LW looking W

fishing boats. The approach is scattered with rock patches up to drying 7.9m and there is drying 4.9m in the entrance. BA chart 3668 and SHOM 7094 give some help.

Porz Guen a small harbour with a breakwater lies ½M N of the entrance to Anse de Kernic. The approach is marked by a port beacon Enez Treas and the entrance by port and starboard beacons. It is used by small fishing boats.

Ile Vierge

178 L'Aber Wrac'h

A popular port of call for the British for many years. A recently extended marina (2007), a number of moorings and just enough facilities for a day or two's stay. Day and night access in all weathers.

Location
8M from Le Corréjou; 6M (by sea) from L'Aber Benoit

Warning
Approaching from the N the flashing red lights on the many wind turbines can be confusing

Shelter
Not very good from the NW

Depth restrictions
4M of deep water to Paluden

Night entry
Well lit, good ldg lts but at least 5M visibility needed

Tidal information
HW Brest +0030
LW Brest +0035

Mean height of tide (m)
HWS	HWN	LWN	LWS
7.7	6.1	2.8	1.0

Tidal streams
The streams start at the following times off the entrance:
HW Brest -0400 ENE-going
HW Brest +0200 WSW-going
Max 3 kts at springs.
Max rate in the river 1½ kts

Berthing
At marina, moorings or at anchor

Charts
BA 1432 (25)
SHOM 7094 (25)

Weather
From Le Stiff on Ch 79 at 0503, 0715, 1115, 1545 and 1915

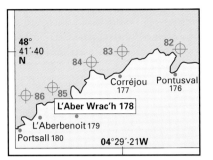

85 L'Aber Wrac'h 48°37'.50N 04°38'.85W

Radio/Telephone
Ch 09 (HW ±2hrs)
Harbourmaster ☎ 02 98 04 91 62

Note:
A simple location plan for the harbours between L'Aber Wrac'h and Camaret may be found on page 192.

PILOTAGE

Approaches

Grand Chenal (Line D)

From ⊕85 or La Libenter W cardinal buoy identify the first leading line which is Ile Wrac'h (square white tower with red top on white house (Q.R), *Front*; Lanvaon (white square tower with orange triangle on top (Dir.Q), *Rear*) 100° (Line D). Plouguerneau belfry is also on this line and there is a rectangular tower just to the N of it. When La Libenter buoy is abeam look for Le Trépied buoy which is ½M away and the minimum limit of visibility to proceed further in safety.

Proceeding down the line leave Le Trépied buoy to port, Le Grand Pot de Beurre red beacon, Le Petit Pot de Beurre red beacon tower and Plate Aber Wrac'h port buoy all to port. The latter three are unlit. Just before the last is reached the next leading line on 128° up the channel (Line E) should become visible. This consists of two white towers with red tops (Dir. Oc(2).WRG.6s, red to the N, green to the S) by the lifeboat house and to the right of the yacht

moorings. If the visibility is not that far, Basse de la Croix starboard buoy will give an indication. In the next 1½M up the channel, pass the following as indicated:

** **Breac'h Ver** green beacon tower to starboard.
Ile Cézon with a black and white disc on the NW side of the fort to starboard.
Enez Terc'h port buoy to port.
Roche aux Moines green beacon tower to starboard. From here the way is clear to the yacht moorings, marina or upriver.

Chenal de La Malouine (Line H). By day only

This channel is narrow and the stream sets hard across the outer approaches. However the leading marks are close to the channel and 1½M visibility is enough to identify them before being committed to the passage.

From a position on Line H 1½M W of Ile Vierge lighthouse identify the large rock of La Malouine, and a smaller rock La Pendante to the W of it. In the gap between these two align Le Petit Pot de Beurre cardinal squat beacon tower and the white pyramid on La Petite Ile de la Croix on 176°. The red beacon

L'Aber Wrac'h approach

tower Karreg Bazil will be to the left of the line. Follow this line making allowance for any cross set. This channel carries a least depth of 3m but passes very close to an isolated rock drying 1.7m to the N of La Malouine, and to the NE of La Pendante which has a least depth of 0.7m over it. The sea usually breaks over the latter at all stages of the tide and in heavy weather it breaks right across the channel; in this event Le Grand Chenal should be used.

The line leaves the following marks on the sides shown:

La Malouine rock 100m to port.
Karreg Bazil port beacon tower to port.
Réau Bras port buoy 100m to port.
When the latter comes abeam leave the line and head between Le Petit Pot de Beurre E cardinal beacon tower and Plate Aber Wrac'h port buoy. From the latter the next leading line 128° can be followed up the river as from ** above.

Chenal de La Pendante (Line J). By day only

Departure in good conditions is preferable to entry for the first time with this channel. The marks are further away than for La Malouine and more difficult to identify. Dangers lie close on each side and the line must be held precisely. The set across can be considerable until S of Le Petit Pot de Beurre.

From a position 2½M W of Ile Vierge lighthouse identify Ile Cézon, a small stone fort on an island with a black and white circular mark painted on the wall of the fort, and Amer de La Pendante black tower, with a white stripe and an orange conical top among trees on the skyline. The latter is roughly midway between the conspicuous white fishery school building and a water tower on the skyline. These marks in line 136° mark Chenal de La Pendante (Line J). This channel carries a least depth of 3.6m but passes very close to drying rocks on the NE side of La Libenter and the SW side of Plateau de La Pendante. It leaves La Pendante an anvil shaped above-water rock painted white 200m to port.

Shortly after this, when Le Grand Pot de Beurre starboard beacon bears 175° leave the line and head for Bar ar Bleiz port buoy. Shortly after Le Petit Pot de Beurre E cardinal beacon tower will come into transit with Ile de la Croix white pyramid (Line H) when alter to pass between Le Petit Pot de Beurre and Plate Aber Wrac'h port buoy. Thence follow the next leading line 128° up the river as from ** above.

Anchorage

The anchorage for large vessels between Roche aux Moines and the lifeboat slip in 12–17m is somewhat exposed from the NW. Shallower anchorages can be found in Anse des Anges clear of the oyster beds.

Anchorage above the lifeboat slip is not allowed in favour of yachts using the many moorings available.

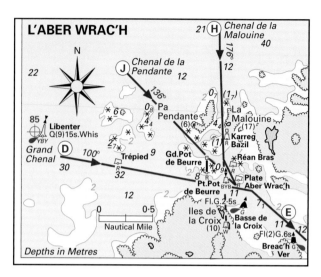

85 L'Aber Wrac'h 48°37'.50N 04°38'.85W

Moorings

There are up to 40 moorings extending from the marina almost up to Perros. Report to the Harbourmaster if picking up a vacant one. The charges are the same for a mooring as for a berth but the launch service comes free (Call on Ch 09). It is common practice for several boats to raft up on each buoy which are well spaced out (max 18m) and substantial. However it an uncomfortable situation in northwesterlies and wind over tide.

Berthing

Maximum length is 12m in the marina although longer may be accommodated on request. There is 2m+ at the outer end but it shallows towards the shore. The practice is to find a berth and then go to the office. Reserved private berths are often roped off.

Warnings

Do not go between the W cardinal beacon and the starboard buoy just upstream of the end of the pontoon where there are rocks.

The E side of the pontoon is more sheltered but both sides are uncomfortable in a northwesterly.

L'Aber Wrac'h marina. *Cécile Le Quintrec*

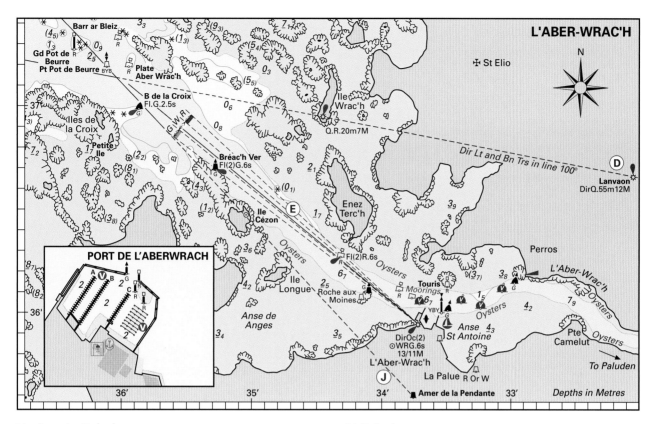

Upriver to Paluden

There is a quay at Paluden with 0.5m alongside it and a slip. It is possible to dry out on the outer face of the quay where the bottom is flat, but there is only one ladder and a couple of bollards, and there are several tractor tyres hanging down on chains which are mostly submerged at HW. This quay is occasionally used by coasters. There are some visitors' moorings off the quay mostly of the dumbbell type. There is a slip on the other side of the river at the Rowing Club. Harbour dues are collected at Paluden Masted navigation ceases at the bridge above Paluden village.

Ashore in L'Aber Wrac'h & Paluden

The village at L'Aber Wrac'h is also known as La Palue.

At La Palue

Water and electricity on the pontoons (included in the charges); fuel on the quay; showers and heads at the yacht club; chandler and chart agent near the pontoon; repairs, engineer and electrician available, ask at the office; the lack of provision shops nearby is the one disadvantage of L'Aber Wrac'h. The nearest is 2km up the hill at Landeda (seasonal bus service). Only oysters and other crustaceans available by the quay, with milk and bread from the souvenir shop just to the E of the quay. A taxi service to Landeda runs sometimes in the season at 0900, 1000, 1100, 1700 and 1800; hotels and restaurants several by the quay and along the road to Anse des Anges where there is a post office.

At Paluden

Water and heads on the quay; shops a twenty minute walk up the hill to Lanillis which has a good selection; showers may be solicited from the Rowing Club opposite; restaurants two round the bay towards the bridge.

L'Aber Wrac'h. Approaching Perros upstream from L'Aber Wrac'h

L'Aber Wrac'h. Paluden
Paluden quay, slip and dumbbell mooring

179 L'Aber Benoit

An unspoilt estuary with deep water and pretty anchorages for 2M to Stellac'h. Can be entered at any state of the tide and reasonable visibility. Few facilities.

Location
6M from L'Aber Wrac'h (by sea); 6M from Portsall (by sea)

Shelter
Good inside the river

Depth restrictions
3m+ to Stellac'h

Night entry
No lights

Tidal information
HW Brest +0025
LW Brest +0030

Mean height of tide (m)

HWS	HWN	LWN	LWS
7.8	6.1	2.9	1.1

Tidal streams
The streams start as follows outside the entrance:
HW Brest -0515 ENE-going flood
HW Brest +0100 WSW-going ebb

Berthing
Anchoring or mooring

Facilities
Long way to few shops

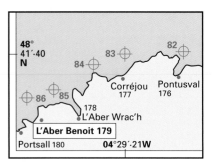

Charts
BA 1432 (25)
SHOM 7094 (48)

Radio/Telephone
None

PILOTAGE

Approaches

From N

From ⊕85 or La Libenter buoy identify La Petite Fourche W cardinal buoy and leave it to port making good a track of 168° *(Line C)* to leave Rusven Est starboard buoy to starboard. Continue on this track until Basse du Chenal port beacon bears about 125° and the highest point of Ile Guénioc is abeam to port. ** Then head 134° to leave Basse du Chenal port beacon 150m to port, Karreg ar Poul Doun port beacon 200m to port and Men Renead starboard buoy 30m to starboard.

With Men Renead buoy abeam alter to starboard to leave the conspicuous La Jument rock, marked with a patch of red paint and a port beacon 40m to port, whence follow the channel on 142° marked by Ar Gazel and Kervigorn starboard buoys and Le Chien isolated danger beacon tower which should be left to port (See photograph next page).

After passing Kervigorn starboard buoy and leaving the small craft moorings in Kervigorn bay to starboard, the channel is subsequently between the moorings on either side. Depths in the channel are unpredictable due to dredging but 3m or more at LW can be expected as far as Stellac'h.

There are oyster beds as far as Stellac'h on the N bank and on both sides above there. The main channel turns S at Stellac'h and a drying bank extends half way across the river from the E bank S of the quay.

From W

This is the best approach in bad weather. See page 169 for approach from Portsall.

Approach Rusven Ouest buoy on a track of 103° (Line X) and identify the line Landeda spire (79) and Basse du Chenal red beacon on 103°. Leave Rusven Ouest close to port, Rusven Sud close on either side and when 200m short of Basse du Chenal beacon turn to 134° and proceed as for the N approach from ** above.

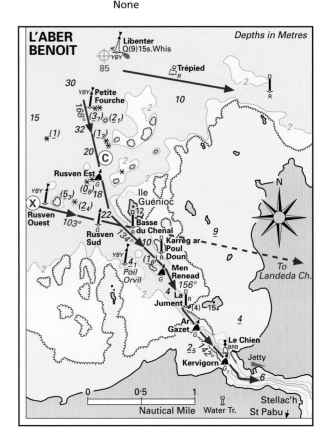

85 L'Aber Wrac'h 48°37'.50N 04°38'.85W

Anchorages and Moorings

Anchor anywhere in the river clear of moorings which now extend above Stellac'h, or pick up a mooring. There is a wide fairway between the lines of moorings in the lower reaches. There are also anchorages to the N of Kervigorn in deep water more suitable in offshore winds. There is a landing at Stellac'h at all stages of the tide.

Berthing

There is a substantial jetty at Stellac'h with a smooth outer side and two ladders; it dries, is used by the occasional fishing boat and a berth may be found here. ½M above this is a slip and a boatyard. There

L'Aber Benoit looking SE

is also a dinghy landing on S side about half-way along the first reach.

There is also a new jetty with a depth gauge on it on the N bank just inside the entrance large enough to take a 35 footer alongside, together with a slip close by. There is little ashore on this side of the estuary.

Ashore in L'Aber Benoit

Facilities

Water tap, heads and telephone on the jetty at Stellac'h; small shops, garage, chemist, cafés and small restaurant to the W and at top of hill in village of Tavenn ar Reut; restaurant and créperie in village of St Pabu above Stellac'h.

Leisure

Good beaches. The island of Guénioc near the entrance to the estuary has prehistoric building remains and a balanced stone that many visitors have tried unsuccessfully to dislodge.

L'Aber Benoit Boatyard   *Peter Taylor*

L'Aber Benoit Anchorage   *Peter Taylor*

180 Portsall Inner Passages

Not for the faint-hearted and only in good visibility. It is an interesting exercise in pilotage but only saves one mile in ten over the outside passage. Access to Portsall harbour from either end but the SW half is the easiest.

Location
6M from L'Aber Benoit (by sea); Le Four lighthouse is at SW end

Shelter
Very little

Warning
Strong streams and narrow rocky channels leave very little room for mistakes

Depth restrictions
Least depth 1.8m but much shallower close to the lines

Night entry
Few lights

Tidal information
HW Brest +0015
LW Brest +0020

Mean height of tide (m)
HWS	HWN	LWN	LWS
7.5	5.9	2.7	1.0

Tidal streams
The streams start at the following times in the channel:
HW Brest -0500 NE-going flood
HW Brest +0130 SW-going ebb
Spring rates 3–5 knots in either direction; the rate accelerates in the narrower parts and towards LW

Charts
BA 1432 (25)
SHOM 7094 (25)

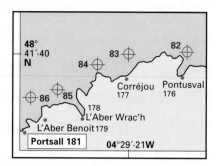

Weather
From Le Stiff on Ch79 at 0503, 0715, 1545 and 1915

Radio/Telephone
None

Lifeboat
An all weather lifeboat is kept at Portsall

PILOTAGE

The optimum time for the identification of marks is when the tide is 3.6m above CD. The back marks tend to disappear behind the front ones any earlier on the tide.

5M is the least visibility to see the leading marks. The passage westward is easier navigationally. An approach from the SW and Chenal Méridional allows an opt out to the open sea via Chenal de Men Glas if the visibility closes down bound NE.

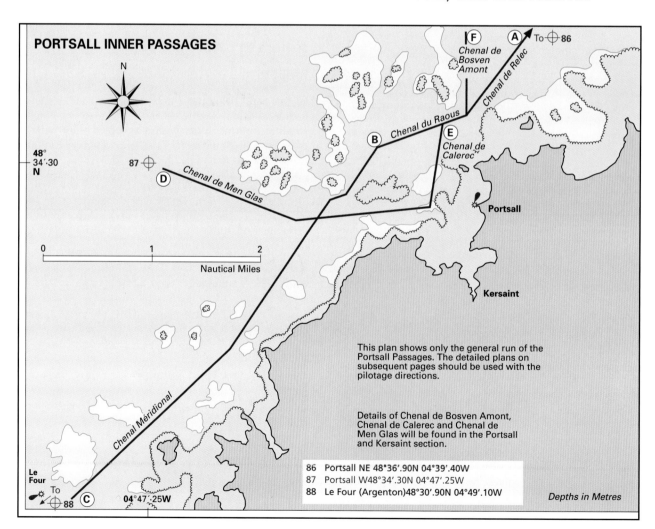

86 Portsall NE 48°36'.90N 04°39'.40W
87 Portsall W48°34'.30N 04°47'.25W
88 Le Four (Argenton)48°30'.90N 04°49'.10W

This plan shows only the general run of the Portsall Passages. The detailed plans on subsequent pages should be used with the pilotage directions.

Details of Chenal de Bosven Amont, Chenal de Calerec and Chenal de Men Glas will be found in the Portsall and Kersaint section.

Depths in Metres

Approaches

From NE Chenal du Rélec (Line A)

Le Rélec buoy or ⊕86 should be approached on a track of not less than 190° to avoid the Queyn-an-Treis 1.8m shoal to the N which breaks in any swell below half tide.

From ⊕86 or Le Rélec E cardinal buoy identify the Chenal du Rélec leading marks bearing 218°. There is a tall white beacon on the N side of Petit Men Louet islet (*Front*). (Grand Men Louet is a squat unpainted beacon 200m to its right). The rear mark, distant 5M is a white beacon with a red top on Pointe de Landunvez (see lower adjacent plan) just W of the ruins of a semaphore building. The visibility is not good enough if these marks cannot be identified and a passage outside should be chosen. Leave Le Rélec buoy close to starboard, Le Trépied shoal (dries 2.5m) close to port and the line of rocks Gouren Gourou close to starboard; there is plenty of water to port of the transit to borrow on at this stage. Leave Ile Longue (3m) 300m to port and when abeam alter to 249° on to the transit for Chenal du Raous.

Chenal du Raous (Line B)

The line here is Bosven Kreis (a rock with two apexes and a white beacon) in line with the southernmost high rock (15.8m) of Le Gremm group. When about 500m from Bosven Kreiz alter to 228° and keep Le Four lighthouse just open LEFT of Bosven Aval (a rock with one apex and white beacon). The stream will now be at its strongest, not necessarily in line with the track in the narrowest part of the passage. The line should be held precisely. Only towards LW will the rocks be uncovered and the channel clearly seen. The immediate dangers are to starboard with Karreg Luth shoal drying 5.2m, to port the shallows to the W of Ile Verte, the extension of Bosven Aval 100m to the E (0.4m) and Seledran rock (dries 0.7m) on the opposite side of the channel. To avoid these look astern and when Bosven Kreiz is in line with Barrou Nèvez (almost covers at HW) 025° alter on to the reciprocal 205° and follow this line clear of the passage leaving Bosven Aval 120m to starboard. Navigation then becomes much easier.

Turn to port to on to the Portsall leading line 085° if bound there.

If continuing W, align Bosven Aval and Bosven Kreiz astern on 036° and maintain 216° until W of Pointe de Landunvez 1½M SW. (Identify Le Yurc'h rock in passing). This transit should be held exactly in the later stages before turning on to the Chenal Méridional track of 229°.

Chenal Méridional (Line C)

When the beacon on Grand Men Louet which is painted white on its SW side (Petit Men Louet 200m to its Eis grey on this side) is in line with the cleft on top of L'Yurc'h bearing 049°, alter to make good the reciprocal 229°. The cleft is like a gunsight and

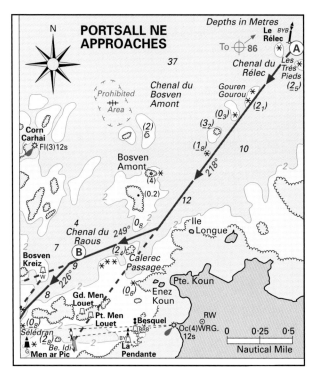

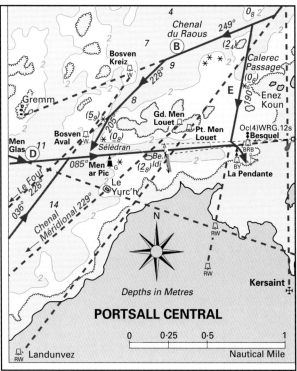

except perhaps at HW, the beacon is lost with any deviation off the line.

This line leads about 200m N of the prominent Ile d'Yoc'h, about 200m S of Grand Chateau rock (3m) and leave Le Taureau W cardinal beacon tower 200m to port. After Le Taureau there is clearer water S of the line. The line then leads into open water about 0.3M S of Le Four lighhouse. Note that there will be extensive overfalls in this area in wind over tide conditions.

IV. TREGUIER TO ILE D'OUESSANT

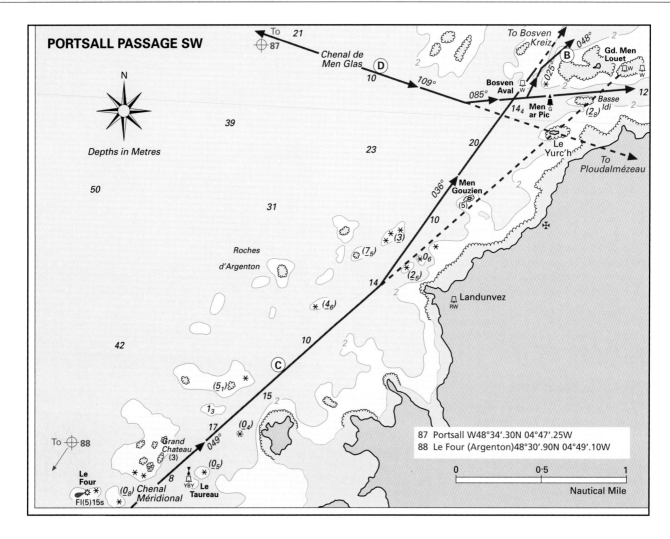

PORTSALL PASSAGE SW

Depths in Metres

| 87 | Portsall W48°34'.30N 04°47'.25W |
| 88 | Le Four (Argenton)48°30'.90N 04°49'.10W |

Nautical Mile

Approaches

From SW

The advantage of an eastbound passage is that it can be taken on a rising tide and usually a favourable wind. Also there is a clear passage seaward via Chenal de Men Glas at the half way stage if conditions deteriorate.

5M is the least visibility to see the leading marks.

Chenal Méridional (Line C)

First identify le Grand Château rock (3m) lying about 0.4M NE from Le Four, and Le Taureau W cardinal beacon tower 0.6M E by N from Le Four. The track lies midway between them bearing 049° with Grand Men Louet beacon, painted white on its SW side, in line with the cleft in the top of Le Yurc'h. The cleft is like a gunsight and except perhaps at HW the beacon will be lost with any deviaton from the line. A help is to keep Men Gouzian (5m) which is easily distinguished just open W of Le Yurc'h.

Approaching Pointe de Landunvez, Bosven Aval and Bosven Kreiz white beacons will come into line bearing 036°. Follow this track until about 500m from Bosven Aval when make a bold alteration to starboard to align the E side of Men Gouzian with the tip of Pointe de Landunvez bearing 205°, then

back to the reciprocal 025° and maintain this line exactly. This will leave Séledren rock (dries 0.7m) close to starboard and Bosven Aval 120m to port. With Bosven Aval abaft the beam, alter slightly to starboard to avoid Karreg Luth (drying 5.2m) and bring Bosven Kreiz in line with Barrou Nevez (almost covers at HW) bearing 025° (see previous page). Follow this line until Le Four lighthouse is just open of Bosven Aval astern bearing 228° and hold this stern transit to make good 048°. This is the narrowest part of the passage with the strongest streams and the transits should be held exactly.

Chenal du Raous (Line B)

Chenal du Rélec (Line A)

When the southernmost rock of Le Gremm is in line with Bosven Kreiz on the port quarter bearing 249°, alter to make good 069° and then follow the directions for Chenal de Raous and Chenal du Rélec on the previous page in reverse.

Note that when Le Rélec buoy and ⊕86 are reached the departure track from there to ⊕85 or to La Fourche buoy for L'Aber Benoit must be less than 010° to clear Queyn-an-Treiz shoal (1.8m) which breaks in any swell below half tide.

Above: Portsall inner passage. Le Rélec E cardinal buoy at E entrance. Le Rélec rock breaking right

Right: Portsall Inner Passage. Chenal Méridional. Le Four lighthouse and Le Grand Château rock bearing WNW

Petit Men Louet/P. de Landunvez   Gd Men Louet   Le Yurc'h

Above: Portsall inner passage. Chenal du Rélec leading marks looking SW

Men Gouzain   Le Yurc'h/Gd Men Louet   Ile d'Yorc'h

Below: Portsall inner passage west entrance looking E. Chenal Méridional

Portsall inner passage eastbound, looking N. Bosven Aval (front) and Bosven Kreiz, the second pair of marks

Relic of a past disaster. Amoco Cadiz's broken anchor at Portsall

181 Portsall and Kersaint

A pretty, drying harbour with drying berths alongside the quay. The deep water anchorage is exposed and a long way from shore. A few facilities.

The data is the same as for Portsall Inner Passage on page 168 with the following exceptions:

Warnings
The drying line is just inshore of La Pendante beacon and all hard sand from there in. Grounding and floating off in NW weather can be very uncomfortable.

Depth restrictions
Dries 4.0m at the quay

Night entry
A sectored light leads up to but not in to the harbour
An all weather lifeboat is kept here on a mooring when there is not enough tide to reach the lifeboat house by the breakwater root.

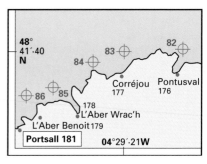

86   Portsall NE 48°36'.90N 04°39'.40W

PILOTAGE

Approaches

Chenal de Men Bras (Line D)

From ⊕87 identify Ploudalmézeau church spire and L'Yurc'h rock; the latter is just S of Men ar Pic starboard beacon tower. Align these on 109° and make good this track down the transit leaving the first group of the Portsall Rocks ¼M to port. There is deep water to the S on this approach.

When the conspicuous Bosven Aval rock with a white beacon on top (see photograph on previous page) bears 070°, identify the next leading marks 085°. They are two beacons with rectangular columns on the land; the front is white with a silver radar reflector on top and the rear is white with a red top (Oc.WRG.12s; white sector 4° wide, Red to N, Green to S) they are not easy to distinguish amongst the houses. Note that the light is obscured at bearings greater than 088° so that a more southerly approach at night from ⊕87 may be needed to pick it up early.

This transit (085°) leaves Men ar Pic starboard beacon tower 150m to starboard and Ile Verte a similar distance to port. The danger on this approach is Bass Idi to the E of Men ar Pic parts of which dry 2.8m; the leading line and the centre of the white sector leave Basse Idi 80m to starboard.

Anchorage

There are now no further navigational lights so an anchorage as indicated on the plan will be needed at night, sounding in as far as depth will allow to get out of the stream.

Towards neaps up to 2m can be found to the SE of La Pendante and clear of fishing boat moorings.

Entrance

** Identify La Pendante N cardinal beacon tower to the right of Besquel isolated danger mark masonry beacon and when it bears 180° alter to 165° between the two. Leave the above water rock (6m) to the SW of Ile Ségue Bras 100m to port and continue to the end of the breakwater.

Chenal de Bosven Amont (Line F)

By day only This approach passes to the E of the sunken remains of the Amoco Cadiz which caused such devastating pollution on this coast in 1978.

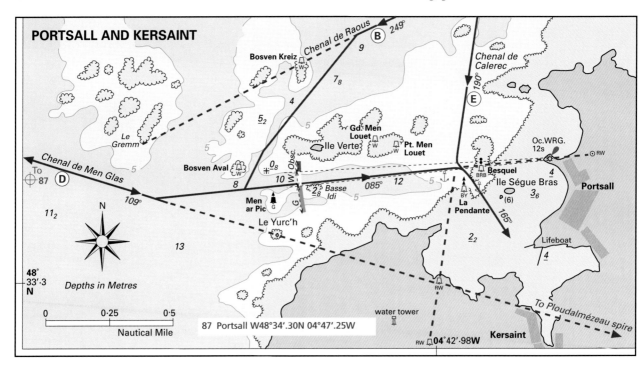

From a position 1M W of Le Rélec E cardinal buoy identify the leading line of the tower of Kersaint church between Pointe Koun and Enez Koun islet (16m) bearing 180°. This transit leaves Bosven Amont rock (7m) 300m to starboard but there are some outlyers a bit closer to the line.

0.4M past Bosven Amont turn to starboard on the Chenal du Raous line with the southernmost of Le Gremm rocks in line with the white pyramid on Bosven Kreiz bearing 249°. The harbour may now be entered either continuing via Chenal du Raous (see page 169) or via Chenal de Calerec.

Chenal de Calerec (Line E)

By day only

When entering from the NE this passage provides a narrow but well marked short cut to the harbour. The least depth is drying 0.6m but there are drying 1.0m rocks very close to the line.

About 0.5M W of Ile Longue when on the Chenal du Rélec or Bosven Kreiz/Le Gremm transits identify two pyramids (both white with red tops) bearing 190°. Turn down this line and follow it precisely with La Pendante N cardinal beacon tower on the port bow. When Besquel isolated danger beacon tower is abeam turn between the two and proceed as from ** Entrance on the previous page. This channel is considered better locally than Chenal du Raous which involves a detour where seas can be unpleasant, provided the leading marks can be identified and held exactly.

Berthing

Alongside the E side of the jetty where it dries about 4.0m but check at the Sailing School as fishing boats use it. The bay is open to the NW and is all hard sand. Grounding and floating off even with the protection of the jetty can be uncomfortable if not dangerous. In these conditions berth around HW and move out before taking the ground.

Ashore in Portsall and Kersaint

Facilities

Water tap and heads on the jetty; showers in the sailing school; card operated fuel pump on jetty; supermarché and garage at Barr ar Lann between Portsall and Kersaint; restaurant and cafés at both villages.

Leisure

The 12th-century château outside Kersaint is worth a visit.

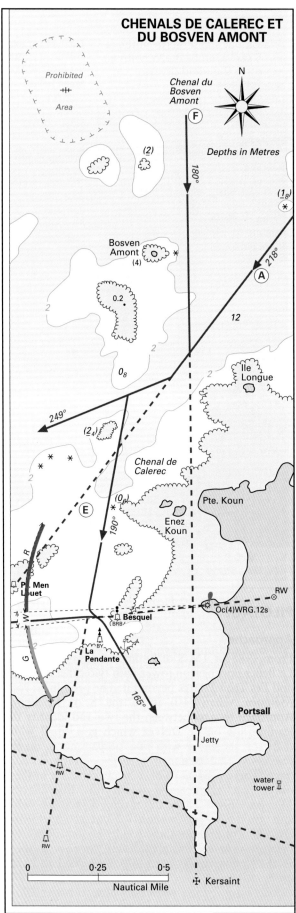

Portsall looking SW at LW

IV. TREGUIER TO ILE D'OUESSANT

Chenal du Four looking SE. Grande Vinotière centre, Kermorvan and Le Conquet far left, Pte St-Mathieu far right

Chenal du Four, steering S past Les Vieux Moines beacon tower and Pointe de St-Mathieu lighthouse

Chenals du Four et de la Helle

From S

The directions bound N are for those bound S but on the reciprocals and may be followed in reverse. If using Chenal de la Helle at night beware of the unlit St Pierre and Luronne buoys which are close to the transit.

Anchorages

Directions for anchorages or berths at the following:
Ile d'Ouessant (Lampaul, Le Stiff, Porz Darland, Porz Penn ar Roc'h) (pages 188)
Ile Molène (page 185)
Le Conquet (page 181)
Anse des Blancs Sablons and Porz Illien (page 181)
L'Aber Ildut (page 178).

Timing of passages

The best time to arrive off Pointe de St Mathieu going S is at LW slack or HW Brest +0600. A fair stream will have been carried from the N and will still be fair up Le Goulet to Brest. It will be foul across L'Iroise if going S but by the time Raz de Sein is reached it should be turning fair again. In strong southerly winds or heavy swell this timing, or a little later, will minimise wind/swell conditions off St Mathieu.

The choice going N is not so clearcut. In heavy northerly weather the main consideration will be to minimise the wind over tide conditions N of Kermorvan and it would be prudent to arrive off Kermorvan as the stream turns to the S at HW Brest, and face 6 hours foul stream but easier seas. In good weather and no excessive swell an arrival off St Mathieu at LW slack (HW Brest +0600) will give six hours fair stream and allow L'Aber Wrac'h at least to be reached before HW there.

89 L'Aberildut 48°27'.90N 04°49'.05W
90 Chenal du Four N 48°25'.69N 04°49'.62W
91 Le Conquet 48°21'.30N 04°47'.75W
92 Chenal du Four S 48°19'.25N 04°47'.75W

187 Ile de Molène

The largest island between Ouessant and the mainland with a charm of its own. Limited shelter for deep draughts at springs. One well marked final approach to the harbour.

Location
8'M WNW of Pointe de St Mathieu; 4' SE of Ile d'Ouessant

Shelter
Some from S, W and E

Warning
Very strong streams around the island

Depth restrictions
From 2m to drying 1.1m in harbour

Night entry
Directional light in N entrance

Tidal information
HW Brest +0005
LW Brest +0005

Mean height of tide (m)

HWS	HWN	LWN	LWS
6.9	5.3	2.6	1.0

Tidal streams
In NW channel to N of island the streams start as follows:
HW Brest −0615 ENE-going
HW Brest −0015 WSW-going
Maximum rates 6 knots, up to 9 kns in Passage du Fromveur

Berthing
Visitors' moorings or at anchor

Facilities
Small *supermarché*, no fuel

Charts
BA 2356 (50)
SHOM 7122 (25), 7123 (20)

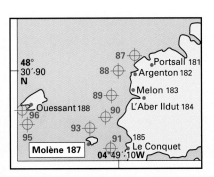

Weather
From Le Stiff on Ch 79 at 0503, 0715, 1115, 1545 and 1915

Radio/Telephone
None

PILOTAGE

There are two practical deep-water outer approaches; from the N and from the W via Chenal NW de Molène.

Approaches

From N

From ⊕93 make good a track of 200° keeping Les Trois Pierres (White column, Iso.WRG.4s) bearing about 180° in its white sector until Men Real E cardinal beacon tower (unlit) and Roche Goulin W cardinal buoy (VQ(9)10s) can be identified.

** By day

Position the white telecommunications mast (to the left of the church spire) between the two on 200°; by night get on to the E edge of the green sector of the directional light on the old breakwater end on 200°. After passing between Men Real and Roche Goulin continue on 200° leaving a line of rocks that never cover close to port and the breakwater to starboard. The tidal stream will be setting hard across this line except at LW slack well in to the anchorage.

From E via N entrance

From ½M to the N of Le Faix N cardinal lighthouse (VQ) make good 270° to leave the distinctive solitary rock La Helle (8) about ½M to port with Les Trois Pierres (White column Iso.WRG.4s) well on the port bow. Pass ¼M to the N of Les Trois Pierres (passing successively through its red, white, green and red sectors into the next white one) and turn down the approach line of 200° as at ** above.

From W via Chenal de Molène or Chenal de la Chimère

Both these offer narrow but deep water routes to the final N channel approach. They are however indifferently marked and have no formal transits. Using BA 2694 or SHOM 7123 they would be an interesting exercise for the skilful navigator well off LW springs, near slack water and in good visibility.

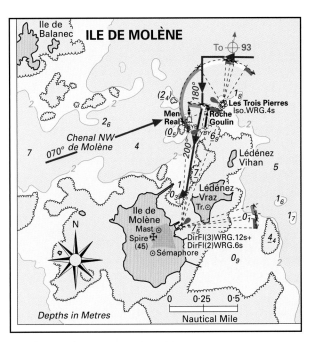

93 Molène 48°25'.80N 04°56'.50W

Chenal de Laz

This is the direct approach from the E in the white sector of the old mole light bearing 271°. It crosses the bar at the S end of the channel drying approximately 5m and local knowledge is needed to find the narrow boat channel through this which would only be negotiable near HWS with any draught. See photograph on page 186.

Moorings

There are 10 white visitors' moorings in between 0.9m and 0.3m to the SSW of the end of the N breakwater to the W of the lifeboat mooring. There are substantial fronds of weeds around them which may make the depth appear less than it is.

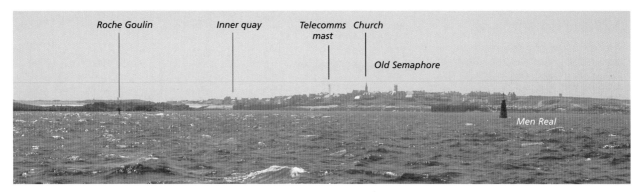

Ile de Molène north entrance looking SSW

Anchorage

In the pool about 200m SE of the N breakwater head in about 1.9m. Depths decrease to the S of this but it may be possible to creep further in at neaps. The moorings at the S end dry 1.3m.

Berthing

There are drying 0.9m and 1.1m alongside the outer end of the main piers and there is a slip on the S side of the S arm. A drying or alongside berth over HW is a possibility here if not occupied by fishing boats.

Ashore in Ile de Molène

The houses above the harbour are close packed so that it looks a town of substance from the approach. The islanders are supported by kelp gathering and fishing and visitors are catered for.

Facilities

Water scarce; fuel none, nearest at Le Conquet; shops a good *huit à huit supermarché*, a Post Office and chandlery from the co-operative; a café and restaurant.

Travel

Occasional ferries run to Le Conquet, Ile d'Ouessant and Brest whence road, rail and air connections may be made with the rest of France.

History

The principal buildings are the church and the old semaphore tower. The clock in the former was a gift from England in the recognition of the services of the islanders when the SS Drummond Castle returning from South Africa was wrecked on Les Pierres Vertes.

Out of 400 on board only 3 were saved; the bodies of 29 of the passengers are buried in the cemetery and others elsewhere around the island. A cistern for water which the island lacked was also built and a richly jewelled chalice for the church was presented by the English in grateful memory of the kindness of the fisherfolk of Ile de Molène on this tragic occasion. There is a small museum about the shipwreck, and the curator gives occasional talks on the subject. Not for those in a hurry.

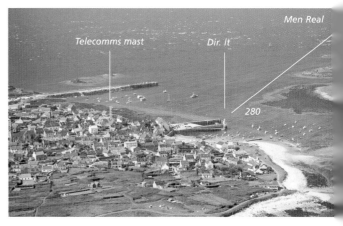

Ile de Molène looking N

Ile de Molène looking S

188 Ile d'Ouessant

Swept by fierce tidal streams and Atlantic storms, there is shelter in fine weather for the visitor, modest facilities and a fascinating island to explore.

Location
12M WNW of Pte de St Mathieu

Shelter
Adequate

Warning
Very strong streams and heavy overfalls around the island; fog is prevalent

Depth restrictions
None of significance in anchorages

Night entry
Anchorages not lit

Tidal information
HW Brest +0005
LW Brest ±0000

Mean height of tide (m)

HWS	HWN	LWN	LWS
6.9	5.3	2.5	1.0

Tidal streams
See below

Berthing
At moorings in Lampaul, also at anchor there and elsewhere

Facilities
Shops and restaurants

Charts
BA 2356 (50)
SHOM 7123 (20)

Weather
From Le Stiff on Ch 79 at 0503, 0715, 1115, 1545 and 1915

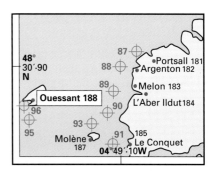

Radio/Telephone
Le Stiff coastguard Ch 16
Mairie ☎ 02 98 48 80 06

Lifeboat
An all weather lifeboat is kept here.

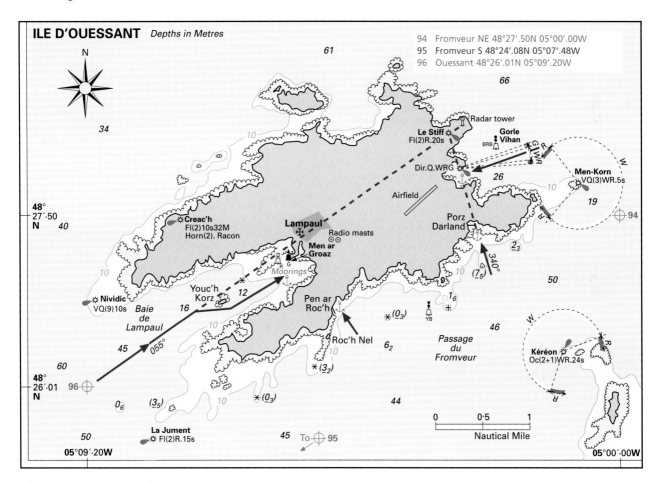

ILE D'OUESSANT *Depths in Metres*

94 Fromveur NE 48°27'.50N 05°00'.00W
95 Fromveur S 48°24'.08N 05°07'.48W
96 Ouessant 48°26'.01N 05°09'.20W

The island is at one of the major maritime turning points on the world's shipping routes and has some of the brightest lighthouses. There is a Separation Zone for commercial shipping to the N and W of the island which is strictly controlled from a centre at Corsen to the N of Le Conquet. There is no requirement for vessels under 300grt rounding Ouessant to report to Ouessant Traffic Control but they should either pass outside the Separation Zone or through the Inshore Route.

Ouessant Traffic Control will, if asked give position and navigational assistance on Ch 13.

Tidal streams

Tidal flows are complex especially to the SW of the island where the direction can change in a short distance and there are many overfalls. Generally the risng tide sets to the NE, falling to the SW. Streams start at the following times from HW Brest:

½M NW of Nividic -0550 NE-going Max 5½ kns
+0045 SW-going Max 5½ kns
At La Jument +0435 NW-going Max 4½ kns
-0045 S-going Max 4½ kns
P. du Fromveur -0515 NE-going. Max 9 kns
+0045 SW-going. Max 8 kns

189 Baie de Lampaul

This is the main yacht anchorage with a number of moorings despite being open to the SW. It is not used by the ferries unless conditions in Baie du Stiff make the conditions there impossible. The lifeboat is housed here.

PILOTAGE

Approaches

From ⊕96 an approach line of either Le Stiff lighthouse or the taller radar tower behind it open to the left of the prominent Youc'h Korz (34) in the middle of Lampaul Bay bearing 055° clears all the outer dangers. The transit should be observed closely to counteract the strong and variable streams outside.

Entrance

Once inside the tidal streams become negligible. Pass Youc'h Korz to the S (an outlyer extends 100m to the N of it) and then approach the moorings/anchorage/harbour with Men ar Groas green beacon tower bearing 050° or less to clear the rocks in the N corner of the bay.

Moorings

There are 24 substantial visitors' moorings in the bay to the S of Men ar Groas beacon tower and a vacant one will nearly always be found.

Anchorage

There may be room and water to anchor inside the two beacon towers where some shelter from the sea and swell may be found. There is 2.3m between the beacons shoaling to 0.8m near the jetty but there are many rocky patches.

Outside the beacons water may be found to the E of the moorings in up to 5m sand and mud. Otherwise anchor outside the moorings in generally good holding. The SE side of the bay is much encumbered with fish farms.

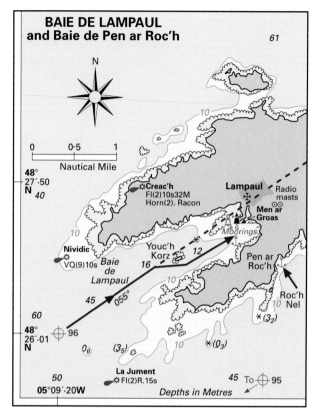

95 Fromveur S 48°24'.08N 05°07'.48W
96 Ouessant 48°26'.01N 05°09'.20W

Berthing

There is a small inner harbour (Porz Pol) 400m to the ENE inside the beacon towers which dries 3.5m with an entrance less than 8m wide. It is cluttered with local boats and mooring lines and the quays, like that on the outer side are rough and uneven. Its use by deep draught yachts is not recommended but it might be possible to dry out inside after a prior recce. A number of small boat moorings obstruct the approach.

See page 189 for pilotage directions for Baie de Pen ar Roc'h.

Ile d'Ouessant. Lampaul

190 Baie du Stiff

Although apparently sheltered from the S through W to NW, heavy weather from any quarter sends in a large swell which makes the anchorage untenable. The holding is poor but there are some visitors' moorings. There are no facilities nearer than Lampaul apart from a café/bar.

PILOTAGE

Approaches

From ⊕94 leave Men Korn E cardinal beacon tower (VQ(3)WR.5s) at least 200m to port when the bay will open up. At night continue through the red sector of the breakwater light (DirQ.WRG) in to the white sector and turn down it on 259°. Leave Gorle Vihan isolated danger beacon tower (unlit) 200m to starboard.
Note that anchoring is prohibited in the bay N of the breakwater due to cables.

Moorings

There is a heavy white mooring buoy for the supply vessel to the S and W of the jetty. Some smaller moorings have been laid inshore of this for visitors, also in the bay S of the jetty.

Anchorages

The holding is poor with rocky patches and the area between the ferry mooring and jetty must be kept clear for the ferries to manoeuvre. Otherwise anchor where there is water but it would not be wise to leave a yacht unwatched except in very settled weather.

191 Porz Darland

A small inlet on the S side of the island to the S of Baie du Stiff. It has a breakwater with a slip inside it in the NW corner which has 3m at the outer end. It is sometimes used by the supply vessel in N winds. See plan above right and photograph on next page.

Approaches

Approach with Le Stiff lighthouse bearing 340° but this disappears when ½M off so continue on the same track towards the breakwater end. Avoid the rock and patches extending from the NE shore.

Anchorage

Anchorage may be found in 5m, sand 100m S of the breakwater. A mooring buoy is sometimes laid here for the supply vessel.

There is a landing slip on the N side of the jetty and a track runs from here to Baie du Stiff.

Ile d'Ouessant. Baie du Stiff looking NNW. Visitors' moorings in foreground

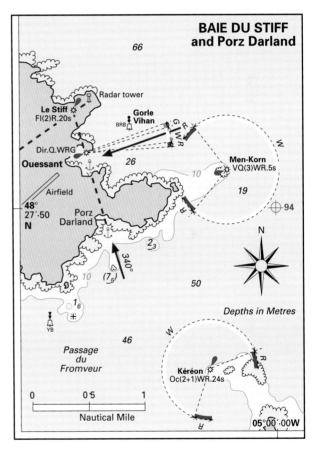

94 Fromveur NE 48°27'.50N 05°00'.00W

192 Baie de Pen ar Roc'h

A wide bay on the S side of the island offering little shelter except from the N and NW when it is sometimes used by the supply vessel. There is a landing slip usable at all states of the tide at the W side, and a track to Lampaul.
See plan on page 188.

Ile d'Ouessant. Porz Darland near LW

Approaches and Anchorage

Approach with the slip and track bearing 330°and anchor as close in as possible between the slip and Roc'h Nel to the S in 5m. See charts BA *2694* and SHOM 7123.

Ashore in Ile d'Ouessant

Facilities

At Lampaul

Water tap on the quay; fuel from garage 1 km; dinghy landing at lifeboat slip; shops two small *supermarchés*, banks and a post office; a number of bars and restaurants, also a disco in season; engineer at the garage; various outlets for bicycle hire.

At Baie du Stiff

A small café open above the jetty in summer; bicycle hire from the café; dinghy landing at jetty.

Leisure

Apart from walks and bicycle rides round the island, the small museum at Creac'h lighthouse is worth the journey and the island's last windmill has been restored. Le Stiff lighthouse, originally built by Vauban in 1695 is sometimes open with only 126 steps to the top.

Travel

Ferries from Le Stiff to Le Conquet, Brest and Ile de Molène. Daily flights to Brest (Guipavas).

History

Qui voit Ouessant, voit son sang may overstate the island's reputation although not in a winter storm at spring tides.

The legends about the island are widespread since it was first mentioned by Pytheas of Marseille in 400BC. It has long been regarded as the resting place of the souls of the departed. The island was scattered with dolmens, cromlechs and other remains of Druidic or pre-Druidic worship until many were used in the construction of the lighthouses. In the 6th century the Welsh monk St Paul Aurelian landed in the bay that still bears his name, Lan Paul or Porz Pol, and built the first Christian church on Ouessant before continuing eastwards to continue his mission in the Roscoff area. In 1388 the English landed and massacred all the inhabitants. In 1788 a French fleet beat an English squadron under Admiral Keppel nearby. At the turn of the century Chateaubriand, returning from America was wrecked off the island, one of the innumerable shipwrecks that the rocks of Ouessant have claimed over the centuries. The graveyard in Lampaul contains many of the victims.

Ile d'Ouessant. Baie du Stiff looking SW

Beyond Le Four

Note When proceeding south of Le Four consult
Imray/RCC Pilotage Foundation book *North Biscay*. As
Camaret-sur-Mer is a convenient stop-over port, after
exiting Le Four, extracts from *North Biscay* are given
on page 192.

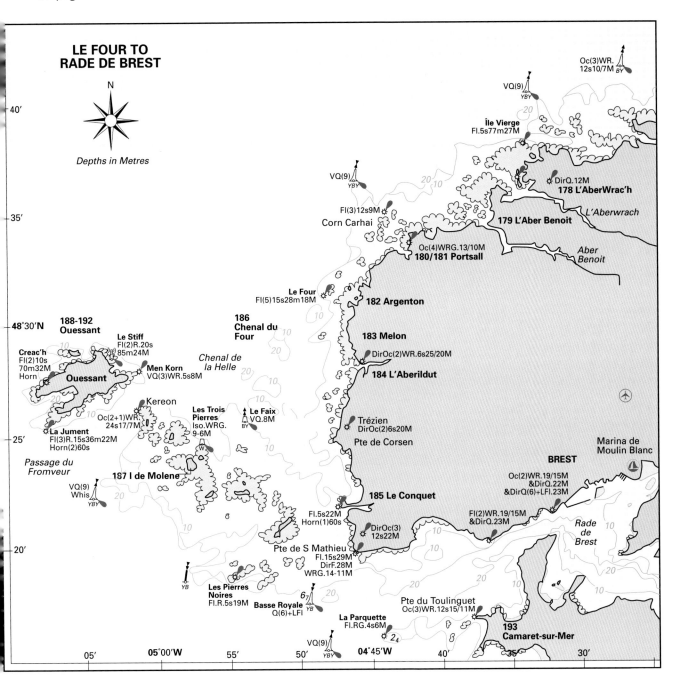

**LE FOUR TO
RADE DE BREST**

N

Depths in Metres

Oc(3)WR.
12s10/7M *BY*

VQ(9) *YBY*

Île Vierge
Fl.5s77m27M

DirQ.12M
178 L'AberWrac'h

L'Aberwrach

VQ(9) *YBY*

Fl(3)12s9M
Corn Carhai

179 L'Aber Benoit

*Aber
Benoit*

Oc(4)WRG.13/10M
180/181 Portsall

40'

35'

Le Four
Fl(5)15s28m18M

182 Argenton

**186
Chenal du
Four**

183 Melon
DirOc(2)WR.6s25/20M

48°30'N

**188-192
Ouessant**

Le Stiff
Fl(2)R.20s
85m24M

184 L'Aberildut

Creac'h
Fl(2)10s
70m32M
Horn

*Chenal de
la Helle*

Men Korn
VQ(3)WR.5s8M

Ouessant

Trézien
DirOc(2)6s20M

Pte de Corsen

Marina de
Moulin Blanc

Kereon
Oc(2+1)WR.
24s17/7M

**Les Trois
Pierres**
Iso.WRG.
9-6M

Le Faix
VQ.8M

BREST
Oc(2)WR.19/15M
&DirQ.22M
&DirQ(6)+LFl.23M

25'

La Jument
Fl(3)R.15s36m22M
Horn(2)60s

*Passage du
Fromveur*

187 I de Molene

Fl(2)WR.19/15M
&DirQ.23M

185 Le Conquet

VQ(9)
Whis *YBY*

Fl.5s22M
Horn(1)60s

DirOc(3)
12s22M

*Rade
de
Brest*

20'

Pte de S Mathieu
Fl.15s29M
DirF.28M
WRG.14-11M

**Les Pierres
Noires**
Fl.R.5s19M *YB*

Pte du Toulinguet
Oc(3)WR.12s15/11M

Basse Royale
Q(6)+LFl *YB*

La Parquette
Fl.RG.4s6M

**193
Camaret-sur-Mer**

VQ(9) *YBY*

05'   **05°00'W**   55'   50'   **04°45'W**   40'   35'   30'

IV. TREGUIER TO ILE D'OUESSANT

193 Camaret

Location
48°17'N 4°35'W

Shelter
Good except from NE

Depth restrictions
3m in outer harbour
2m shoaling to 0·4m in inner harbour

Night entry
Well lit

HW time
Brest HW–¼

Mean height of tide (m)

	HWS	HWN	LWN	LWS
Camaret	6·6	5·1	2·5	1·0

Tidal streams
Weak in the bay

Berthing
Two marinas
Visitors' moorings

Fuel
Port Vauban wave breaker

Facilities
Some repair facilities, many shops, bars and restaurant

Charts
BA 2350 (50), 3427 (22·5)
SHOM 7401 (22·5)
Imray C36 (large scale)

Radio
Camaret port VHF 09

Telephone
Capitainerie ☎ 02 98 27 89 31
Tourist Office ☎ 02 98 27 93 60

Attractive fishing port with excellent facilities

Camaret is an ideal stopover when bound north or south through the Chenal du Four. It is an attractive fishing port that has successfully transformed itself into a yachting and tourist centre. There are shops, seafood restaurants, excellent coastal path walking, good beaches and some history.

PILOTAGE

Approaches

From exiting Le Four (⊕92) track 103°/8M to N of Pointe du Grand Gouin (⊕93) then 102°/0.8M to approach Camaret (⊕94).

Berths and Anchorage

Anchoring is not allowed. There may be free visitors' buoys (white) with 3m or more in the Bay SE of the N mole. Otherwise larger boats should seek a berth in Port Vauban, smaller boats will benefit from the greater shelter in Port du Notic.

Ashore in Camaret

Facilities

Camaret has chandlers, a shipbuilder, a sailmaker, supermarkets, laundrettes, restaurants, bars and a wide variety of leisure shops.

There is a bus service to Le Fret, from where there is a fast ferry to Brest.

Leisure

A walk in Camaret is likely to take you along the breakwater to or from Sillon Point.

The rotting fishing boats are much photographed but the more enduring buildings are also interesting. The church with the broken tower is Notre-Dame de Rocamadour. It is so called because pilgrims from Ireland and Britain used to disembark at Camaret and set out overland to Rocamadour. The church has some fine wooden statues as well as a collection of votive offerings. Sailors brought these, in thanks for narrow escapes at sea.

The rugged Vauban Tower was built just in time to successfully repulse an Anglo-Dutch landing attempt at the end on the 17th Century. There are another two forts near Camaret, one at the Pointe de Toulinguet and the other at Pointe du Grand Gouin. They are not accessible but on a fine day the walking is wonderful.

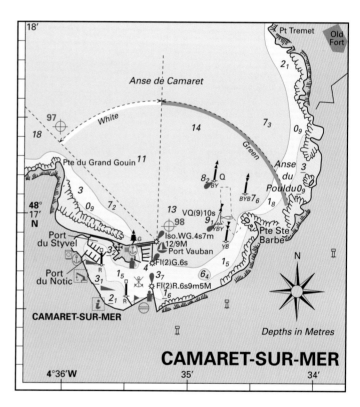

97 Camaret   48°17'.44N 4°36'.08W
98 Camaret 1 48°16'.92N 4°35'.19W

Appendix

1. LIST OF LIGHTS

Cherbourg
1454 **Pointe de Barfleur** Fl(2)W.10s72m**29M**. Grey tower, black top
1462 **Cap Lévi** Fl.R.5s36m**22M**.Grey square tower, white top
1469 CH1 buoy Fl.W.10s. Red ball on red and white striped buoy
1470 Fort d'Ile Pelée Oc(2)WR.6s19m10/7M. Red and white pedestal on fort. 055°–W–120°–R–055°
1471.5 Q.W.9m13M Passe de l'Est ldg lts 189° White metal pylon on hut
1471.51 *Rear* Q.W.16m13M White column, black bands, white top
1476 Fort de l'Est Iso.G.4s19m9M. White pylon, green top
1478 Fort Central VQ(6)+LFLW.10s.N cardinal marker. Vis 322°–032°
1480 **Fort de l'Ouest** Fl(3)WR.15s19m**24/20M**. Grey tower, red top on fort. 122°–W–355°–R–122°
1482 Digue de Querqueville Fl(4)G.15s8m4M. White support, green top
1484 P.de l'Ouest outer ldg.lts 141°
Front DirQ.W.5m17M
1484.1 Gare Maritime *Rear* Dir.Q.W35m19M. White triangle on grey pylon Intense 141°
1486 Inner ldg lts 125°*Front* F.G.10m8M. White support, green top
1491 Avant Port pierhead Q.R.11m6M. White pylon, red top
1499 Marina mole head Fl(3)G.12s7m6M. Green pylon
1499.5 Wavescreen pontoon head Fl(4)G.15s4m2M. White post, green top
1504 Darse de Mielles. Car Ferry Mole F.Vi. Purple column
THERE ARE OTHER LIGHTS IN THE NAVAL AND COMMERCIAL HARBOURS WHICH ARE NOT LISTED

Omonville–la–Rogue
1508 Omonville Iso.WRG.4s13m10/7/7M. White pylon, red top. 180°–G–252°–W–262°– R–287°
1512 **Cap de la Hague (Gros du Raz)** Fl.W.5s48m**23M**. Grey tower, white top
1514 La Plate Fl(2+1)WR.10s11m9/6M. Octagonal N cardinal beacon tower

Goury
1513 La Foraine VQ(9)W.10s12m6M. W cardinal beacon tower
1516 Ldg lts 065°*Front* Q.R.5m7M. Red square in white square on pier
1516.1 *Rear* Q.W.11m7M. White pylon on masonry hut.

Diélette
1632 Breakwater W. Iso.WRG.4s12m10/7/7M. White tower, green top. 070°–G–135°–W–140°–R–180°
1632.2 N. head Fl.R.4s8m5M. White metal tower, red top
1632.3 Basin corner Fl(2)R.6s6m1M. Metal post
1632.4 Fl(2)G.6s6m1M. White metal post, green top
1638 **Cap de Carteret** Fl(2+1)W.15s81m**26M**. Grey tower, green top

Carteret
1640 Jetée Ouest Oc.R.4s7m7M. White metal post, redtop
1641 Training wall head Fl.G.2.5s4m2M. White metal post, green top
1642 Fl(2)R.6s5m1M. Red pylon
1642.2 Fl(2)G.6s5m1M. Green pylon
1643 Marina entrance Fl(3)R.12s. Red pylon
1643.2 Marina entrance Fl(3)G.12s.Green pylon

Portbail
1644 Ldg lts 042°*Front* Q.W.14m10M. White pylon, red top
1644.1 *Rear* Oc.W.4s20m10M. Belfry
1646 Training wall head Q(2)R.5s5m1M. White mast, red top

Iles Chausey
1654 **Grande Ile** Fl.W.5s39m**23M**. Grey square tower

Granville
1660 **Pointe de Roc** Fl(4)W.15s49m**23M**. Grey tower, red top
1662 Jetée Ouest head Fl.R.2.5s12m4M. Red pylon
1664 Jetée Est head Fl.G.2.5s11m4M. White pylon, green top on hut
1666 Le Loup Fl(2)W.6s8m11M. 2 black balls on black tower, red band
1668 Hérel marina. Digue Principale Fl(2)R.6s12m5MHorn(2) White metal post, red top
1668.2 Secondary mole Fl(2)G.6s4m5M. Green structure
1668.4 Entrance to basin W Oc(2)R.6s4m2M. Grey pylon, red top
1668.6 Entrance to basin E Oc(2)G.6s4m2M. Grey pylon, green top

Cancale
1670 **Pierre d'Herpin** Oc(2)W.6s20m**17M**. White tower, black top and base
1672 Cancale pier head Oc(3)G.12s12m7M. White pylon, green top on green hut

Alderney
1532 **Casquets** Fl(5)W.30s37m**24M**. White tower, 2 red bands, the Horn (2) 60s highest and NW of 3 towers
1536 **Quenard Point** Fl(4)W.15s37m23M. White round tower, black band
1537 Chateau l'Etoc Iso WR.4s20m10/7M. On roof of building. 071°–R–111°–W–151°. **Quenard Point and Chateau l'Etoc in line 111°**
1538 Braye ldg lts 215°*Front* Q.W8m9M. Orange triangle
1538.1 *Rear* Q.W17m12M. Orange triangle
1538.5 Breakwater head LFl.W.10s7m3M
1539 Quay head 2 F.R(vert)8m5M
1539.1 Inner harbour N F.G.5m2M
1539.2 Inner harbour S F.R.5m2M

Guernsey
1548 Platte Fougère Fl.WR.10s15m16M. White octagonal tower, black band. 155°–W–085°–R–155°
1548.5 Tautenay Q(3)WR.6s7m7/6M Black and white beacon. 050°–W–215°–R–050°
1548.8 Petite Canupe Q(6)+LFl.15s. S cardinal
1549 Beaucette Marina *Front* F.R Red stripe on white patch
1549.1 Beaucette Marina *Rear* F.R White stripe on red board
1550 Platte Fl.WR.3s6m7/5M Green conical stone tower. 024°R–219°–W–024°
1552 Roustel Q.W8m7M White metal framework column
1558 St Sampson Ldg line 286°*Front* F.R 3m5M Post *Rear* F.G 13m
1559 Brehon Iso.W.4s19m9M Beacon on round tower
1560 St Peter Port Ldg lts 220°Castle BWater head Al WR.10s14m16M Dark round granite tower, white on NE side. Horn 15s
1560.1 Belvedere *Rear* Oc.W.10s61m14M White square on white tower.
1562 White Rock Pier Oc.G.5s11m14M Round stone tower
1569 Victoria Marina Ldg lts 265°*Front* Oc.R.5s10m14M White framework tower, red lantern
1569.1 *Rear* Iso.R.2s22m3M Tall square white building
1570 Queen Elizabeth Marina. Dir. 270° Dir.Oc.WRG3s5m6M 258°– G–268°–W–272°–R–282°
1574 St Martin's Point Fl(3)WR.10s15m14M Flat–roofed white concrete building
1580 **Les Hanois** Fl(2)W.13s33m**20M** Grey round granite tower, black lantern

Herm
1546 Alligande Fl(3)G.5s. Orange A on black mast. Ra Refl.
1546.2 Petit Creux Q.R. Pole with red fluorescent C
1546.4 Epec Fl.G.3s. Black E on green mast

Appendix

1546.6 Vermerette Fl(2)Y.5s. Orange V on beacon
1546.65 Harbour Quay. N end 2 F.G. Green square on green beacon
1546.7 Percée Q(9)W.15s. W cardinal

Sark
1544 Point Robert Fl.W.15s65m**20M** White octagonal tower
1545 Bec du Nez Fl(4)WR.15s14m8M White wooden structure on rock 057°–W–230°–R–057°
1545.5 Big Russel. Noire Pute Fl(2)WR.15s8m6M On rock. 220°–W–040°–R–220°

Jersey
1622 Grosnez Point Fl(2)WR.15s50m19/17M. White concrete hut. 081°–W–188°–R–241°.
1620 La Corbière Iso.WR.10s36m18/16M. White round stone tower. Shore–W–294°–R–328°–W–148°–R–Shore
1616 Noirmont Point Fl(4)W.12s18m10M. Black tower, white band.
1614 St Aubin Harbour Iso.R.4s12m10M Metal column Dir 254°DirF.WRG5m Same structure 248°–G–253°–255°–R–260°
1608.6 Elizabeth Marina entrance Oc.R.4s4m2M On stone embankment
1608 Fort Charles E Q(3)W.5s2m1M E cardinal
1606 Platte Fl.R.1.5s6m5M
1604 Red and Green Passage Ldg lts 023° *Front* Oc.G.5s10m11M Red board on metal framework on dolphin.
1604.1 *Rear* Oc.R.5s18m12M Red board on metal framework tower
1598 Demi de Pas Mo(D)WR.12s11m12/9M Black tower, yellow top 130°–R–303°– W–130°
1594 Western Passage Ldg Lts 082°*Front* Oc.W.5s23m14M Red board on white metal framework tower
1594.1 *Rear* Oc.R.5s46m12M White metal framework tower
1588 Gorey ldg.lts 298°*Front* Oc.RG.5s8m12M White framework tower
1588.1 *Rear* Oc.R.5s24m8M White square, orange sides on wall
1586 St Catherine B.Water Fl.W.1.5s18m13M White framework tower
1584 Sorel Point LFl.WR.7.5s50m15M Black and white chequered round concrete tower. 095°–W–112°–R–173°–W–230°–R–269°–W–273°.

St Malo and La Rance
1674 Les Courtis Fl.G.4s.14m7M Green tower
1675 La Plate Q.WRG.11m 10/7/7M. N cardinal. 140°–W–203°–R–210°–W–225°–G–140°
1676 Le Grand Jardin Ldg Lt Fl(2)R.10s24m15M. Grey tower, red top 089°*Front*
1676.1 Rochebonne *Rear* Dir.F.R.40m**24M** Grey square tower, white face, red top
1680 Le Buron Fl(4)G.15s.15m7M.Green tower
1682 Mole des Noires head Fl.R.5s.11m 13M.White tower, red top. Horn(2)20s
1686 Les Bas Sablons Ldg Lts Dir.F.G.20m**22M**. White square tower, black top 129°*Front* Intense 127°–130°(24 hours)
1686.1 La Balue *Rear* Dir.F.G69m**25M**. Grey square tower. Intense 128°–130°
1686.2 Ferry terminal pier head VQ.G 6M
1687 Ecluse du Naye Ldg lts 070°*Front* F.R 7m3M. One at each end of lock
1687.1 *Rear* F.R.23m7M. White spot, red border on white column
1688 Les Bas Sablons. Marina Fl.G.4s.7m5M. Grey mast Mole head
1692 La Jument Fl.G.4s.6m4M. Green tower.
1692.5 Tidal Barrage Fl.W.4s.11m3M. Signal mast. Synchronised with 1692
1693 NW wall Fl(2)G.6s.6m5M. Green pylon.
1693.2 NE wall Fl(2)R.6s. 6m5M. Red pylon on dolphin.
1693.4 SW wall Fl(3)G.12s.
1693.6 SE wall Fl(3)R.12s

St Briac
1695 Embouchure du Frémur Dir.Iso.WRG.4s10m13/11/11M. White mast on hut. Dir. 125°121°–G–124°–W– 125°–R–130°

St Cast
1697 Mole head Iso WG.4s.11m11/8M. Green and white structure. 204°–W–217°–G–233°–W– 245°–G– 204°
1698 Cap Fréhel Fl(2)W.10s.85m**29M**.Grey square tower, green lantern Horn(2)60s

Erquy
1701 Mole S end head Fl(2)WRG.6s11m7/5M. White tower, red top. 055°–R–081°–W–094°–G–111°–W–120°–R–134°
1702 Inner jetty head Fl(3)R.12s10m3M. Red and white tower.
1703 Le Rohein VQ(9)WRG.10s.13m10/7/7M. W cardinal tower. 072°–R–105°–W–180°–G–193°–W–237°–G–282°–W–30 1°–G–330°–W–072°

Dahouët
1704 La Petite Mouette Fl.WRG.4s.10m9/6/6M. Green and white tower. 055°–G–114°–W–146°–R–196°
1705 Entrance Fl(2)G.6s.5m1M. Green pylon.

Le Légué
1708 Point à l'Aigle VQ.G13m8M. White tower, green top.
1708.1 VQ.R. 4M
1709 Custom House jetty Iso.G.4s6m2M. White column, green top

Binic
1710 Mole de Ponthièvre Oc(3)W.12s12m11M. White tower, green lantern.

St Quay–Portrieux
1712 N. Mole head Fl.G.2.5s11m2M.White and green octagonal metal tower
1713 S. Mole head Fl.R.2.5s8m2M.White mast, red top.
1713.5 NE Mole head Fl(3)G.12s10m2M. Green tower.
1713.55 N. Mole elbow. Dir 318°Dir.IsoWRG.4s16m15/11M. Concrete tower. 159°–W–179°–G–316°–W–320°–R–159°
1713.6 SE. Mole head Fl(3)R.12s10m2M. Red tower

Roches de St Quay
1714 Ile Harbour Oc(2)WRG.6s16m10/8M. White tower and dwelling, red top. 011°–R–133°–G–270°–R–306°–G–358°–W –011°
1714.5 Herflux Dir.Fl(2)WRG.6s10m8/6M. S cardinal.115°–G–125°– W –135°–R–145°.
1716 Le Grand Lejon Fl(5)WR.20s17m 18/14M. Red tower, white bands. 015°–R–058°–W–283°–R–350[3]–W 015°
1720 L'Ost-Pic Oc.WR.4s20m11/8M. Two white towers, red tops. 105°–R–221°–W–253°–R–291°–W–329°

Paimpol
1722 Porz Don Oc(2)WR.6s13m15/11M. White house. 269°–W 272°– R–279°
1723 48°47.2N, 03°02.4W Q.G. 2M. Starboard green beacon
1724 Kernoa Ldg Lts. 262°*Front* Q.R5m7M.White and red hut.
1724.1 *Rear* Dir.Q.R12m 14M. White pylon, red top.Intense 260°–264°
1726 La Horaine Fl(3)W.12s13m11M. Grey octagonal tower on black hut
1730 Barnouic VQ(3)W.5s15m7M. E cardinal on octagonal tower.
1731 Roche Gautier VQ(9)W.10s2M. W cardinal buoy
1734 Roches Douvres Fl.W.5s60m24M. Pink tower with green roof on dwelling. Siren 60s
1738 Les Heaux de Bréhat Oc(3)WRG.12s48m15/11M. Grey tower. 227°–R–247°–W–270°–G–302°–W–316°–R–348°.

Ile de Bréhat
1740 N end. Le Paon Oc.WRG4s22m 11/8M. Yellow tower. 033°–W–078[3]–G–181°–W–196°–R–307°–W– 316°–R–
1742 Rosédo Fl.W.5s29m20M. White tower, green lantern
1744 Men Joliguet Iso WRG.4s6m 13/11M. E cardinal beacon tower. 255°–R–279°–W–283°–G–175°

1745   Roc'h Quinonec Dir.Q.WRG12m10/8M. Grey tower.
        254°–G–257°–W–258°–R–261°
1745.4 Kermouster Dir.Fl.WRG.2s16m10/8M. White
        structure. 267°–G–270°–W–272°–R–274°

Lézardrieux. Rivière de Trieux
1748   La Croix Ldg. lt. 225°*Front* Q.W15m18M. 2 grey
        round towers, white on NE side, red tops.
1748.1 Bodic *Rear* Dir.Q.W55m22M.White base, green top.
        Intense 221°–229°
1752   Coatmer Ldg. lts 219°*Front* Q.RG.16m7M. White
        gable. 200°–R–250°–G–053°
1752.1 *Rear* Q.R.50m 2M. White gable. Vis 197°–242°.
1758   Les Perdrix Fl(2)WG.6s5m6/3M. Green tower.
        165°–G–197°–W–203°– G–040°

Rivière de Tréguier
1760   La Corne Fl(3)WRG.12s14m8/6M. White tower, red
        base. 052°–W–059°–R–173°–G–213°–W–220°–R–052°.
1762   Grande Passe Ldg lts 137°Port de la Chaine *Front*
        Oc.W.4s12m11M. White house
1762.1 Sainte Antoine *Rear* Dir.Oc.R.4s34m15M. Red and
        white house.

Port Blanc
1768   Le Voleur Dir.Fl.WRG.4s17m14/11M. White tower.
        140°–G–148°–W–152°–R–160°

Perros Guirec
1770   Passe de l'Ouest.Kerjean
        Dir.Oc(2+1)WRG.12s78m15/12M. White tower, black
        top. 144°134°–G–143°–W–145°–R–154°
1774   Passe de l'Est. Ldg lts. 224° *Front*
        Dir.Oc.(4)W.12s28m15M. White house Le Colombier.
1774.1 Kerprigent *Rear* Dir.Q.W79m 21M. White tower
1780   Jetée est Fl(2)G.6s4m9M. White pile, green top
1782   Mole Ouest Fl(2)R.6s4m9M. White pile, red top

Ploumanac'h
1784   Men Ruz Oc.WR.4s26m12/9M. Pink square tower.
        226°–W–242°–R–226°

Les Sept Iles
1786   Ile aux Moines Fl(3)W.15s59m24M. Grey tower and
        dwelling.

Les Triagoz
1790   Rocher Guen Bras Oc(2)WR.6s31m14/11M. Grey
        stone tower, red lantern. 010°–W–339°–R–010°.

Trébeurden
1791   Pointe de Kerellec Iso.WRG.4s15m8/5M. Grey tower.
        058°–G–064°–W–069°– R–130°
1791.7 Trébeurden breakwater head Fl.G.2.5s8m2M. White
        column, green top.

Lannion
1792   Beg-Léguer Oc(4)WRG.12s60m12/9M. West face of
        white house, red lantern.
        007°–G–084°–W–098°–R–129°

Locquémeau
1794   Ldg. lts 121°*Front* F.R.21m6M. White pylon, red top
1794.1 *Rear* Oc(2+1)R.12s39m7M.White gabled house, red
        lantern.

Primel
1796   Ldg. lts 152°*Front* Q.R.35m7M. White square, red
        stripe on white pylon
1796.1 *Rear* Q.R.56m7M. Red stripe on white wall.
1796.4 Marina jetty head Fl.G.4s6m7M. White column,
        green top on hut.

Baie de Morlaix
1799.9 Ile Noire Ldg. lts 190°*Front* Oc(2)WRG.6s15m11/8M.
        White square tower, red lantern.
        051°–G–135°–R–211°–W–051°
1800   La Lande Common *Rear* Fl.W.5s85m23M. White
        square tower, black top.
1800.1 Ile Louet. Ldg. lts. 176°
        Front Oc(3)WG.12s17m15/10M. White square tower,
        black top. 305°–W–244°–G–305°.
1804   Le Menk Q(9)WR.15s6m6/4M. West cardinal. 160°–
        W–188°–R–160°.

Bloscon
1805   Jetty head Fl.WG.4s9m10/7M. White tower, green
        top. 200°–W–210°–G–200°.
1808   Ar Chaden Q(6)+LFl.WR.15s14m8/6M. S cardinal.
        262°–R–290°–W–293°–R–326°–W–110°

1810   Men Guen Bras Q.WRG 14m9/6M.N cardinal.
        068°–W–073°–R–197°–W–257°–G–068°.

Roscoff
1811   Astan buoy VQ(3)W.5s. E cardinal. Ra refl.
1812   Ldg. lts Mole N 209°*Front* Oc(3)G.12s7m7M. White
        column, green top
1812.1 *Rear* Oc(3)W.12s24m15M. Grey square tower, white
        on NE side.
1813   Jetty head Q.W.5m1M. N cardinal
1816   Ile de Batz Fl(4)W.25s69m23M.Grey tower, black
        lantern.
1816.3 Slip. S. end VQ(6)+LFl.W.10s. S cardinal.

Moguériec
1818   Ldg. lts 162°Jetty. *Front* Iso.WG.4s9m11/6M. White
        tower, green top.
1818.1 *Rear* Iso.G.4s22m7M. White column, green top
        Pontsuval
1820   Pointe de Beg Pol Oc(3)WR.12s16m10/7M. White
        tower, black top white dwelling.
        Shore–W–056°–R–096°–W–Shore.

Le Corréjou
1821.3 Lizen–ven–Ouest buoy VQ(9)W.10s5M. W cardinal
1822   Ile Vierge Fl.W.5s77m27M. Grey tower. Horn 60s.

L'Aber Wrac'h
1826   Ldg. lts. Ile Wrac'h. 100°. *Front* Q.R.20m7M. White
        square tower, orange top, dwelling
1826.1 Lanvaon *Rear* Q.W.55m12M. White square tower,
        orange triangle. Intense 090°–110°. Synchronised
        with front.
1831   N breakwater. Dir. 128°Dir.Oc.WRG.6s5m13/11M.
        White structure. 126°–G–127°–W–129°–R–130°
1832   Breac'h Ver Fl(2)G.6m3M. Starboard beacon tower.

Portsall
1836   Corn Carhai Fl(3)W.12s19m9M. White octagonal
        tower, black top.
1838   Portsall Oc(4)WRG.12s.9m13/10M. White column,
        red top. 058°–G–084°–W–088°–R–058°.
1854   Le Four Fl(5)W.15s28m22M. Grey truncated tower.

L'Aber Ildut
1856   L'Aber Ildut DirOc(2)WR.6s12m 25/20M. White
        building. 081°–W–085°–R–087°.

Chenal du Four N
1859   Valbelle buoy Fl(2)R.6s5M. Red can
        Les Plaitresses Fl.RG.4s15m9/6M. White octagonal
        tower. 343°–R–153°–G–333°.

Chenal de la Helle
1862   Le Faix VQ.W.16m8M. N cardinal tower
1870   Les Trois Pierres Iso.WRG.4s15m9/6M. White column.
        070°–G–147°–W–185°–R–191°–G–197°–R–213°–R–07
        0°.

Le Conquet
1872   La Grande Vinotière LFl.R.10s15m5M. Red octagonal
        tower
1873   S. Mole head Oc.G.4s5m6M.Green mast

Ile Molène
1871   Old Mole head Dir 191°
        DirFl(3)WRG.12s6m9/7M.Column on hut. 183°–G
        –190°–W–192°–R–203°.
        Chenal des Laz Dir 261°DirFl(2)WRG.6s. Same
        structure. 253°–G–260°–W–263°–R–270°

Chenal du Four S
1873.9 Trézien Dir.Oc(2)W.6s84m20M.Grey tower, white on
        S side. Intense 003°–011°
1874   Kermorvan *Front* Fl.W.5s20m22M. White square
        tower. Front leading light 138°for Chenal de la Helle
        with no. 1880.
1874.1 St Mathieu Ldg. Lts Fl.W.15s.56m29M. White tower,
        red top 158°*Rear* Dir.FW.54m28M. Intense 157°–159°
1875   291°Q.WRG26m14/11M. White tower.
        085°–G–107°–W–116°–R–134°
1876   Corsen Dir.Q.WRG.33m12/8M. White hut.
        008°–R–012°–W–015°–G–021°.
1880   Chenal de la Helle Lochrist
        DirOc(3)W.12s49m22M.White octagonal tower, red
        top. Intense 135°–140°. *Rear* ldg. lt for Chenal de la
        Helle with no. 1874

1884 Les Vieux Moines Fl.R.4s16m5M. Red octagonal tower.
1886 Les Pierres Noires Fl.R.5s.27m 19M.White tower, red top. Horn(2)60s.

Ouessant
1842 Le Stiff Fl(2)R.20s85m24M. White tower; radar tower 340m NE.
1843 Port du Stiff. Mole head Dir.Q.WRG11m10/7M. White tower, green top. 251°–G–254°–W–264°–R–267°.
1844 Creac'h Fl(2)W.10s70m32M. White tower, black bands. Horn (2)120s.
1846 Nividic VQ(9)W.10s28m10M. Grey octagonal tower.
1848 La Jument Fl(3)R.15s36m22M. Grey octagonal tower, red top. Horn(3)60s
1849 Pierres Vertes buoy VQ(9)W.10s. W cardinal
1850 Kéréon Oc(2+1)WR.24s38m17/7M. Grey tower. 019°–W–248°–R–019°. Horn (2+1)120s
1852 Men Korn VQ(3)WR.5s21m8/8M. E cardinal. 145°–W–040°–R–145°.

2. WAYPOINTS

There are clear direct tracks carrying at least 2m to a width of 400m between adjacent waypoints unless the space between is marked with - - - - -. Nevertheless the waypoints and the tracks between them must be plotted and checked on an up-to-date chart before being used for navigation.

⊕01	Barfleur	49°42′.90N	01°15′.50W
⊕02	Rénier	49°45′.00N	01°22′.00W
⊕03	Cherbourg E	49°40′.75N	01°35′.40W
⊕04	Cherbourg	49°40′.75N	01°39′.30W
⊕05	Bréfort	49°44′.00N	01°51′.00W
⊕06	Plate	49°44′.40N	01°55′.60W
⊕07	Hague	49°44′.00N	01°58′.00W
⊕08	Foraine	49°43′.00N	01°59′.00W
⊕09	Jobourg	49°38′.80N	01°59′.00W
⊕10	Diélette	49°33′.37N	01°52′.17W
⊕11	Flamanville	49°32′.50N	01°55′.00W
⊕12	Carteret	49°21′.20N	01°48′.06W
⊕13	Portbail	49°17′.50N	01°45′.40W
⊕14	Catheue	48°57′.80N	01°41′.50W
⊕15	Granville	48°49′.50N	01°37′.70W
⊕16	Cancale	48°40′.06N	01°49′.40W
⊕17	Herpin	48°44′.50N	01°48′.00W
⊕18	Rochefort	48°43′.50N	01°58′.40W
⊕19	St Malo	48°41′.50N	02°07′.25W
- - - - -			
⊕20	Alderney NE	49°45′.19N	02°09′.93W
⊕21	Alderney NW	49°44′.84N	02°12′.09W
⊕22	Swinge	49°42′.74N	02°15′.79W
- - - - -			
⊕23	North Race	49°45′.80N	02°04′.30W
⊕24	South Race	49°41′.50N	02°06′.20W
⊕25	Schôle	49°36′.60N	02°16′.20W
⊕26	Fougère	49°31′.24N	02°27′.77W
- - - - -			
⊕27	Jersey NW	49°14′.20N	02°18′.00W
- - - - -			
⊕28	Jersey N	49°16′.55N	02°04′.90W
- - - - -			
⊕29	Roustel NNE	49°29′.45N	02°28′.68W
⊕30	St Peter Port	49°27′.37N	02°31′.36W
⊕31	Musé	49°26′.24N	02°27′.53W
- - - - -			
⊕32	Lower Heads	49°25′.74N	02°28′.53W
⊕33	St Martins SE	49°24′.72N	02°31′.37W
⊕34	Hanois SW	49°25′.69N	02°44′.08W
- - - - -			
⊕35	Doyle N	49°31′.94N	02°31′.60W
- - - - -			
⊕36	Beaucette	49°30′.25N	02°30′.08W
- - - - -			
⊕37	Aligande (Herm)	49°27′.95N	02°28′.88W
- - - - -			
⊕38	Percée (Herm)	49°27′.75N	02°27′.37W
⊕39	Forquies (Herm)	49°27′.38N	02°26′.45W
- - - - -			
⊕40	Gouliot (Sark)	49°26′.15N	02°22′.88W
- - - - -			
⊕41	Sark N	49°27′.48N	02°22′.00W
- - - - -			
⊕42	Sark S	49°23′.79N	02°22′.48W
- - - - -			
⊕43	Maseline (Sark E)	49°26′.14N	02°20′.48W
- - - - -			
⊕44	Jersey SW	49°10′.24N	02°16′.08W
- - - - -			
⊕45	St Helier	49°09′.94N	02°07′.33W
- - - - -			
⊕46	Jersey SE	49°07′.80N	01°57′.16W
- - - - -			
⊕47	Gorey	49°11′.94N	02°00′.78W
- - - - -			

⊕48	Minquiers NW	49°00′.00N	02°23′.08W
⊕49	Minquiers SW	48°53′.50N	02°20′.00W
- - - - -			
⊕50	Minquiers NE	49°01′.40N	01°54′.50W
⊕51	Minquiers SE	48°53′.00N	01°58′.61W
⊕52	Banchenou (for St Briac, St Jacut and St Cast)		
		48°42′.00N	02°11′.42W
⊕53	Fresnaie	48°40′.00N	02°15′.40W
⊕54	Fréhel	48°42′.00N	02°18′.80W
⊕55	Les Justières	48°40′.20N	02°26′.50W
⊕56	Chenal d'Erquy	48°39′.15N	02°29′.00W
⊕57	Erquy	48°38′.24N	02°30′.05W
⊕58	Plateau des Jaunes	48°37′.16N	02°36′.10W
⊕59	Dahouet	48°35′.40N	02°34′.90W
⊕60	Légué (St. Brieuc)	48°34′.20N	02°41′.10W
⊕61	Binic	48°36′.30N	02°46′.15W
⊕62	St Quay-Portrieux	48°38′.90N	02°48′.45W
⊕63	L'Ost-Pic	48°47′.10N	02°53′.80W
⊕64	Paimpol	48°47′.90N	02°53′.80W
⊕65	Lézardrieux	48°53′.30N	02°58′.60W
⊕66	La Gaine NW	48°55′.50N	03°01′.50W
⊕67	Jument	48°55′.48N	03°07′.20W
⊕68	Tréguier	48°54′.34N	03°11′.61W
⊕69	Port Blanc P. Guirec	48°52′.20N	03°20′.01W
⊕70	Ploumanac'h Sept I.	48°51′.05N	03°29′.20W
⊕71	Triagoz	48°49′.90N	03°38′.75W
⊕72	Trébeurden	48°46′.06N	03°37′.31W
⊕73	Lannion	48°44′.35N	03°37′.60W
⊕74	Locquirec	48°42′.75N	03°37′.80W
⊕75	Les Chaises	48°44′.57N	03°46′.72W
⊕76	Primel	48°43′.50N	03°49′.92W
⊕77	Morlaix	48°43′.35N	03°53′.50W
⊕78	Duons	48°43′.25N	03°55′.40W
⊕79	Roscoff. Bloscon	48°43′.80N	03°57′.20W
- - - - -			
⊕80	Ile de Batz W	48°44′.45N	04°03′.00W
⊕81	Moguériec	48°43′.50N	04°05′.45W
⊕82	Pontusval	48°41′.60N	04°19′.20W
⊕83	Le Corréjou	48°41′.40N	04°29′.21W
⊕84	Vierge	48°40′.05N	04°34′.10W
⊕85	Libenter (for L'Aberwrac'h and L'Aber Benoit)		
		48°37′.50N	04°38′.85W
⊕86	Portsall NE	48°36′.90N	04°39′.40W
- - - - -			
⊕87	Portsall W	48°34′.30N	04°47′.25W
⊕88	Le Four (Argenton)	48°30′.90N	04°49′.10W
⊕89	L'Aber Ildut	48°27′.90N	04°49′.05W
⊕90	Chenal du Four N	48°25′.69N	04°49′.62W
⊕91	Le Conquet	48°21′.30N	04°47′.75W
⊕92	Chenal du Four S	48°19′.25N	04°47′.75W
- - - - -			
⊕93	Molène	48°25′.80N	04°56′.50W
⊕94	Fromveur NE	48°27′.50N	05°00′.00W
⊕95	Fromveur S	48°24′.08N	05°07′.48W
⊕96	Ouessant (Lampaul)	48°26′.01N	05°09′.20W
⊕97	Camaret	48°17′.44N	04°36′.08W
⊕98	Camaret 1	48°16′.92N	04°35′.19W

Overfalls in the Fromveur to the the SE of Ouessant

3. CHARTS
British Admiralty Charts
60	Alderney and the Casquets	25
807	Guernsey and Herm. Beaucette	25/15
808	E Guernsey, Herm and Sark	25/15
1106	Approaches to Cherbourg	50
1136	Jersey – N coast	25
1137	Jersey – Approaches to St Helier	25
1138	Jersey – E coast	25
1432	Le Four to Ile Vierge. L'Aber Wrac'h	25/15
2356	Goulet de Brest to Portsall including Iles d'Ouessant	50
2602	Cherbourg	10
2643	Ouessant to Pointe Penmarc'h	200
2664	Ouessant to Ile de Batz	150
2668	Ile Vierge to Plateau des Roches Douvres	150
2669	Channel Islands and adjacent coasts	150
2700	Approaches to St Malo	15
2745	Roscoff and Morlaix	20
2845	Alderney Harbour	6
3140	St Peter Port	6
3278	St Helier	6
3345	Chenal du Four	25
3653	Guernsey to Alderney and adjacent	50
3654	Guernsey, Herm and Sark	50
3655	Jersey and adjacent coast of France	50
3656	Plateau des Minquiers and adjacent	50
3659	Cap Fréhel to Iles Chausey	50
3668	Le Four to Anse de Kernic	50
3669	Anse de Kernic to Les Sept Iles	50
3670	Les Sept Iles to L'Ost-Pic	50
3672	Tréguier; Granville; Erquy; Port Blanc; Perros Guirec; St Quay-Portrieux	25/15
3673	Ile de Bréhat; Paimpol; Lézardrieux	20
3674	L'Ost-Pic to Cap Fréhel. Le Légué	50

Leisure Folio – SC 5604 Channel Islands
5604.1	Isle of Wight to Guernsey
5604.2	Plymouth to Guernsey
5604.3	Cherbourg to Guernsey
5604.4	Guernsey to Jersey
5604.5	St Malo to Jersey
5604.6	SW approaches to Jersey
5604.7	Alderney
5604.8	Alderney Harbour
5604.9	Guernsey, Herm and Sark
5604.10	Approaches to St Peter Port
5604.11	St Peter Port, Beaucette, Casquets
5604.12	Sark
5604.13	Jersey
5604.14	Approaches to St Helier
5604.15	St Helier; Les Ecrehous
5604.16	E coast of Jersey
5604.17	Plateau des Minquiers

Imray charts
C18	**Western Approaches to the English Channel and Biscay**	1,000
C33A	**Channel Islands**	120
	Plans – St Peter Port, Omonville; Goury;Portbail; Diélette; Carteret; Gorey; Alderney; Beaucette; Creux; St Sampson; Little Russel.	
C33B	**Channel Islands (South) and North coast of France**	120
	Plans: St Helier; St Malo; Granville; Erquy; Binic; Dahouet; Pontrieux; St Helier approaches; St Malo approaches; Port du Légué	
C34	**Cap d'Erquy to Ile de Batz**	110
	Plans: Binic; St Quay; Pontrieux; Tréguier; Primel; Le Légué; Ile de Bréhat; Anse de Perros; Paimpol; Port Blanc; Lézardrieux; Dahouet; Perros Guirec; Port Clos; Port de la Corderie; Trebeurden; Ploumanac'h.	

C35   **Baie de Morlaix to L'Aber Ildut**   77
       Plans: Ile de Batz; Approaches to L'Aber Wrac'h and
       L'Aber Benoit; Argenton; Pontusval; Moguériec;
       Portsall; l'Aber Ildut; Port de Marlaix; Roscoff.
C36   **Ile d'Ouessant to Raz de Sein**   80
       Plans: Le Conquet; Port de Brest; Lampaul

2500 CHANNEL ISLANDS FOLIO

2500.1   **Alderney to Iles Chausey** 1:220 000
2500.2   **Alderney to Guernsey** 1:80 000
          Plans Alderney Harbour to Longy Bay, Beaucette
          Marina, St Peter Port
2500.3   **Guernsey, Herm and Jethou** 1:50 000 *Plan* Herm
          Harbour and Rosière Anchorage
2500.4   **Guernsey to Jersey** 1:100 000
          Plans La Maseline and Creux Harbour, Havre Gosselin,
          Little Sark, La Corbiére Boat Passage, St Helier
          Harbour
2500.5   **Jersey (St Helier) to Carteret** 1:85 000 *Plans* Les
          Écrehou, Gorey Harbour, Brett Boat Channel and
          Violet Channel
2500.6   **Alderney to Jersey** 1:120 000
          Plans St Catherine's Bay, Diélette
2500.7   **Jersey to Granville** 1:120 000
          Plans Maîtresse Île, Sound of Chausey, Granville
2500.8   **Jersey to St Malo** *Plan* St Malo approaches 1:120 000
2500.10   **Approaches to the Channel Islands** 1:400 000

SHOM charts

4233	La Rance – De St Malo à l'écluse du Chatelier	15
5636	Du Nez de Jobourg à la Pointe de Nacqueville	50
6903	Guernsey et Herm. Beaucette	25
6904	Guernsey E, Herm et Sark	25
6930	Des Roches des Portsall au Plateau des Roches Douvres	150
6934	Alderney et les Casquets	25
6938	Abords de St Helier	25
6939	Jersey – Cote Est	25
6966	Des Heaux de Bréhat au Cap Levi	156
7086	Rade de Cherbourg	15
7094	Du phare du Four à l'Ile Vierge; L'Aberwrac'h	25
7095	Baie de Morlaix; Ports de Morlaix et Roscoff/Bloscon	20
7120	Abords de Cherbourg	25
7122	St Mathieu au phare du Four; Chenal du Four; Le Conquet	25
7123	Ile Molène; Ile d'Ouessant; Passage du Fromveur	20
7124	Baie de Lannion. Primel à l'Ile Grande; Lannion; Trébeurden	25
7125	Abords de Perros Guirec; Sept Iles; Ploumanac'h	20
7126	De l'Ile Balanec aux Heaux de Bréhat; Tréguier	20
7127	Abords de l'Ile de Bréhat; Lézardrieux; Paimpol	20
7128	Baie de St Brieuc; St Quay-Portrieux; Binic	20
7129	Du Cap Fréhel à St Briac	20
7130	Abords de St Malo de Hébihens à Pointe de la Varde	15
7131	Du Havre de Rotheneuf à Cancale; Cancale	20
7133	Abords de Goury, Diélette, Carteret; Port Bail; Régneville	15
7134	Iles Chausey	15
7150	De Portsall à l'Anse de Kernic	48
7151	De l'Anse de Kernic à l'Ile Grande	49
7152	De l'Ile Grande à l'Ile de Bréhat	49
7153	De l'Ile de Bréhat au Plateau des Roches Douvres	49
7154	De l'Ile de Bréhat au Cap Fréhel; Le Légué	49
7155	Du Cap Fréhel à la Pointe de Grouin;	49
7156	De la Pointe du Grouin à la Pointe d'Argon; Mont St Michel	49
7157	De la Pointe d'Argon à Carteret; Passage de la Déroute	49
7158	Cap de Carteret à Cap de la Hague	50
7159	Guernsey, Herm et Sark à Alderney et Bancs de Casquets	50
7160	De Jersey à Guernsey	50
7161	Iles Chausey à Jersey; Plateau des Minquiers	49
7341	Abords de Granville	15

4. Bibliography

Admiralty Sailing Directions - English Channel
NP27
Admiralty Tide Tables Vol I NP201
Admiralty List of Lights Vol A NP74
Admiralty List of Radio Signals for Small Craft
NP289
Admiralty Tidal Stream Atlases NP250, 264, 265
Votre Livre de Bord Manche/Atlantique. Bloc
Marine
Rough Guide to Brittany
Brittany in a Week Frank Dawes
Mariners of Brittany Peter Anson
Naval Biography John Marshal
Secret Anchorages of Brittany Peter Cumberlidge

5. The Breton Language Glossary

By Nick Heath

It is of interest, and sometimes actually of value to the navigator, to know the meanings of some of the more common Breton words which appear in place names. Those who have cruised on the Celtic fringes of Britain will recognise some of them; the Irish inish corresponds to the Breton inis, and those who have cruised in West Highland waters will know the meanings of glas and du. I have no pretensions to a knowledge of Breton, but set down here the results of a few investigations.

The pronunciation is, or should be, more like English than French, with the final consonants sounded. The letters c'h represent the final sound of Scottish loch or Irish lough (but not English lock); there is indeed a word loc'h, meaning a lake or pool; ch is pronounced as in shall. The French books and charts do not always distinguish between these, and there may be some errors in this book in consequence. In France, as in England, mobility and the radio/TV are killing regional differences and Raz is now usually pronounced Rah; Penmarc'h, pronounced Penmargh a generation ago, is now often Painmar, and Bénodet has gone from Benodette to Bainoday and collected an accent in the process. The most misleading example of this process is porz, which means an anchorage, possibly quite exposed and/or lacking in all shore facilities, not a port. This gets frenchified into port, and the French word port does mean a port, and not an anchorage, which is anse or rade.

A Breton glossary is hard to use because initial letters are often mutated into others, following complicated rules, depending on the preceding word. I have tried to meet this by suggesting, after the relevant letters, other(s) from which the initial might have come. Suppose that one wants to find the meaning of I. er Gazek (which is quite likely since The Mare seems to be the commonest name given to an islet). There is no word gazek in the glossary, but after G it says 'try K'; kazek means a mare; it mutates into gazek after er. Mutations of final letters also occur, but these do not usually cause difficulty in finding a word.

aber	estuary
anaon	the dead
al, an, ar	the
arvor	seaside
aven	river
B (try P)	
balan, banal	broom
bann, benn	hilltop
barr	summit, top
baz	shoal
beg	point, cape
beniget	cut, slit
benven, bosven	above-water rock
bian, bihan	small
bili, vili	shingle
bir, vir	needle, point
bran	crow
bras, braz	large
bre, brenn	small hill
breiz	Brittany
bri, brienn	cliff
C (try K)	
D (try T)	
daou	two
don, doun	deep
dour	water
du	blac k
ell	rock, shallow
enez	island
er a, an	the
fank	mud
froud, fred	strong current
freu	river
G (try K)	
garo, garv	rough
gavr	goat
glas	green
goban	shallow
gromell, gromilli	roaring
gwenn	white, pure
hir	long
hoc'h, houc'h	pig
iliz	church
izel	shallow
inis	island
kan(iou), kanal	channel
karn	cairn
kareg	rock
kastel	castle
kazek	mare
kein	shoal
kel(ou)	large rock
ker	house, hamlet
kern	summit, sharp peak
kleuz(iou)	hollow, deep
koad, goad	wood
kornog	shoal
koz	old
kreiz	middle
kriben	crest
lan, lann	monastery
marc'h	horse
melen	yellow
men	rock
mor, vor	sea, seawater
nevez	new
penn	head, point
plou, plo	parish
porz, porzig	anchorage
poul	pool, anchorage
raz	strait, tide race
roc'h	rock
ros	wooded knoll
ruz	red
ster	river, inlet
stiv, stiff	fountain, spring
teven, tevenneg	cliff, dune
toull	hole, deep place
trez, treaz	sand, beach
V (try B, M)	
W (try Gw)	
yoc'h	group of rocks

Index